JAMES P. PFIFFNER

*Politicians use experts the way
that drunks use lampposts:
for support, not illumination.*

D1279999

The Politics of Expertise

Second Edition

The Politics
of Expertise

Second Edition

Guy Benveniste
University of California, Berkeley

boyd & fraser publishing company
san francisco

Guy Benveniste
The Politics of Expertise, second edition

Library of Congress Catalog Card Number: 77-9200

ISBN: 0-87835-060-8 paper
      0-87835-067-5 cloth

1 2 3 4 5 · 0 9 8 7

Contents

Preface to the Second Edition

SINCE THE PUBLICATION of the first edition of this volume, interest in planning and policy analysis has continued unabated. Accountability and evaluation have emerged as important components of administrative processes. Experts are in demand, and everyone wants to know why and how they influence decisions. The main purposes of this book are still to explain why experts are in demand, to clarify the nature of the relationships they have with the clients that hire them and with the implementers and beneficiaries of the programs they champion, to highlight how the game is played successfully and how influence is exercised, and lastly to discuss the consequences of the rise in importance of experts in modern society.

This new edition has been expanded to include a number of topics which did not receive sufficient attention in the first edition: the growing importance of policy analysis as prelude to programming and planning, the growth of evaluation and accountability, and the choice of strategies of implementation.

I am grateful for the comments of many colleagues and those of our students in the policy program in the Graduate School of Education at Berkeley who have contributed to this new edition. I wish to thank in particular Eugene Bardach, Charles Benson, Burton Clark, Sandra Elman, and Arnold Meltsner.

Lastly, I wish to thank Joan Killeen, Ann Nishizawa, and Jo-Ann Work for producing the manuscript, and Bill Rock for editing it.

GB
Berkeley, California

Preface to the First Edition

IN RECENT DECADES, faith in rationality has dominated our notions of public and private administration, not only in the United States but in Europe, in many "developing" nations, and in the socialist countries. This faith in rationality emerged unquestioned along with faith in modern technological development and economic growth. We believed that Western notions of progress and the use of science had become the universal and dominant mode of political thought, and that modern technological societies had become increasingly similar because they were all subject to the same universal technical constraints. This was to be an age of technocracy where reason and fundamental technical demands would somehow displace old-style politics and the confusion of competing ideologies.

In many western countries, in all the socialist countries, and in most developing nations, various forms of national, regional, or organizational planning were instituted. Everywhere the systems approach to problem-solving was proclaimed the new rule of the day. The systems approach with its call for rationality, measurements, accountability, and optimization seemed so eminently logical that it was only surprising that it was not adopted spontaneously. Yet the call for planning implied a better and more coherent order beyond the realm of politics.

Recently a reaction has begun to set in. Our faith is not as secure, and a malaise prevails. A new generation has begun to evolve new political movements, involving an anti-technocracy stance seen in the graffiti on the walls of Paris during the student uprising in May 1968: "When the last technocrat and the last bureaucrat are hung by their tripes will we still have problems?"

The experts whose advice has had no impact on public policy probably far outnumber those whose influence is as discernible as they expected it to be. Moreover, some technocrats have been surprised by the countermovement and in their fear of it, or at least in their ignorance of its causes, have sometimes become the advocates of repression instead of solutions. Thus expertise is going through a crisis of its own.

The original purpose of this book remains straightforward: to understand why and how experts influence public and private policy. In the effort, however, a second purpose emerged: to explain the limits of technocracy and highlight the danger of excessive reliance on accountability and all other forms of rationalization.

Thus, this book clarifies the role of systems experts and planners in government and industry in the context of the rapid changes taking place in technological societies. The book explains that it is a new social role combining political and technical dimensions, a role that cannot be devoid of value judgments and political commitment.

The idealistic students and others who espouse the cause of renovation of society assume that expertise is an evil used to maintain the status quo, insensitive to human needs and aspirations. Thus they reject a potential tool for intervention and accomplishment within the system. But expertise is a political action and as such need not be disdained by those on the left on the assumption that it suits those on the right.

Those experts who still believe they are responsible only for a narrow spectrum of technical knowledge and who fail to assume their political responsibility become agents of bureaucratic sterility. I hope that this book will awaken their political consciousness, and challenge them to understand their own purposes and commitments.

THIS BOOK IS intended primarily as a text to be used in schools where systems experts are trained. It is for students of engineering, business and public administration, economics, public health, welfare, education, community, and city and regional planning and programming.

Yet the book will be useful to the practitioner, the layman, and even the anti-technocrat who distrusts the systems people.

Those who oppose the experts may be fighting the wrong issue, because the systems approach to policy formulation may be only a symptom of the present malaise.

I AM INDEBTED to many, but special thanks are due to Eugene Bardach, Robert Biller, Warren Ilchman, Martin Krieger, Peter Marris, and Laura Sanders who commented extensively on earlier drafts. The editorial genius of the Glendessary Press provided structure and design for the book: special thanks go to C. H. Gustafson and Don Hansen, and to Loralee Windsor Lowe and Bill Rock for their contributions as manuscript editors.

Miss Helen Rudy and Miss May Kawamoto have typed the manuscript with diligence and, together with the manuscript editors, a critical eye on the sentence structure and literary style of an ex-Frenchman.

GB
Berkeley, California

The Politics of Expertise

Second Edition

one

The Prince
and the Pundit

"THE PRINCE OUGHT always to take counsel but only when he wishes, not when others wish; on the contrary he ought to discourage absolutely attempts to advise him unless he asks it," says Machiavelli, for "it is an infallible rule that a prince who is not wise himself cannot be well advised..." (Machiavelli 1952 ed., p. 127).

But times have changed. Modern Princes* governing modern technological societies do not dispose of experts as they wish. They cannot avoid expert advice because modern technological societies are vastly complex sets of interacting subunits, and no modern Prince can comprehend the complexities of his domain. A modern Prince is highly dependent on the quality and reliability of the information, advice, and guidance he receives. In fact, he may appear to be a prisoner in the hands of his advisors, the specialized experts in his retinue.

Of course he resents it. Monsieur Pompidou is reported to

---

*The reader will understand why we have not attempted to refer simultaneously to the masculine and feminine genders of the word "Prince." Obviously, women occupy positions of power, and our use of the term "Prince" in this book refers to all occupants of such positions.

3

have quipped, when he was prime minister of France, that there were three ways for a politician to ruin his career: chasing women, gambling, and trusting experts. The first, he said, was the most pleasant and the second the quickest, but trusting experts was the surest. The bon mot is amusing, but there is no question that experts play an increasingly predominant role in the French public administration. For that matter, they play significant roles in all nations, and they are ubiquitous in any large organization.

This is the age of experts: the briefings, the flip chart, facts and figures from computer output, forecasts and trend analysis, the invention and use of social measurements for policy formation and feedback evaluation, programming of sequential action programs, management information and control systems, PERT (program evaluation and review technique), CPM (critical-path method), cost-benefit analysis, models and simulation, regional and national planning, accountability. In short, this is the age of the multidisciplinary, large-scale approach to systems research for policy-making.

Dependence on expertise arises from, and is accentuated by, the rate of change in the social system. The environment is being changed not so much by factors outside the control of man—weather, earthquakes, or new diseases—as by man-made inventions—expanding economies, new products, new patterns of living, new values, and emerging goals. The malaise arises from what Alvin Toffler (1970) dramatically called "future shock."

Problems are generated faster by societies that spend increasing resources to reinvent their cultures. The percentage of the gross national product of the United States spent on all forms of research and development jumped from less than 0.2 percent in 1920 to 1 percent around 1940, to 2.74 percent in 1959, to a peak of 3.0 percent in 1964, and then down to 2.3 percent in 1975 and about 2.2 percent in 1976 (Dedijer 1965, p. 483; Greenberg 1969, p. 112; National Science Foundation 1976). Resulting social and economic costs include constant organizational readjustments, the increasing severity of the unforeseen consequences of technological inventions, and the cost of articulating all the components of a complex production system with its consumption system (Benveniste 1977, Mishan 1967, Stanford Research Institute 1959).

Therefore, the call for experts and the corresponding demand for increased levels of rationality in policy-making do not arise from the emergence of a more profound or better scientific understanding of society. They are the result of the excessive social dislocations and uncertainty fostered by science and technology.

The modern Prince, if he is wise, is aware of his increasing ignorance. Since his policies can have unforeseen consequences, he seeks to understand the implications of his actions or inactions. The social system is so complex and so interdependent that he has to rely heavily on analysis to discover the implications of alternative courses of action. Even if he is only interested in a short-term future corresponding to his stay in office, he is forced at least to contemplate changes that will take place as long as he holds power.

Yet, while any political regime is dependent on the allegiance of its intelligentsia, the intelligentsia is also dependent on the political regime to provide resources and access to the centers of decision-making. When new political regimes take over they require the support of the cadres, of managers, technicians, and experts who operate the technological structure. When the Bolsheviks took over on November 7–8, 1917, they did not have the support of the engineers and technicians, who were supporting the Provisional Government (Azrael 1966, p. 28). The bourgeois specialists were both threatened and cajoled. In time they were replaced by a new planning elite. But even now in the Soviet Union the suspicions and mutual distrust continue as the ideologists in the party, the *apparatchiki,* confront a rising elite of technocrats who have infiltrated the party.

It is a questionable, though sometimes fashionable, assumption that technocrats in the Soviet Union, Europe, the United States, and elsewhere control politicians, or that politicians control the technocrats. There may never be a clear victory either for those who generate or defend a political ideology or for those who claim that their access to knowledge permits them to displace or eliminate the importance of ideology. Each depends on the other, and this mutual dependency sharply limits the power of either side.

In fact, both politicians and technocrats are genuinely confused about the nature of their respective roles. The current popular belief is that the domain of politics is the exclusive responsibility of the politician, while the expert is exclusively concerned with facts and rationality. But the actual behavior of experts is more complex and does not fit these expectations. We find in practice that experts do exercise power of their own. A modern Prince does not completely control his experts, even though they depend on him since he hires and fires them. But there exist many subtle ways to evade and influence a Prince, and these subtleties are not unknown to the successful pundit.

The Actors

IN THIS BOOK the Prince is the conventional client in the client-expert relationship. He or she is a politician or a manager in search of advice. At times the Prince is a single individual; for example, the president of the United States who hires a multitude of experts to advise him. At times the Prince might be a group; for example, a management group, a council of ministers, or a city council establishing a planning commission. Since experts depend on someone to hire them in the first place, the Prince is central to our discussion.

The pundit, the expert, the man or woman of knowledge, is a new breed of advisor. In contrast to the men of wisdom who have always walked the corridors of power, the new breed of experts usually works within a large group of professionals. These may be in the Department of Defense and other departments, the executive office of the president, planning agencies, state governments, and other organizations, but they all have certain characteristics in common.

These men and women are, first and foremost, staff people with a concern for policy. They are concerned with the future, with what is to be done next; they are willing to provide advice; they have a domain of expertise. Their professional ideology is apolitical. The canons of their approach include team work, interdisciplinary research, a penchant for problems that can be quantified, and continued long-term involvement in policy, evaluation, and planning. They have been called "the new utopians" by a sociologist interested in planning (Boguslaw 1965), but I would describe them as inventors of images of the future (Polak 1973) that are sometimes implemented, or as inventors of utopian or trivial plans that serve to legitimate or excuse the failures of their Prince. At times they seem to succeed and influence policy; often they seem to fail.

But the Prince and the pundit are not the only actors in this play. We talk also about the Prince's lieutenants, the men and women of administration who surround the Prince and control the machinery of implementation. Though experts often disregard them, these implementers are an important group. They are the members of the bureaucracies who sometimes succeed and sometimes fail to bring about the policies the experts help elaborate.

The Prince, the experts, and the implementers are only part of the cast. There are also the beneficiaries: those whose lives and purposes are affected by expert designs. These are the people for whom the plans are made in the first place, the people who may support or fight planners and who may be peaceful or violent depending on the way the play unfolds. In this book we call them beneficiaries. At times they are victims, in the sense that the recommendations of experts run contrary to their interests. But whatever the outcome, the experts rarely know them. In most policy situations the experts do not have the time, the resources, or the know-how to communicate with their beneficiaries.

A Few Definitions

SEVERAL ROLES PLAYED by experts are the subject of this book: policy analyst, programmer, evaluator, and planner. We are also interested in forecasters, systems analysts, budget analysts, futurists, or whatever name our pundit has adopted. Each of these roles can be played "in house," that is, the expert works inside a single organization and advises management; or "outside," that is, the research is undertaken for many organizations and for the general public even if the expert is hired by a single agency.

"In house" experts work for a Prince who controls the organization. For example, a long-range planner in a steel company provides management with policy alternatives. Management controls the company and the planner knows that recommendations to the management can become choices and ultimately be translated into directives to the staff of the company.

"Outside" experts work for a Prince who only partially controls the many organizations and the public affected by the exercise. For example, a city planner advises the mayor and the city council, but the mayor and the city council control only the city staff. They do not control private property owners, the federal and state agencies, the school board, etc.; yet, these independent decision-makers may still be influenced by experts and this influence is central to the success of the experts' intervention.

Policy analysis is the research and other actions needed to examine and decide upon alternative courses of action dealing with broad policy problems. It is research undertaken prior to taking decisions to specify the comparative feasibility, costs, consequences, and long-term benefits of specific actions and programs undertaken to pursue a policy objective (Etzioni 1971, p. 8). Policy analysts use a wide variety of methodologies, some of which will be briefly mentioned here. Policy analysis is always an integral component of programming and planning.

Programming is the research and other actions needed to select specific programs among alternatives, the setting of targets for action, and the specification of the necessary steps to bring about implementation. Programming involves policy analysis but goes beyond it. It includes not only research on choice among alternatives, but also specification of desired targets and study of implementation steps. Programming can include a legislative dimension when bills have to be enacted, but it usually refers to the more detailed work undertaken after the passage of bills authorizing specific programs. In its narrower definition it is the translation of enacting legislation into specific activities to be undertaken by an administration.

Evaluation is the research and other actions needed to assess the success or failure of specific actions and programs for the purpose of deciding whether these should be continued, modified, or terminated. Evaluation is also widely used to determine compliance with governmental regulation; for example, compliance with consumer safety requirements. Evaluation is often part of policy analysis, programming, and planning; that is, most policy analysis, programming, and planning has an evaluation component, first to determine how previous attempts to solve a problem have worked out and second to obtain information on the success or failure of new programs. Evaluation research is usually a main component of activities undertaken under the general rubric of "accountability." But "accountability" can also include more prosaic forms of control, such as determining that an agency spends its funds as intended.

Planning is the research and other actions needed for the elaboration of a complex set of articulated programs designed to achieve the goals of an organization, a city, a region, a nation, or several nations. Planning usually requires a considerable level of effort in policy analysis, evaluation, and programming. Plans are specifications of future events that are set ahead of time for less than one, five, or even ten to twenty years. These specifications are usually for the output of organizations (e.g., the factory will produce fifty percent more steel in the course of the next three years). Rolling plans are continuous planning exercises in which planners evaluate the results of the ongoing plan and modify the future targets to reflect accomplishments to date. Planners are concerned with the selection of policy alternatives, the articulation of different programs (i.e., assuring that all components of the system for which the plan is elaborated are meshed together), the setting of targets, and the study of legal, administrative, or financial steps necessary for implementation.

In this book we often use the words "planners" and "planning" to refer, generally, to experts involved in any or all of these four dimensions: evaluation, policy analysis, programming, and planning.

Futurism is the research undertaken about events in the more distant future that cannot be properly programmed or planned. Whereas planning is usually limited to nearer time horizons, futurism deals with twenty years, fifty years, or even further time horizons. Futurism is less concerned with implementation and more concerned with depicting possible or probable future "scenarios" as a tool for deciding desirable courses of action in the present. Long-term futurist scenarios are often used in policy analysis or in programming and planning to provide a longer-term perspective for current decisions.

Systems analysis is the use of conceptualizations and procedures to study complex processes. Basically, systems analysts are interested in (1) defining systems (for example, an analyst may define the "learning system" of a child as consisting of the schools, television, books, records, libraries, museums, plays, movies, other children, adults, etc.); (2) defining goals (for example, what the child should learn); (3) understanding the processes involved in reaching goals (the analyst wants to know how the child learns from teachers, television, books, etc.); (4) assessing resources (how many books, what kind of television programming, how many schools, etc., do we have?); and (5) choosing preferable ways to use resources to reach desired goals (should we spend more on books, television, or schooling?). Step 3—understanding the processes—is most important. Analysts may have theories about what goes on or use models or simulations to replicate reality and also process data. Systems analysis rose in importance when computers became commercial in the early 1950s and large volumes of data could be processed rapidly and economically. Systems analysis is used in policy research, programming, evaluation, and planning.

Optimization techniques refers to techniques of systems analysis designed to find the "best way" to undertake a task and reach a desired goal given a set of constraints. For example, a typical optimization exercise would be to find out the least expensive way to build a power line from a hydrosite to a load center 100 miles away, given a set of constraints such as: the line must not cross dense population centers, the towers cannot be taller than a certain height, the right-of-way cannot be acquired in certain areas, the line has to be able to withstand given wind characteristics, etc. The typical optimization program specifies a variable for which the minimum (or maximum) is sought (here, it was the minimum cost) and a set of constraints that need to be met.

Cost-benefit analysis is used in two ways. First, it is used to provide a systematic comparison of alternative ways of reaching a goal. Second, it is used to justify the undertaking of specific programs (i.e., if and when expected benefits exceed expected costs). In contrast to optimization techniques, cost-benefit analysis does not necessarily provide the "best way" to undertake a task, because the technique does not provide a way to search for unknown solutions and find the best solution. Basically, it only provides ways of comparing known alternative options of reaching goals on a similar basis. For example, if we want to decide whether to use air, rail, or car transportation for a vacation trip across the country (assuming all three forms of transportation are adequate to our goal), we may compare costs by giving a dollar value to the extra time needed for rail and car travel and thus be able to compare the desirability of paying a higher fare on the plane against rail fares or the lower gasoline costs and maintenance plus depreciation costs of driving. We might also use this methodology to justify or cancel the trip. We would show that the expected cost of the trip (expressed in dollars) is less or more than the expected benefits (also expressed in dollars). Cost-benefit analysis is widely used in policy analysis, programming, evaluation, and planning.

Forecasting is undertaking studies of probable future events that can be anticipated with some degree of confidence. For example, we can forecast the probable college population five years from now because this population is already born and is in school. Using past data and trends, we can predict what proportion of the population of young adults who will be of age to enter college five years from now will probably do so. Forecasting is either deterministic or policy-determined. It is deterministic when nothing can be done to alter future conditions; for example, we cannot increase and probably cannot decrease the total population of young adults who will be of age to enter college five years from now because they have already been born. Forecasting is policy-determined when there are options open to policy-makers. For example, the total population of young adults who might go to college in five years cannot be altered, but the proportion of secondary-school leavers who go on to college depends, in part, on the availability of college space and of fellowships. We can therefore make different forecasts, assuming that we adopt different policy options regarding college construction and the availability of fellowships. Forecasting is widely used in policy analysis, programming, evaluation, and planning.

Budgeting is the specification of available resources for a given time span (usually one year). Budgets are usually elaborated in terms of monetary resources but can also be elaborated in terms of any resource (for example a manpower budget). Budgets are conventionally used to control the inputs of organizations (the legislature approves the budget which tells the administration what resources it can count on in the next fiscal year). In contrast to programming and planning, which usually deal with the output of organizations (you will increase steel production by fifty percent in the next three years), conventional budgeting focuses on inputs (you can hire ten more drivers, build two new factories, etc.). Recurrent budgets refer to expenditures the organization incurs in normal operation (salaries, materials used year after year). Development budgets refer to expenditures the organization incurs only from time to time for facilities that will last a long time (for example, the construction of new schools).

Program budgeting is the application of systems analysis to budgeting so that resources used as inputs are justified in terms of specific program goals (outputs). Instead of providing a list of all the items needed by an organization (e.g., it needs 50 employees, two dozen cars, 25 telephones, etc.), a program budget sets objectives (the organization will increase sales by 10 percent via promotion: telephone promotion will take 30 percent of the effort; door-to-door, 40 percent; advertising, 30 percent; telephone promotion will contribute a 3 percent increase in sales and for this they need 15 employees, 15 telephones; door-to-door will need 15 employees and 15 cars—they are expected to contribute x percent to increased sales, etc.). Program budgeting was very popular in the sixties, but its utility has been questioned in social sectors where goals and targets are not easily specified and measured (what is "good" education?) and where specifying goals tends to distort the purposes of the organization (if we specify that a school must increase the scores of its pupils on tests, the staff of the school is going to prepare students to take tests instead of teaching other important content). But when goal specification is desirable, program budgeting is still in vogue. It is sometimes used as part of programming and planning exercises (Schick 1973, Worthley 1974).

Zero base budgeting is budgeting based on the assumption that all programs have to be rejustified anew (i.e., we start anew each year with zero budget and justify all activities). Therefore, in theory at least, zero base budgeting should rely on evaluation to provide justification that each program and activity is achieving the desired objectives. Zero base budgeting can be used in programming and planning.

Management information and control systems are the sum of all the intellectual tools management can use to establish what the organization is doing and how it can reach desired goals. They include statistics, reports, evaluations, data storage and processing, sampling, quality controls, etc. The basic idea used in control systems is that of feedback: management information and control systems provide monitoring of the outputs of the relevant organizations or subunits of organizations to determine how well they are doing what they are supposed to be doing. This output data is analyzed and fed back to policy-makers to determine how policies might be altered, innovated, and pursued. Control systems consist essentially of evaluation and of analysis components which, together, translate evaluation results into desirable new policy options. Control systems are used in programming and are central to rolling plans.

PERT (program evaluation and review technique) and CPM

(critical-path methods) are programming or planning implementation techniques concerned with future time. Given a goal that needs to be accomplished at a future time, the analyst works backwards to determine when and how activities have to be undertaken to achieve the goal. For example, if a book is to be out in the spring (goal), it must be typeset and the proofs have to be checked beforehand. This means that the final edited copy needs to be ready in January, which means that the second draft has to go to the typist in December, etc. Complex projects usually require initiation of simultaneous streams of activities that gradually come together as the components of the project are integrated. The timing of research and development, the bidding and awarding of contracts, getting contractors to work together require time. An important aspect of these techniques is lead-time analysis; for example, finding out how much time has to elapse between the day the appropriation for a program is approved and the day the agency is able to initiate implementation, how much lead time before contractors can respond to bids, can be selected, and can complete the tasks. What is the average rate of delay in contract completions, etc.? This analysis relies on data about existing capabilities and on the past performance of agencies and contractors. Since these techniques focus on implementation, they are most important to programming and planning.

THESE FEW DEFINITIONS highlight a number of significant differences and similarities:

—First, there exist varieties of expert roles, but all experts share a common professional ideology: they are concerned with providing rational ways of thinking about complex future issues.

—Second, these roles are related: policy analysis, programming, evaluation, and planning are part of a continuum and to a considerable extent overlap.

—Third, there exists an important distinction between "in house" and "outside" experts. As we shall see in subsequent chapters, the relations between expert and Prince are quite different and the consequences for implementation are also different.

—Fourth, all these expert roles use methodologies of analysis that are relatively recent. While some go back to the nineteenth century, their widespread application is a phenomenon of the twentieth century. In the United States, planning was initiated during World War I and during the New Deal in the late thirties. But the widespread use of systems analysis, the growth of policy analysis, programming, evaluation, and planning are phenomena of the 1950s, and their practice is still evolving and will continue to evolve. As a result, what is considered acceptable research for analysis at one historical time may no longer be considered sufficient later on.

—Fifth, analysis, evaluation, and planning are competitive endeavors and the competition among those who use or do this research has much to do with the ways the norms of what is considered acceptable research change.

—Sixth, for the moment at least, this new profession has not yet developed all the trappings of conventional professions. There do not exist, as yet, well-established definitions of what is desirable professional behavior, nor is there a code of professional ethics, nor is there any professional court that defines standards of professional work. The profession is evolving and we can expect many new developments in the coming decades.

Invention of New Social Roles

THE ROLE OF "social architect," "social engineer," or "man of knowledge" has been suggested and even described in several social accounts and ideologies of the past (Mannheim 1935, Znaniecki 1940). But its widespread operational implementation is a phenomenon of the second half of this century. The new breed of experts actually plays roles that are still in the process of creation. They are being invented by the extension and adaptation of two existing roles in the repertoire, by a combination of political *and* scientific roles, which are generally understood as separate and distinct.

We take existing role definitions for granted. It is only when social circumstances are markedly changed and we grope desperately for ways to behave that we intuitively understand the extent to which the existing role repertoire is a finite cultural resource.

Roles are a principal social asset because they give us the ability to cope with the uncertainty of social encounters. For example, you and I know what to expect when we meet, we know how to behave at the death of friends, and we know what is expected of us in countless social situations. Without this shared set of mutual expectations and trust we would not be able to function.

Role definitions are changed continually. They are changed when certain actors begin to behave differently and when actors in counter-roles begin to have different conceptions of the ways each role should be played. But we change roles or define new roles very slowly because trust and mutual expectations of behavior can only be built up over time.

In moments of acute social crisis—for example, when a revolution takes place—certain roles are abolished, new roles are created, and the prerogatives associated with certain roles are changed dramatically. But even in revolutionary periods, the actors are constrained by the existing role repertoire and cannot transform the social order radically. Fundamental changes in social relations take place after a revolution, just as they take place after a strike or after the reorganization of a bureaucracy.

In any social crisis there is a constraining time element. The crisis indicates a change of direction or a break with the past, but the actual implementation of the break is gradual, because much of the social order has to depend on mutual trust, and trust is acquired by continued experience and reinforcement.

The present malaise is related to the acceleration of the rate of change, the rapid increase in the numbers of agencies and groups involved in decisions, the growth of government regulation, the rising deterioration of work in organizations, and the difficulty of predicting what will happen next. Since most social life takes place in the context of formal organizations (firms, universities, churches, unions), the deterioration of bureaucracy influences all of us. As a leading exponent of the sociology of organization puts it:

> The older and more complex organizations in our society—business firms, governmental bureaus, city government, labor unions, churches, hospitals, schools and universities—appear to be deteriorating. With every passing day, the human and material costs of providing a product or service seem to be going up, while the resulting quality is either wavering or going down. Organizations are becoming increasingly rigid and difficult to change; it is almost impossible to induce them to re-examine and renew themselves. (Argyris 1970, p. 1)

Rapid and accelerating technological changes with their economic, social, and psychological consequences are an important factor in creating excessive bureaucratic uncertainty, which in turn results in bureaucratic fear. As the future becomes more uncertain, the bureaucracy becomes more rigid and rule-ridden. It therefore performs less well, and this accelerates the spread of the malaise. At that point, planning, accountability, and systems analysis appear to be palliatives, and the call for experts becomes generalized (Benveniste 1977).

Therefore, just as a traditional society evolves the roles of warriors and shelter builders to deal with constant, if uncertain, elements in its environment, we are now evolving the new roles of experts in response to the threat posed to individual decision-makers confronted by choices in situations where the outcomes are too uncertain and the penalties are too heavy.

As it turns out, experts do not always solve these problems; indeed, they sometimes accentuate them. Insistence on performance, accountability, efficiency, and planning does not always fit the realities of organizations. Sometimes it results in goal conflict and goal displacement. The more exactly goals are specified, the more difficult it is to reach agreement about them. Moreover, measurements themselves can become the new goals and displace what they are supposed to measure.

At first the experts may seem to be useful, but in time their domain of expertise suddenly appears terribly limited and constrained. The political mood turns to distrust. New ideologies claim that the essential qualities of life are being lost. The experts are attacked because they appear unable to deal with many essential qualitative issues. The ideologues rediscover that rationalization is by definition a schema or simplification, and therefore fails to deal with emerging values. They accuse the experts of spending too much time counting what is not important and thus failing to deal with what is essential. They may even accuse the experts of inventing measurements that distort or displace accepted values. But disenchantment with the systems approach or with planning does not resolve the problems of technological societies. The doubt serves only to increase insecurity and alienation.

Leaving these fundamental issues aside, at least for the moment, the new experts still face the challenge of inventing and playing a new role that is not generally perceived as such. During these formative years, they encounter serious difficulties because they have to use an existing role—that of the social scientist—to attempt to fill needs they consciously or unconsciously recognize. But they are forced to do this under severe constraints. These constraints are the result of the differences between the existing roles, i.e., on one side the scientist who, within the discipline, attempts to pursue a politically value-free role, and on the other side the politician who spells out the values to be pursued.

Experts may be lulled into believing that they are more scientists than politicians because of the way they conceptualize problems. They often see themselves as problem-solvers and not as arrangers of solutions. They are concerned with models, but any model of a social situation is an abstraction, a simplification of that situation. Policy experts and planners are able to study problems and make recommendations because they have access to or have invented a way of conceptualizing the problem that tells them how to derive one or more solutions. In other words, given a problem to solve, the systems experts invent or have access to a system of conceptualization that allows them to make recommendations.

The conceptualizations and the conceptualizers are also a part of social reality. Yet most models, including economic models, do not include the effects of the model itself within the model, because the discipline does not provide an easy way to attribute effects to the model. Nor has there been much research on how different ways of providing advice influence outcomes.

The present traditions of policy expertise and planning have been bred in intellectual environments where there was little opportunity to think about the process of providing expert advice rather than about its content. Urban, regional, economic, educational, and community development planners have all tended to spend their intellectual resources on studying solutions without giving much thought to the effects of their own actions on the situations in which they worked.

Clearly, a national planning body or high-level policy experts in visible and public positions have an influence that arises not so much from their intellectual work as from the impact of their statements about the future. For example, a team of experts in such a position can alter the expectations of other decision-makers or even alter the subjective probabilities other decision-makers associate with the course of future events, thus altering the substance of the problem and indeed the rules of the game they took for granted when they started looking for a solution.

This process dimension of planning tends to be disregarded within the conceptualizations of experts. To be sure, many experts intuitively perceive the difference between their conceptualization and the way their statements may alter reality. When economic planners consider whether production targets should be raised above expected output to create an additional incentive for the producing units, they are no longer constrained by their own model of the situation; instead they are considering how the model will be perceived and how it will be manipulated and used to advance certain programs and downgrade others. This notion of the production system is expanded to include the guidance apparatus of the system, how the information the guidance system transmits is received, and how the original system is transformed by this fact. But these intuitions are not easily systematized.

In other words, ignorance of the political sociology of their own role and the limitations of their own disciplines tends to orient the experts to conventional role definitions. They tend to view themselves as men or women of knowledge even if their behavior does not always fit that definition.

Dysfunctions of the Conventional
Definition of the Expert's Role

T HE MAJOR DYSFUNCTION of the conventional role definition is that experts are confused about the relevant political actors. They do not perceive the difference and relative
importance of implementers and beneficiaries, while they pay
too much attention to the Prince. But even if experts recognize
the political aspects of expertise, other actors do not. If experts
play the political dimension of their role at all, they are forced to
do so under the guise of searching for information or consulting
knowledgeable practitioners. They are not able to devote much
time to these political activities since they are not expected to
carry them out.

The conventional role definition obscures the relative importance of the political actors with whom experts could negotiate.
The professional assumption that they serve a client makes
them lose sight of the fact that the Prince who hires them does
not always control, or is not always a representative of, the
implementers and beneficiaries. The experts therefore fail to
see the linkages of their own intervention to the client-
implementer-beneficiary system.

They tend to consider implementers as enemies: dull bureaucrats who see only the trees and fail to find the forest; bureaucrats who are going to have to be coerced into changing their
ways; people of little significance whom one may seek out when
gathering facts but whose sensitivities one disregards. If experts
originate consultations with them, it will be only with those
whose experience they consider valuable for undertaking the
necessary research.

The beneficiaries are perceived to have no importance. They
probably do not understand the complexities of the problem,
their technical awareness is minimal, and who has the time to
worry about them? To consult them is to subject oneself to the
indignities of political pressure. It is not atypical for experts to
avoid contact with the ultimate beneficiaries of their recommendations.

The beneficiaries resent it; they feel manipulated or unable to deal with their own future. If they can organize and exercise political pressure, they may hamper implementation. The implementers who deal on a daily basis with the beneficiaries become aware of the fragility of the experts' knowledge and doubt the validity of their recommendations.

Moreover, this raises the issue of participation in policy analysis and planning, and in this respect we must recognize that beyond these attitudes and role mystification, there also exist very real structural constraints. In other words, even if experts understand the political implications of their actions, they are still limited in their ability to encourage participation. There are limits to the time and resources that can be spent for that purpose.

This does not eliminate the problem: for many experts the only relevant actor is the Prince, who happens to pay wages, supply office space, provide status, and offer access to the substance of research; these evident attitudes make the Prince an attractive target for experts' attention.

This means that in many instances experts tend to emerge as the equivalent of selective filters for communication and decision in the social system. They use their available time to consult in selected circles. Since they limit participation, they permit information and influence to flow only within a restricted portion of the body politic.

While experts usually limit the level of participation in policy-making, they can also enlarge it. They can provide means to change the entourage of the Prince. The relevant issue, therefore, is the nature of this selective process: who participates, and who does not. The conscious recognition of this political dimension of planning requires that the time budgets of experts be designed accordingly. That is, if experts are to play political roles, they need time to consult, organize political support, and seek acceptable solutions. Of course, this is exactly what is difficult to do because of the underlying role mystification. Experts are not expected to play such a role, yet sometimes they find they have to.

The net result of all this seems to be either failure or excessive success. Failure takes place when experts discover that their reports and recommendations simply gather dust and excessive success when their tentative advice is translated into hard-and-fast rules which turn out to be undesirable.

Failure is usually associated with experts who serve a Prince who does not control the relevant implementers; for example, national planning. In the post–World War II period, hundreds of national development plans were elaborated, more than 125 central planning offices were established in both rich and poor countries, and about a hundred specialized training centers gave courses in national and regional planning. Yet with more than thirty years of experience behind them, national planners talk more about failures than about successes (Caiden and Wildavsky 1974, Levine 1972, Martin 1969). "Why are experts left out of policy decisions?" they ask. Why don't politicians, experts, and administrators work together? Why is planning failing? The experts are aware that their own training and orientations are deficient and that their own tendency to downgrade political action is a source of frustration:

> [The planner] must persuade others that he serves a useful purpose and is not a fifth wheel to the coach. He may also have to spend more time learning how to make friends and influence people than how to make models. (Martin, p. 41)

Failure also leads to discouragement. The experts are prone to assume that if planning does not work it means that rationality cannot prevail in society as presently constituted. The apparent inability of the political mind to comprehend professional technical issues depresses them. The way politicians disregard their recommendations astonishes them. At most they assume that planning does not fit with politics:

> Could it be that the aims and methods of many planners are at variance with those who have the final say in the determination of policy or who are responsible for the day-to-day implementation of proposals? In the march forward who is the one out of step? Do most planners understand the problems involved in running a government, are they capable of handling day-to-day crises and, to paraphrase the words of Rudyard Kipling, can they keep their heads when all about them are losing theirs and blaming it on them? (Martin, p. 41)

Ultimately, the revolt of beneficiaries who do not seem to

understand the subtleties of the economic or social situations in which they find themselves, leads the experts to believe that planning has to be imposed from the top because the beneficiaries at the bottom cannot perceive the outcome of their own actions. The experts become increasingly impatient with democratic politics and insist that in times of crisis leadership has to be reaffirmed.

By then, the unwitting political actor is calling for large-scale centralized power to force implementation and acceptance of his or her recommendations. The mild liberal reformists have become conservative and dogmatic; they act as if systems expertise has to be elitist and manipulative:

> The liberal majority among city planners have lately defined planning as the act of getting the cities "back under control." By this they mean organizing the social life of the modern city into a single unit so that conflicts can be handled centrally. Control seems to them the primary problem: once the cities are made susceptible to central planning by a few in the name of the many, *what* is to be planned can then be described as the "first necessary step" in dealing with the city's woes. Without a Master Plan drawn by professionals, the city's planners tell us, the substance of New York problems have a "meaningless context" and cannot be solved. . . . Dissenters on both the left and right have called into question the fitness of planning by an elite which is often out of touch with its constituents. (Sennett 1970)

The opposite is excessive success. This happens when the Prince who hires experts has considerable power over implementers; for example, when federal agencies mandate obligatory evaluations of the programs they fund (Guttentag and Struening 1975, Suchman 1967). The experts are often unaware of the threat they represent. Since they need output measures to evaluate programs, they plunge ahead urging that organizations collect output measures. But as is often the case, output measures only capture a limited aspect of the tasks undertaken by organizations. Nevertheless, once the measures are collected, they become important in their own right, the staff is obliged to produce "good" measures if they want continued funding, and the outside experts discover they are unwittingly altering the organization. By then, it is too late to back off, the success of the programs can be jeopardized, the staff of the implementing agency is sullen; the experts begin to see them in adversary roles, and sometimes the ultimate outcome is deterioration of service.

Experts as the New Elite

A DILEMMA OF complex interdependent technological societies can be summarized by two opposing needs: (1) the need for technology, which implies increasing specialization, interdependence, expertise, and the funneling of planning information through societal control systems that reduce the accessibility of decision-makers; and (2) the need for individual and group self-expression and self-determination, which calls for higher levels of effective political participation.

The role dilemma of our modern-day expert is symptomatic of the underlying structural problem. Can modern social structures be adapted to maintain desirable individual and group needs for effective political participation while at the same time fulfilling the rigidities imposed by technology?

This question is not without theoretical significance, since an important and respected school of thought in American political science had been demonstrating both theoretically and empirically that political development goes hand in hand with modernization and, more particularly, with the development of a worldwide political culture (Almond and Verba 1965), a political culture that James S. Coleman summarizes as:

> . . .the prevalence of a scientific and rational outlook, the primacy of secularity in human relations, "at least a formal acknowledgment of humane values," the "acceptance of rational-legal norms for governmental behavior," and "deference to democratic values . . . at least in the minimum sense of encouraging mass involvement in political activities." The quintessence of the political character of this emerging world culture is a "political culture of participation" which leads to the concept of the modern "participatory state." There are two models of the latter: the totalitarian with its subject political culture, and the democratic with its civic political culture. (Coleman 1965, pp. 14–15)

A natural optimism seemed to prevail in this literature. But it appears to be misleading. Undoubtedly it is pleasant to believe that a wider diffusion of the amenities of life—shelter, food, education, and health protection—leads to a more reasonable political culture of participation. But as we see only too clearly, there also exist structural constraints: not everyone can participate in all the decisions that affect one's life; there is not enough time, not to mention capability. As a result, experts have acquired a new social role: they have become a social class in its own right. As a social class, experts can be expected to protect their own interests—which need not be representative of those of the general public (Armstrong 1973; Bell 1973, pp. 375–78; Thoenig 1973, pp. 197–279). The question, then, is far more complicated. We must ask how social structures can be modified to allow the process of technological change without impairing, beyond limits acceptable to citizens, the level of their participation in important decisions that affect them. In addition, what kinds of institutions are needed to allow this kind of participation? Ultimately we have to ask what rates of technological change can be sustained without impairing social structures. But before we can ask these questions, we need to perceive that policy analysis, evaluation, and planning are both politics and technique and that the role of experts involves both dimensions.

The Anti-Expert Reaction

EXPERTS FACE OPPOSITION (1) when they disclose facts tending to invalidate political ideologies; (2) when they seem to be acquiring political power; and (3) when scientists begin to fear repression of their disciplines because of a reaction against experts.

When the planners confront conventional party ideologies with facts, they may alter the influence of these ideologies. The search for facts and the repercussions of facts on ideology are not problems for policy analysts only. Any social scientist dealing in politically sensitive areas must be concerned. But policy research is always oriented to sensitive areas, and therefore there are more opportunities for analysts to uncover unwelcome facts.

In the more common situation, analysis is sponsored by an agency which expects to obtain a report supporting a given policy option, but the data is inconclusive or points the other way. Often the sponsor attempts to suppress such reports, since the agency might be damaged by it. For example, the 1966 study sponsored by the U.S. Office of Education, the so-called Coleman Report, was expected to show gross inequalities in resources reaching black and white students. The study used data and analysis that did not make these inequalities as clear as was expected, and, as a result, the study remained relatively inaccessible, for some time at least, until it was picked up in Congress and by the mass media (Coleman 1972, p. 13). Many other examples can be mentioned, but the more visible and interesting cases usually take place abroad when policy research or even social science research undertaken by Americans is embarrassing to foreign governments. The reason foreign cases are more visible is simply that it is much easier for a government to object to research undertaken by non-nationals than it is to object to the work of local social scientists. Conversely, foreigners are often quite insensitive to local situations (Beals 1969, Berreman 1969, Horowitz 1967). For example, a typical case is that of the anthropologist Oscar Lewis, whose books on the culture of poverty in Mexico were attacked by the Mexican Geographical and Statistical Society (Beals 1969, pp. 11–19). The reason is simple: Oscar Lewis, in his well-known studies of the life style in poor urban neighborhoods in Mexico (Lewis 1959, 1961), provides material for anthropologists and sociologists concerned with the culture of poverty. He also provides a ready source of ammunition for opponents of the dominant political party in Mexico.

Experts who are insensitive to the ideological repercussions of their work are always surprised when they encounter opposition. But they should not be; they should expect such reactions and plan for their occurrence.

The second source of opposition emerges when experts begin to influence decisions. As long as no one pays any attention to their recommendations, no one cares who they are. But when experts influence decisions, the question arises: by what right is their voice to be heard? If the experts on the staff of a government agency charged to protect consumer interests insist on certain safety standards, the question immediately arises: by what right do these unelected bureaucrats insist on measures that imply additional costs to industry? Who is to say that one life saved because of improved safety standards should cost a company and ultimately the consumer an extra thousand or million dollars? Who is to define what is right and wrong? To succeed, experts need more than analysis, they also need political support.

The more experts acquire power of their own, the more they become suspect to politicians. Since experts are supposed to be technicians, the Prince is suspicious when they do not seem to be playing their expected role. If, in addition to gathering indiscreet facts, they also appear to be fomenting political action, the Prince will be convinced that his experts have gone beyond the bounds of good conduct. At some point he will want to eliminate these undesirable competitors. Thus, the role of experts is difficult to play and opposition is unavoidable.

Finally, to compound difficulties, experts face opposition from other social scientists because these scientists fear the repercussions of generalized reactions against all policy experts on their own work. The anti-expert reaction—"do not bother me with facts, damn the experts"—can quickly become an attack against all social sciences and ultimately against all scientists and intellectuals.

Bona fide scientists and other intellectuals are not ready for this attack and they seek to dissociate themselves from it. As a result, an additional anti-expert or anti-technocrat movement is generated by scientists and intellectuals who rapidly become concerned that the anti-rationality movement will result in penalties to them and will be detrimental to the general advance of the arts and sciences.

Since the social sciences are most vulnerable and the most closely associated, they are the first to generate this kind of anti-technocrat reaction. Their call for value-free social sciences becomes louder when the social sciences fear political intervention.

Politicians' suspicions are a perennial problem in the United States (Lyons 1969), in Western Europe (Dogan 1975, Meynaud 1964), and particularly in the Soviet Union (Gehlen 1969) where the boundaries between party dogma and the domains of expertise are continually challenged. The dissociation of bona fide scientists emerges from these reactions but the anti-expert stance of scientists is no less real and no less obstructive to the playing of expert roles.

Academic suspicions about the think tanks, such as the RAND Corporation or the Stanford Research Institute (Neiburg 1966), are not limited to suspicions about the quality of the research that takes place in those institutions or to the dislikes of the political objectives pursued; they can also arise from genuine concern about the political costs incurred by all social scientists when the think tanks engage in policy work, particularly in programs that are unpopular with the clientele of universities. Within the universities, fear of involvement breeds strange alliances between those who decry the evils of the institutions of government and reject the establishment and those who seek to divorce the university from action-oriented policy research. Thus, the university finds it increasingly difficult to engage in policy research, and this results in shifts of research funds from universities to the more tightly controlled think tanks.

All of these problems emerge in part from the absence of role definition between science and political action in the context of science. It is one of the growing pains of the creation of a new social role. But awareness of this problem can also be the basis of a solution. As experts begin to perceive the political dimensions of their role and as politicians and social scientists come to expect our pundits to make political commitments and take political actions, the growing pains of the new profession may be alleviated.

The Political Dimension of Expertise

EXPERTS ARE INVOLVED in politics, and politics are never devoid of ideological content. Therefore our pundits are, wittingly or unwittingly, involved in ideological issues. They cannot escape making commitments to normative definitions of the good life.

As long as this new profession remains uncommitted to political ideologies, the effect is to make each and every technocrat the overt or covert agent or fomenter of his or her own private ideology. In such circumstances, the systems experts, the policy analysts, the evaluators, programmers, and planners are no more than accidental political agents in a fragmented social order.

My question, therefore, is not whether technocrats might animate a world of robots, but whether experts accept the responsibility of their potential political role in society. It is evident that a fragmented profession cannot hope to accomplish political acts as long as experts behave as if they were not involved politically and as long as they sharply limit the domain of their political norms and values.

To organize experts requires the conscious selection of a limited yet diversified domain of values where a professional consensus can be achieved. If technocrats in Western democracies are to be useful, i.e., able to reduce uncertainty to desirable or tolerable levels without bringing about totalitarian regimes, they cannot remain unconscious of their social function and they cannot remain fragmented. If they are inevitably involved in politics, they had better know it, organize themselves, and become both experts and committed political actors. Their role mystification may have been inevitable initially, but the time has come to shed the mask, at least among members of the profession. If all or part of the profession shares even a minimum set of values, it should find out what those values are and defend them. If experts are to espouse causes, if they want to support this or that group, champion the needs of beneficiaries, defend the interests of their Prince, or simply protect their own jobs, they need, at the very least, to be aware of the political dimension of their role.

two

Uncertainty and Implementation

TECHNOLOGICAL CHANGE creates uncertainty and uncertainty brings about a need for experts. Why? Because policy analysts, programmers, and planners deal with future events. Even evaluators are concerned with the future: evaluations of past programs are used to choose among future options.

Some scientists suggest that the rate of technological change will slow down but it will not stop:

> Many technological changes are now approaching certain natural limits. The "S curve" is beginning to level off. We may never have faster communications or more TV or larger weapons or a higher level of danger than we have now. This means that if we could learn to manage these new powers and problems in the next few years without killing ourselves by our obsolete structures and behavior, we might be able to create new and more effective social structures that would last for many generations. We might be able to move into that new world of abundance and diversity and well-being for all mankind which technology has now made possible. The trouble is that we may not survive the next few years. (Platt 1969)

Kenneth Boulding suggests that mankind suffers from "agoraphobia," the fear of the marketplace of ideas:

> There seems to be a fundamental disposition in mankind to limit
> agenda, often quite arbitrarily, perhaps because of our fears of
> information overload. We all suffer in some degree from agora-
> phobia; that is, *the fear of open spaces,* especially *open spaces* of the
> mind. As a result, we all tend to retreat into the cozy, closed
> spaces of limited agendas and responsibilities; into tribalism,
> nationalism, and religious and political sectarianism and dogma-
> tism. (Boulding 1966, p. 167)

If mankind fears excessive uncertainty, it also fears excessive
certainty. We avoid totally closed spaces. While we differ about
what is stimulating and what is not, we fear the malady of ennui;
we retreat from absolute routines as well as from lack of chores.
More significantly, we retreat from total certainty, because chal-
lenges are necessary for self-awareness and self-determination.
Georges Sorel, in his analysis of violence in social life, quotes
Ernest Renan: "People die for *opinions* and not for *certitudes*"
(Sorel 1950 ed., p. 45).

Technology creates uncertainty by providing many new options for action: the more we have new ways of doing things, the
more it is unclear which course of action we will adopt, and our
behavior becomes more uncertain. Moreover, technological
societies are composed of many subunits that are articulated
among themselves. What an individual or an organization does
creates consequences for many other individuals and organizations. Therefore, when the rate of technological change accelerates, when options for action multiply, and when social systems
become complex, interrelated, and integrated, a need to see
ahead emerges:

> When the change-rate was slower, policy could be largely cor-
> rective, acting after the event. With a faster change-rate, it has to
> become more anticipatory, acting before the event. This relates
> it to planning. The task of government now extends from regu-
> lating the present to creating the enabling conditions for the
> future. (Trist 1970, p. 302)

Two Varieties of Uncertainty

WE MAY BE UNCERTAIN about what will happen next. We
may want to know how our environment will change or
how we, ourselves, will change. This is one type of uncertainty.

Or we may want to know what to do next: how we should act, what course of action we should pursue. This is a second type of uncertainty. Policy analysts, evaluators, programmers, and planners are always answering two kinds of questions: what might happen? and what might we do?

Experts scan and analyze existing information to make probabilistic statements about future events: for example, a group of experts undertakes a forecast of the probable range of energy consumption and production to the year 2000; or they analyze all relevant information to provide a basis for determining a reasonable course of action: experts determine the potential for alternative sources of energy and recommend investments in research on solar, wind, and nuclear energy; they study ways to save on energy consumption and to foment exploration for conventional sources.

The fact that experts deal with uncertainty has two important consequences. First, it means that experts are in demand in crisis conditions when there exists much uncertainty. In the next pages we examine how planning was initiated in a Communist country (the Soviet Union) and a capitalist country (France), and we see how certain historical events created acute conditions which necessitated initiation of nationwide planning.

Second, and more importantly, it means that experts have to deal with people's beliefs about the future. In other words, it is not rationality per se that matters but power or trust. Experts can reduce uncertainty to the extent that they are perceived to have power and/or are trusted. They are trusted to the extent that they succeed in reducing uncertainty.

Origins of Planning in the Soviet Union and France

PLANNING WAS NOT included in the initial ideological commitments of the Russian Revolution. Very little was said about planning by any of the Marxist writers. Planning took place after the revolution; it arose independently of the ideology. It arose from the problems of taking control of the production apparatus; in fact, it followed that takeover.

A large portion of trade and industry had remained in private hands after the 1917 revolution. The bourgeois managers were kept for a number of years and many economic institutions were not taken over until 1927. The Supreme Council of National Economy, an operational organization, was established in December 1917, and it gradually acquired control and responsibility for running industry and trade. But this monolithic, bureaucratic attempt to organize production and distribution was short-lived. Yet even during its short life span, the council had to make difficult decisions on resource allocations between the competing units within its own structure. Therefore, it created an internal planning bureau. This bureau elaborated the first five-year plan for 1928–1933. This was nearly ten years after the revolution.

Meanwhile, the agency that was to become the principal planning body, the Gosplan, had been established in 1921. At first it was only a minor planning group attached to the Council of Labor and Defense and therefore some distance from the operational controls of the Supreme Council and its own planning bureau. It undertook more theoretical and longer-range planning studies and did not draft the first five-year plan.

A Planning Academy was founded in 1930 to train young but seasoned party members for senior executive posts in the rural areas, and the Gosplan's own Institute of Economic Research and other institutes began to train an elite of planners. By the time the Supreme Council was abolished in 1932, the Gosplan had acquired control of the Central Statistical Office. It therefore became a central and principal source of planning capability.

One year before, in 1931, the Gosplan was reorganized and was divided into eleven sections, dealing with energy, industry, agriculture, construction, consumption, distribution, labor, culture, science, statistics, and the organization of planning itself, and it began to coordinate the planning taking place within the various and more decentralized ministries that acquired operational responsibilities formerly held by the monolithic Supreme Council of National Economy.

This early period of Soviet planning went through two phases:

(1) the creation of a formal institution of production and distribution, i.e., the Supreme Council, and the creation within that formal organization of a policy research and planning capability; and (2) the creation of a decentralized formal apparatus of production and distribution with a strong external planning institution to help articulate and orient the economy.

The research undertaken during the initial years of Soviet planning was not very sophisticated. Nevertheless, the Gosplan helped to make decisions on priorities for resource allocation, and it provided some benchmarks for future developments.

Early Soviet planning was a response to the needs of a government that had abolished one basis for making economic decisions, i.e., private incentives and market mechanisms. As control of the economy passed from private hands to those of an emerging state bureaucracy, a major crisis of uncertainty arose from the need for coordination and articulation. The government faced a decision-making overload that planning helped meet. The research may not have been very sophisticated, but it was sufficient to create an image of the future that allowed decision-makers in many different bureaus, agencies, and departments to orient their own action toward it. While the "quality" of the image and the content of the policies the government pursued are important, from my point of view here, it is the act of creating the image which is interesting. Without it the system would not function.

The Soviet case and those of other socialist countries are somewhat different from planning developments in Western Europe or North America, because those socialist governments nationalized most of the means of production and eliminated many of the market mechanisms that still prevail in capitalist economies. But the usual assumption that national planning goes hand in hand with government control of the means of production does not hold. As in the case of France, planning also emerged in capitalist countries when the future had to be made less uncertain.

Planning in socialist countries is sometimes referred to as "imperative" because the government has extensive means of control on the operations of all the firms, communes, government ministries, and other organizations that implement the plan. At present, Soviet firms are directly controlled by ministries of the government, but they have some leeway as to how they operate and how they finance their expansion. The plan spells out the production targets to be reached and sets prices such that when production targets are reached, the firms make a profit. Part of that profit is used to expand production and part is used to pay bonuses to workers and employees. Therefore, there exist direct incentives which make factory managers and workers desirous of having the plan implemented.

In contrast, national planning in capitalist countries is referred to as "indicative" planning because the government does not have, or at least does not appear to have, as much influence on the private sector. Therefore, the plan is an "indication," an orientation as to where to go.

French indicative planning relies on government persuasion and other legal and financial means to orient the actions of the private sectors to goals jointly elaborated by labor, private, and government sector representatives in the context of a national planning institution called the Plan Organization. It partially reflects the distribution of power in French society. Yet the emergence of French planning was very similar to that of the Soviet Union even if the actual conditions were different.

French planning did not follow in the footsteps of a revolution; it grew from the devastation of war. It arose in conditions of crisis caused by the collapse of the French economy. It was conceived during the Second World War and initiated at the time of liberation. The major preoccupation of the Jean Monnet Plan was to rationalize the use of American assistance. An emergency plan to use this aid was drawn up as early as 1944.

Immediately after the liberation, the government initiated a large-scale, yet limited, nationalization program. Electricity, gas, coal, railroads, and some banks and insurance companies were taken over by the state. A Ministry of the National Economy was established to acquire operational responsibility for the nationalized industries. But this particular ministry was short-lived, partially because of the threat it presented to the more traditional ministries (e.g., the Ministry of Finance) and partially because of the opposition of the private sector. The government faced a crisis regarding resource allocation that was similar to the larger-scale crisis in the Soviet Union. Moreover, the private sector feared the government's intervention in the economy, and indicative planning was perceived as a plausible substitute for larger-scale nationalization. It would provide a rationale for the transformation and modernization of the economy without abolishing the private sector. The Plan Organization, a revolutionary idea for France, was suggested by Jean Monnet; it was formally established in 1946, and elaborated a first plan for 1947–1952. In time, planning was institutionalized and its concerns were gradually broadened.

The Plan Organization is still a small ministry, but its influence goes far beyond the numbers employed on the staff. It has become so much an instrument of the administration that a coalition of political parties of liberal tendencies attempted in 1964 to elaborate a counterplan to break the monopolistic position of the Plan (Cohen 1969). As a result, the French parliament insisted that the planners present them with plan options to allow that body to exercise some choices instead of having a single finished, coherent product to deal with, a product that could either be adopted or rejected but could not be modified. But the attempts of the left and of parliament to participate in planning (starting with the fifth plan for 1966–1970) were not particularly successful. During those years the planners were well-entrenched, and had enough support in the private sector and government to ignore the left and leave parliament with the taste of planning but not the reality.

> Perhaps the Parliamentary debates served an educative function in making the issues of planning clearer to the public, but the Government's ability to ram through exactly what it wanted made it quite impossible for anyone to hold the illusion that Parliament had actually *participated* in planning. (Cohen 1969, p. 230)

The French and Soviet models of planning are quite different. The content of the plans, the social policies pursued, the administrative arrangements and the processes of participation in planning reflect the political and administrative realities of each country. But they emerge from similar conditions of uncertainty, and these in turn are the source of the experts' power.

Centralized Power and Implementation

THERE EXISTS A conventional notion that planners and government need strong power to plan; that planning has to be "imperative" in nature; and that short of centralization and strong executive control to impose the plan, it will fail. A distinguished French planner who worked in India in the late fifties made this argument:

> I underline the idea that for genuine economic planning socialisation of the ownership of the means of production is needed. I am bound to say that the attempt towards economic planning in India has completely confirmed this view. (Bettelheim 1959, p. vii)

Gunnar Myrdal reviewed the Indian experience ten years later and came to a more pragmatic evaluation. Myrdal argued that planning in India and Pakistan had not emerged from needs, but as an idea of the elite (Myrdal 1968, p. 739). Therefore, it was programmatic: planning was preceding necessary changes instead of responding to them. But in time, Myrdal believed, planning would take root in the real needs of the situation.

To understand Bettelheim, it is necessary to distinguish between planning and the content of policies and plans; between process and any set of ideological goals, such as rapid economic growth, full employment, and the redistribution of income to achieve equality of opportunity. Bettelheim was not really suggesting that planning would fail in India; he was criticizing the political structure and its ability to achieve the goals of economic development. In other words, his assumption that planning requires complete government centralization and strong controls equates the success of Indian planning with the success of a selected set of policies. Given the political structure of India at the time Bettelheim wrote about it, it was doubtful that the growth policies could ever succeed. But this does not mean that planning fails or does not exist.

In a similar vein, a recent study of eleven non-Communist countries concludes that national development planning should be abandoned:*

> Controlling the future direction of a society—which is what planning, properly interpreted, is about—cannot be the work of a few men called planners or political leaders. (Caiden and Wildavsky 1974, p. 312)

According to the two authors, planning is wasted motion because planners or governments cannot control all aspects of economic life. Given the existing political reality of the countries surveyed, the authors suggest that reforms of the budgetary process, strong control by finance ministries, and focus on the specific projects the government will finance would yield better results.

Without realizing it, Caiden and Wildavsky have joined forces with Bettelheim. They are saying, in effect, that without strong centralized government control of the means of production, plans are not going to be implemented; therefore, governments in poor but democratic countries should not waste time attempting to plan all aspects of economic life, including the private sector. They should concentrate instead on the government budget and on specific development projects.

The argument about the necessity of imperative planning rests on the assumption that experts serve a powerful Prince who can implement the plan. But this assumption is erroneous. Even the most powerful Prince cannot always decide what to do or cannot always impose decisions on all the minions of the kingdom. Experts, whether they be policy analysts, evaluators, or planners, always serve a Prince who has limited power and is therefore attentive to the political environment. If a federal agency sends experts to evaluate a program in a city, if this program is very popular among many clients and has considerable political support among influential leaders in and out of government, the federal agency is going to move cautiously before it listens to experts who want to abolish it.

---

*Ghana and Uganda in Africa; Argentina, Chile, and Peru in South America; Indonesia, the Philippines, Malaysia, and Thailand in Southeast Asia; Ceylon and Nepal in South Asia.

Even when experts work "in house" in a single large organization for a central management that has the necessary authority and therefore considerable power about what is decided and done, there still exist many semi-independent fiefdoms headed by strong department heads, the lieutenants of the Prince who are not going to be easily swayed and who are jealous of their own influence. These fiefdoms are not going to be easily disposed of. Even if experts make sense, management will think twice before it moves against the wishes of these centers of influence.

Moreover, nothing in the structure of centralized organizations guarantees that a Prince has to listen to the advice of experts. The fact that so many intelligence failures have been documented in the past (Wilensky 1967) illustrates how centralization or control of the means of production is no guarantee that the advice of experts will be listened to. The politics of expertise prevail any time there exist different ideas about what might happen in the future and what might be done about it.

The central point that must be understood at the outset is that all interventions of experts take place in a political environment. This is true of the Soviet Union as it is true of General Motors or Afghanistan or of a Quakers' meeting. Experts exercise influence to the extent that they acquire power or are trusted. When experts disregard political reality, they usually fail. Many failures of planning, programming, policy analysis, or evaluation are not failures due to a lack of centralized government power, but failures of experts who are misguided in believing that it was sufficient to conduct research to achieve a consensus about the future.

The suggestion that planning should be abandoned should not be taken literally, and when it is, it is an oversimplified interpretation of the problem. The governments of poor countries face many constraints and cannot afford to make too many mistakes. To be sure, modernization and economic development is a complex process which cannot be totally rationalized. But some coherence and rationality has to prevail. Experts in the employ of a national planning agency have an overall perspective of the way the entire economy is changing and can, to a limited extent at least, articulate government policy and foment private-sector initiatives. Caiden and Wildavsky are correct to urge improvements in budgeting practices, but good budgeting can benefit from the longer time horizon and wider-spectrum perspective of planning. The point is not to abolish planning, but to consider what should be planned and what should not. I emphasize that the real issue of planning consists in determining what can be planned profitably and what cannot be planned ahead of time and should be left to be solved when the problem emerges.

We will return to this issue later in this book. For the moment, it will suffice to mention that this is not an easy problem to quantify. Nevertheless, when experts become aware of *both* the costs and benefits of their interventions, they can decide how to answer these questions.

Power and Images of the Future

INVENTING IMAGES OF the future and reducing uncertainty involves social power. In fact, it is not uncertainty per se that brings about a need for planning, but the absence of sufficient social power to deal with it.

Max Weber defines social power as the ability of persons to carry out their will even when opposed by others (Weber 1947 ed., p. 151). Power can also be understood as the ability to handle uncertainty. A strong dictator has access to many political resources and does not fear uncertain future events. Whatever eventuality arises, he will be able to carry out his will whatever the conditions he encounters in the future.

Strong political actors do not need the advice of well-meaning experts and planners. These Princes care little about planning and optimization because uncertainty does not affect their chances of success. Evidence of this is common. For example, when bilateral and multilateral aid agencies insisted on planning, many strong governments in developing countries accepted foreign experts for prestige reasons or to facilitate aid negotiations. But these acts did not necessarily mean that the governments needed experts to reduce uncertainty. In fact, many highly qualified economic planners in countries under strong governments have served to reaffirm the fact that a strong government has the ability to disregard advice completely. And the more local officials disregard the foreign experts, the more they reaffirm their own independence and power. As a foreign expert told me:

> Here, when the government can do as they fancy, when they disregard the international advisors, they show who is really boss around town. There is no point trying to marshal facts and figures because they will not pay any attention to them . . . in fact they will often do just the contrary of what we propose—because it suits them and at the same time puts us in our place.

Of course, situations arise where the prevailing uncertainty is perceived to be too costly for the policy-makers. Many risks are involved in selecting policy options, the penalties for making erroneous choices are high, and the resources to handle errors are not available. In an interdependent world where the vagaries of world trade, aid, and other exchanges can affect even the strongest political regime, the call for planning is always present in some form or another.

The call for planning is a call for new political resources. For example, government intervention in the economy results in uncertainty. When the market economy is no longer left to the hazards of individual choice because individual decisions conflict with a collective goal, other forms of resource allocation are instituted. The political cost of making these allocations is high. We forget that market mechanisms (the exchange of goods in the marketplace, which sets prices and, therefore, the allocation of resources among competing claims) are inexpensive politically, because they dictate who gets what without having to explain why. As soon as the market is replaced by some form of governmental intervention, political costs are incurred whatever course of action is adopted. If prices are manipulated and production altered, there will be malcontents, and the malcontents will blame those who govern. Therefore, the call for planning is a call to reduce these costs. It is the uncertainty of the choices and the need for political resources that bring about the emergent power of the experts.

If planners create new political resources, they also acquire power of their own. The power of planners comes from many sources, one of which is the performance of functions no one else can perform.

An example from small task groups illustrates the argument. Any small task group confronted by an uncertain environment will value the member who helps other members cope with it. He accrues prestige and status as his advice is sought. If the group needs him more than it needs other members, prestige and status become social power. He is able to set a price for his advice, to demand favors in exchange for his services. As Peter Blau has shown, any time you have a hierarchy in an organization faced with a novel external threat, the hierarchy attempts to handle it, but if others arise who can deal with this threat, these others may replace those occupying positions of authority (Blau 1964, p. 135). Therefore, when planners are called in because they can handle the threat of uncertainty, they also alter the existing power structure.

Evidence of this expert power is not limited to planners. For example, Michel Crozier, in a detailed study of an industrial organization, found that the equipment maintenance people in a factory he studied had considerably more prestige and power among the workers than could be explained by their position or profession. He found that the equipment maintenance "experts" acquired their influence and power from the fact that they were able to repair the production machinery when it broke down, which was the most significant uncertainty faced by the production groups. Crozier singled out two kinds of power arising from this:

> First will evolve the power of the expert, i.e., the power an individual will have over the people affected by his actions through his ability to cope with a source of relevant uncertainty. Second, there will emerge the power necessary to check the power of the expert. (Crozier 1964, p. 163)

As Crozier points out, everyone in the organization is an expert of sorts, though his expertise might be extremely humble; therefore, the power relations between members depend on the extent to which anyone is dependent on anyone else and the extent to which anyone can be substituted for someone else. The maintenance people cannot go too far in exercising their power vis-à-vis the manager for the obvious reason that in the final analysis, they might be replaced. Similarly, a Prince may fire his experts if they go too far astray.

If planners can come and go, the same cannot be said of planning institutions. Any Prince can hire or fire his experts, and most will take care to replace them when their influence becomes excessive; but while single experts may be replaced, the institutions of planning remain, and the power of experts accrues to the institutions instead of the individuals. Since planning tends to be unitary—i.e., it usually takes place as a single centralized activity without competition—the power of this single institution may be appreciable.

In ancient Greece and Rome, the capacity to foresee the future, what the Greeks called *mantikē,* provided a formalized social institution to deal with policy uncertainty. The various oracles, such as those at Dodona or Delphi, helped reduce uncertainty, often by relying on the principle of self-fulfilling prophecy. But the social power of the priesthood affiliated with the oracle was limited by potential competition. Better oracles could be discovered, and had to be discovered once an oracle had been obliged to make too many specific predictions that subsequently failed. *Mantikē* was a talent that certain fortunate people had, and, as Cicero pointed out, any nation, enlightened or grossly barbarous, could believe "that the future can be revealed, and . . . recognize in certain people the power of foretelling it" (Flacebere 1965, p. 1). But this talent could also be lost, and changing fashions provided the equivalent of competitive situations between oracles.

In contrast, monopolistic planning institutions have a distinct advantage over the oracles. Since they cannot be easily replaced, they acquire power—often at the expense of legislatures or the executive—and while staffs can be changed from time to time, there is usually considerable elbow room left between the experts and those who hire them. This elbow room arises from the technical dimension of the role. Since the need for expertise and planning is related to reducing uncertainty, overt policies and plans have an effect of their own, the multiplier effect, resulting from the way decision-makers orient their behavior toward more probable future events. As we shall now see, this multiplier effect is a most important source of political power for the expert.

Principles of Implementation

IMPLEMENTATION IS carrying out, accomplishing, fulfilling, producing, or completing a policy, a program, a plan, or an evaluation (Pressman and Wildavsky 1973, p. xiii).

Given two kinds of uncertainty (what may happen, what should we do?), implementation refers to the second of these. If an expert makes a probabilistic statement about what might happen in the future, this statement may be correct or incorrect, but we do not refer to the event's actually taking place as implementation; we simply state that the forecast turned out to be correct. On the other hand, if an expert is asked, "What should we do?" and this expert provides a solution: "We should build a dam on this site," the actual building of the dam is the implementation of the recommendation.

Implicit in this distinction is the notion of resistance to change. The question "What may happen?" implies that there exists no policy option. We simply want to know what might happen in the future if everyone continues to behave as we can expect them to do. On the other hand, the question "What should we do?" followed by "We should build a dam at X" implies that there exist several alternatives. We might build the dam elsewhere or not build it at all. This implies that the proposal will not be implemented automatically. We may find that the dam should be built but there are not enough resources in the development budget, or the site belongs to an agency that is opposed to the dam, or the people who may be affected by the construction are strongly opposed.

There exist two principles of implementation. First, implementation takes place when a system of reward and punishment operates in such a way that most of the relevant implementers perceive advantage in implementing. They either obey orders or know they will accrue rewards if the dam is built: "There is something for most everyone." In many situations, this requires altering the existing system of reward and punishment.

The second principle of implementation is called the multiplier effect. Implementation takes place when many relevant implementers are convinced that implementation will take place in any case. They shift their own behavior to accommodate to this perception and accordingly bring about implementation. If almost everyone is convinced that the dam will be built, the few opponents may desist and everyone begins to act as if it were a fait accompli.

In most situations, both of these principles operate simultaneously. Implementation takes place because "there is something for many" and because it appears that it is inevitable. But whether one principle of the other dominates depends on circumstances.

The first consideration is whether the existing system of reward and punishment can be altered. This is possible if the Prince has considerable authority over the implementers and if the experts can influence the Prince to manipulate the way implementers are rewarded or punished. Suppose enrollments in higher education are decreasing and the Prince wishes to counteract this trend. Obviously, incentives could be provided to increase the flow of students (these might include fellowships, convenient short-term programs, changed admission criteria, tailoring programs to client needs, etc.). This in turn may require new incentives for the faculty (they may be rewarded when they alter programs so as to increase the flow of students). If the Prince can bring about such changes, the flow of students may increase.

Altering the system of reward and punishment may be feasible when experts work "in house," that is, in a single organization with strong management, or when they work for an agency that has considerable authority over the relevant implementers. "In house" experts can convince the Prince to alter pay bonuses to reward certain behavior, or experts working for an agency that provides funding to another may insist that funding only be provided when certain output measures are achieved.

When experts work for a Prince with limited authority, it is not feasible to alter rewards. In those instances, experts have to rely on the multiplier effect. Since most important world issues involve situations where many implementers have to cooperate and no single Prince has the power to guide action, it follows that the multiplier effect may be far more important.

Altering Rewards and Punishments

LET US FIRST DISCUSS the system of reward and punishment. How is this done? As we suggested above: by providing incentives that are clearly perceived by the implementers to be tied to implementation. This means that we have to be able to measure, in some way or another, that implementation took place, and we must be able to reward (or punish) accordingly. This is usually achieved by setting targets for implementation, establishing measures for each of these, sampling performance, and tying incentives such as pay bonuses or other social awards to the achievement of these specific measures. For example, in the Soviet Union, plant managers are under pressure from workers to achieve the plan production targets because their firm will be able to make a profit and they will therefore be able to pay bonuses to all workers. Take another example: suppose a university announces an affirmative action plan whereby it will seek to hire more minorities and women on the faculty. If the university does no more than announce its intent, the faculty, composed mostly of white men, will continue its customary conventional search procedures whereby trusted colleagues and friends in other universities recommend potential talent. After the announcement, faculty searches will continue to operate as they previously did. Should a woman or a minority member be recommended, his or her candidacy will receive attention, but there is no incentive for the faculty to go out of its way to find women or minority candidates. Now, suppose the university provides incentives to the faculty to seek out qualified minority and female candidates. I purposely say seek out; I do not mean hire. If the incentives are attractive, more minority and female candidates will be considered, and if faculty choices are not biased, we can reasonably expect that a higher percentage of minorities and women will be selected than in the past.

Take another example from evaluation and the interventions of federal agencies on local education systems. As a result of federal funding, experts have introduced many new output measures in education. Many local school systems have been obliged to test their students' achievements in reading, mathematics, and other areas on nationwide standardized tests. In some cases, teacher rewards have been altered to provide them with direct incentives to improve the scores of their students. If teachers are rewarded when their students achieve higher scores on standardized tests, the system of reward and punishment may be very effective, and high scores on the standardized test may become a new and important goal for many teachers. This we can call "excessive" implementation.

Experts are often unaware how powerful the system of reward and punishment can be. At times, they may even underestimate the extent to which they can reorient the behaviors of implementers, and "excessive" implementation can take place.

More often they underestimate the process completely. Their recommendations do not take into account that implementers are being rewarded for not doing what they suggest they should do. If a plan is announced but people continue to be rewarded for doing something else, the plan will probably not be implemented. Many federal programs have failed when no care was taken to create incentives at the local level to permit their implementation. Thus, more often than not, funds intended for good purposes (such as creating new urban housing for poor people on federally owned land) were not implemented because the potential implementers (the mayors and urban developers, the federal agencies controlling land in large cities) did not have anything to gain from these programs (Derthick 1972).

The Multiplier Effect

THE MULTIPLIER EFFECT operates on a different principle. Let us assume that we cannot modify the rewards and punishments that motivate the behavior of implementers. For

example, let us assume that we are national planners hired by
the government and we have no way of altering the profits made
by firms in the private sector.

The multiplier effect is directly tied to the reduction of uncertainty. When independent decision-makers have to decide what
to do about the future, they respond to their preferences (i.e.,
to the existing system of reward and punishment) *and* to their
subjective assessment of what is going to happen in the future
and the way future events affect their preferences. We may
prefer A to B but if we are convinced B will happen and A will
not, we may shift and act as if we really preferred B to A.

Let me be more explicit. You and I usually make decisions in
light of our preferences. These preferences may be determined
by what we think is important, the values we espouse, and the
goals we pursue for ourselves and for the groups with which we
identify. I ask for a raise because I prefer to have more money
than I now receive. You prefer to plan a trip to Florence instead
of spending money on a new station wagon. More often, these
preferences reflect our own assessment of the system of rewards
and punishments in organizations. A government bureau chief
wants to expand her program, and she submits a new budget
request for a twenty percent increase in funds, because she
believes that such an increase will mean rewards for herself, for
her staff, and for her agency and its clients.

Clearly, preferences are not isolated, independent whims of
the mind. If you prefer to plan a two-week trip to Florence
instead of spending money for a new station wagon, it is because
you believe you might possibly go to Florence. Your preferences are related to their possibility. Given more resources, you
might consider a trip around the world, including a month in a
houseboat on the Kashmir lakes and six weeks to discover the
beauties of the Khmer palaces of Cambodia. But you know what
is possible. While you would prefer to take the houseboat, the
trip around the world is not at all probable. You do not even
consider it.

In like manner, policy-makers do not make decisions only on
the basis of their preferences. They also associate subjective
probabilities with the desirable outcomes they pursue. The

government bureau chief prefers to expand her programs three-fold in coming years, but she is not going to request a threefold budget increase because she is already convinced that such a request has little chance of being granted. She requests a twenty percent increase, because she knows there is a high level of probability that she might get at least a ten percent increase if she asks for twenty.

When the subjective probabilities associated with preferences are altered, decisions are also altered. If you hear, via the grapevine, that your rich uncle is seriously considering giving you a large present, you will rush and arrange for the houseboat—just in case—assuming there is a fifty-fifty chance he will come through with the check. If the government bureau chief discovers that the new plan includes a substantial increase of resources for programs such as the one she heads, she initiates a new budget request for a fifty percent increase.

Planners and experts are able to have a multiplier effect on public and private decision-makers when the statements they make about the future are perceived to have a high probability of proving true. Therefore, the way experts present their plan or recommendations provides an additional source of social power.

Two central factors come into play in creating perceptions of the subjective probability that a plan will be implemented: (1) the apparent rational or scientific basis of the experts' statement, and (2) the known supportive commitments of a number of implementers sufficient to create a belief that the plan will become a reality.

It is difficult to oppose a course of action that appears to be inevitable. Few valiant fighters will organize for a losing cause. In some instances the judicious combination of rational logic, elements of scientific determinism, and known commitments by a coalition of supporters places the experts in a powerful position from which is it most difficult to dislodge them.

This is nowhere more evident than in the elaboration of policies of national defense. The logic of deterrence based on a rational "cool-headed" calculus of the way two or more opponents deal with threats, responses to threats, reprisals, counter-reprisals, limited wars, arms races, brinkmanship, and even surprise attacks, provides a theoretical basis for argument that cannot be disregarded short of questioning the fundamental assumptions that underlie it (Shelling 1963). Moreover, the subjective probabilities associated with the probable actions of the opponent and the well-known principle that one cannot disregard the worst possible outcomes, combine to create social situations with a momentum of their own, a pervasive inevitability that alters the mode of thinking of the actors in the situation.

In such conditions, expert access to intelligence, particularly classified intelligence that is difficult to evaluate or question, combined with the known existence of a significant coalition of political supporters, provides experts with an indirect multiplier strength that allows them to exercise more influence than they could achieve directly.

There is, of course, a distinct style to this kind of influence process. Reliance on a considerable body of expertise, and on access to secret information provides a foundation for the apparent knowledge of the experts. "If you knew what I know, you would not think the way you do," gives a ready answer to those who doubt the wisdom of the expert. The large think tanks and the professional consensus that exists within these organizations provide the first elements of a monopolistic condition of expertise. A multiplicity of separate research institutions working for a single government agency adds to the appearances of scientific legitimacy. Moreover, the genuine conviction and dedication of the researchers who work in such institutions add to their credibility. It is not a trivial matter of inventing false intelligence and it is not the work of an elite of warmongers; instead it is the fundamental process of predetermining possible outcomes on the basis of unquestioned assumptions about human behavior. These provide the strong consensual position of this highly qualified and responsible body of experts. It is this consensus that has a strong impact on other decision-makers.

The alliances these experts can establish with significant political forces, both inside and outside government, become a second set of political resources, which are then multiplied by the actions of many other actors who become convinced of the inevitability of the plan.

Moreover, what is overt knowledge to some can still be covert knowledge to others. Both inside and outside an administration, access to decisions and knowledge can be kept selective. A course of action can be kept a partial secret while public opinion is not yet ready for it, as long as those who are privy to the knowledge are convinced that it is the only possible outcome. Mounting a ladder of proof based on its own untested convictions, an elite of experts can acquire far more influence on the course of events than those who hired them ever intended them to have.

As long as experts are generally convinced of the correctness of their methodologies and as long as they refrain from applying value judgments to the courses of action they advocate, there is a strong probability that they can subvert prevailing values in government and private institutions. Planning failures include those of experts who have no influence and are unable to achieve what they believe to be important. They also include those of experts who acquire too much power, happen to make mistakes, and are surprised to discover that the technical and narrow definition of their role was inadequate and led them to disregard widely shared values.

Experts and Implementation

WHY SHOULD EXPERTS be concerned with implementation?

First, because a Prince who hires experts does not usually hire them to dream about impossible futures. When experts are hired to recommend courses of action, they are hired to recommend courses of action *that are feasible.*

Second, because experts are professionally concerned with the consequences of their recommendations. It is not possible to be an expert and not be concerned with the way one's recommendations are received. Are they accepted? rejected? forgotten? or excessively implemented?

How do experts concern themselves with implementation?

Three patterns of behavior have been suggested (Hargrove 1975, p. 32): first, they can build estimates of the feasibility of different implementation strategies; second, they can go a step further and recommend alternative program designs and organizational structures; and third, they can play an active role in the actual implementation process.

This book assumes that experts practice any and all of these three kinds of intervention. To be sure, there exist very real constraints on the amount of time and effort that some experts can spend on actual implementation, and their contribution is only a very small part of what has to be done by implementing agencies. As we saw in the first chapter, planners tend to be more concerned with implementation than policy analysts. Some planning agencies may even have a staff that specializes in implementation design. But all experts are concerned with implementation, and a concern with implementation means that at the outset the expert is asking the following questions:

—What are the various alternative courses of action that can be recommended?

—For each of these alternatives, who stands to gain, and who stands to lose? among implementers? among beneficiaries?

—For each of these alternatives, can we invent or alter existing rewards and punishments for implementers to increase the probability that the alternative will be implemented?

—For each of these alternatives, can we organize a coalition of supporters among relevant implementers sufficiently large to create a generalized belief that implementation will take place and thus generate the multiplier effect?

—For each of these alternatives, can we describe beneficiaries who will want the service, and can we invent or alter existing patterns of communication so that the beneficiaries can know about the service and know how to use it?

—If the implementers and beneficiaries are many and the programs complex, can we invent an administrative structure that will allow the coordination and activation of all the activities that have to take place to make implementation a reality?

—If the programs are new, can we find and train the necessary talent to undertake them? Will this be possible or will it threaten existing staffs of implementers?

—What legal, economic, financial, and administrative steps have to be undertaken to implement programs? Can it be done in reasonable time? What might be the consequences of failure if the program happens to fail?

Asking such questions is not implementation per se, but it is what is called "implementation analysis," an integral component of the research that experts can undertake (Allison 1975, Bardach 1977). As we shall see in this book, implementation analysis can involve more than analysis, and the demarcation line between what is analysis, what is action toward implementation, and what is political organizing is not always clearly defined.

Implementation Design

W E HAVE DISCUSSED implementation analysis, that is, the analysis of the broad political parameters of the feasibility of pursuing one or another course of action. Once a course of action is selected, implementation design is initiated.

Implementation design is a joint responsibility of experts and of implementation agencies. Some of it is initiated by experts; much of it has to be carried out by the implementing agencies as part of their daily activities.

There are several dimensions to implementation design:

—the legal and legislative dimension. Experts find out if existing laws and regulations permit undertaking a proposed program. When the program involves federal, state, and local authorities, rules and regulations at all levels have to be reviewed. Decisions have to be made to review the course of action in light of legal circumstances or to initiate new legislation to fit needs of proposed programs. The time and cost of instituting new legislation have to be weighed against the need for it.

—the financial dimension. Where and how will the necessary budgets be appropriated? How are these appropriations processed? What are the budget procedures? What is the budget calendar of the implementing agencies? When are budgets submitted? How are approvals obtained? What lead times are involved?

—the operating dimension. What agencies will implement the activity? What new staffing will they require? How can this staff be trained? Where and how will facilities to undertake the activity be secured? Who controls these facilities? How can they be obtained for the proposed activity? Who are the potential clients of the program? How will the clients be selected and treated? Should they be assisted to obtain the new service? Should the service be advertised? How can equity in delivery be assured?

—the planning and coordinating dimension. What agency will coordinate federal, state, and local activities? Can one agency undertake this task? Where should it be located? How should it be funded? What controls will it need? Who will staff it? Is legislation needed to establish it?

—the evaluation dimension. How will the activity be monitored? What kind of reporting is useful? For what purpose? What agency will evaluate the results of the proposed activity? On what basis will the evaluation be conducted? Who will evaluate it? Who will fund this dimension?

Experts are not responsible for and cannot undertake all these tasks, but they are responsible for activating and facilitating the work of the multiplicity of agencies whose cooperation is necessary for the success of the endeavor.

In short, the responsibility of experts goes beyond analysis. How much and how far experts become operational and work in implementation depends on the nature of the involvement: who is the Prince, who are the implementers, what purposes do they pursue? In practice, experts find that in some areas the Prince, his lieutenants, or ardent supporters among implementers are ready to carry on; in other areas, everything has to be done and there is no one to do it. It is this reality that spells out just how much implementation they undertake.

three

Legitimation and
Staff Functions

W E DISCUSS in this chapter two secondary functions of experts: first, the legitimation function of expertise; that is, the use of experts to reassure everyone that decisions taken for other motives appear to have been taken for rational, technical reasons; second, the staff function of experts: the extent to which they become the private staff of their Prince, their role in maintaining secrecy when the situation is explosive and the Prince is attempting to gain time before acting, and their role in defining how to think about issues.

The use of knowledge and rationalization to reduce excessive uncertainty is not the only function of experts. Take the example of national economic planning in the Third World. This planning movement arose from two distinct needs. First, events taking place within these countries—in many of them, the result of a post-independence crisis—made planning essential to reduce uncertainties and to create a new bureaucracy with a strong ideological commitment to modernization. In addition, it was required by external factors, particularly the need of donor governments and international agencies to legitimate post-colonial economic assistance.

These secondary functions of planning result in behavior patterns that are different from those we would expect under conventional role definitions. For example, if planning is used to legitimate decisions that have already been made, experts will be looking for and presenting facts that confirm these choices. Yet there also exist situations where experts provide legitimation for decisions and still exercise professional judgment: for example, when no one has the time to influence or control every detail of their plans.

Sometimes experts play an additional role. Instead of being used only as advisors, they are used as the operational staff of a new Prince. They become agents of bureaucratic innovation: they help the Prince acquire control of his empire. They help the Prince gain time or operate in secrecy. One aspect of this function of experts needs more attention: their role in defining what is relevant in making policy choices. Without knowing it, experts are often too conservative, or even wrong, in their approach simply because their technical bias dominates the way the problem is defined. These functions are important. The purpose of this chapter is to make them explicit so as to understand how experts emerge on the political scene and to clarify some of the sources of experts' power and influence.

Legitimation Functions

AS MANY THIRD WORLD countries achieved independence in the fifties and sixties, the notion of bilateral and international economic assistance replaced the colonial policies of the past. In France, the United Kingdom, and Belgium, the bureaucracies of the colonial ministries were transformed to administer aid programs. In the United States new agencies were created to provide foreign economic aid. International institutions created by the United Nations and regional organizations began to channel resources and talent from the wealthier countries. Private and religious institutions continued or expanded their activities.

Conflicts between donors began to take place as many different organizations representing different interests took an active role in the economic development field. The old-time private organizations, including the religious missions and cultural exchange programs that had been working for many years before independence, confronted the new government aid missions of other countries seeking new zones of influence. The missions from international or regional agencies sought to establish their own identity in aid and often competed among themselves. These conflicts between donors were accentuated by conflicts within the fledgling administrations of the new countries. The donors were confronted with long laundry lists of needs from the recipients and with competing claims from different ministries. The wise recipients were able to play one donor against another. Political pressures to give aid sometimes resulted in too evident and discouraging white elephants.

After several years' experience, the donor agencies became aware that competition among themselves (particularly among non-Communist donors) and the resulting overlap, duplication, and large-scale waste would jeopardize public support at home. Taxpayers were not known to favor government programs of this nature. But if it was necessary to coordinate and rationalize the action of the donors, it was also preferable to achieve coordination without appearing to do so vis-à-vis the recipient countries. The donors needed a rationale for aid, and national planning in each country provided it.

Consequently, in the late fifties professionals in donor agencies, particularly in bilateral and international agencies, acquired a strong belief in planning. They called for national centralized planning in developing countries even when such practices did not prevail at home. President Kennedy proposed that all United States foreign aid be extended on the basis of "orderly planning for national and regional development instead of a piecemeal approach." The charter of the Alliance for Progress requested Latin American countries to create or strengthen existing planning capabilities to to prepare long-term plans (Waterston 1965, p. 36). International institutions and other bilateral aid programs made similar demands. As a result of all this pressure, national planning bodies were created in many developing countries.

Some developing countries were by no means convinced that national economic planning fitted their needs, but they responded with the appearance of planning, if not with the realities. Planning commissions could always be created and fulfill other functions, even if they did not actually engage in much policy research and did not influence policy-making. At least one Latin American country, Mexico, went as far as elaborating a secret national plan that had the double advantage of being useful in external aid negotiations without affecting internal political realities, particularly the opposition of its private sector to any notion of national planning (Benveniste 1970, p. 85).

By the end of the sixties this planning movement was receiving considerable support from the international aid agencies, because their international framework allowed a professional and non-ideological basis for giving assistance to planning in developing countries. Among these agencies the World Bank played a leading role:

> We have initiated a new and expanded program of Country Economic Missions in order to assist the developing nations in their formulation of overall development strategies, and at the same time to provide a foundation for the donor nations and international agencies to channel their technical and financial assistance in as productive a manner as possible. Practical planning in the development field calls for current and comprehensive socioeconomic data. The World Bank Group will gather, correlate, and make available this information to the appropriate authorities. As this program gains momentum, we will schedule regular annual reports on the 30 largest of our developing member countries . . . and biennial or triennial reports on another 60 countries. (Robert S. McNamara, "Address to the Board of Governors," World Bank Group, Copenhagen, Denmark, 21 September 1970, p. 4)

As we saw in chapter 1, planning has not always been successful. There have been evident successes and failures. In the sixties, the World Bank spent much time analyzing past experiences and published a most comprehensive and careful review (Waterston 1965).

There is no single explanation for planning failures, but the evidence suggests that in some cases the failure is a direct result of the function served by experts. Although international experts may believe they are being sent to a foreign country to provide advice on how to do things better, they sometimes discover to their dismay that they are being used by a clever politician who knows what he wants and how to manipulate them to get it. The experts expect to undertake a careful professional study of problems and to recommend the most reasonable course of action, but they sometimes find themselves in the confusing situation of recommending courses of action that are imposed on them. I recorded the following account by one expert on an international aid mission to advise on a large-scale development project:

> Our mission was received by the minister in the early days of our arrival. He told us in no uncertain terms the objectives he was pursuing. He made quite clear the kind of report he expected. While he was very gracious, there was little doubt that we were expected to come up with figures to justify his project and the principal purpose of the project was to make him visible nationally or even internationally. . . . The [sponsoring aid agency] was very excited by the project because of its international repercussions and the way it helps it get a foot in the door here. It made little sense to most of us; the costs were known to be high and the benefits most uncertain. We met every day at dinner time and argued what should be done. Some wanted to resign, but the mission was impotent—we knew the minister would go ahead anyway. . . . For us to resign was no solution, it would only jeopardize our relation with [the aid agency] and make it difficult to serve again. . . .

This legitimation function of experts is not peculiar to foreign aid programs. It extends to any situation where, for one reason or another, a Prince can dominate and control his experts. In this respect, it may appear strange that international experts could be easily manipulated by aid agencies or even by host government officials. We easily assume that host governments are more dependent on foreign aid agencies than the agencies are on them. But in terms of sheer bureaucratic survival, most host government bureaucracies can survive even if one of the aid agencies disappears, whereas few aid agencies can continue to exist without host government approval, since most of the agencies depend on resources that will only be voted if their activities in the host countries are carried on. Therefore, the general lack of enthusiasm for aid in the United States and elsewhere greatly weakens the aid agencies' position in relation to host governments. With the exception of agencies, such as the World Bank or foundations, that rely on their own sources of financing, most aid agencies have to deal with both host governments and political pressures at home. This is not only true of foreign aid; it is also true of many federal and state programs within the United States.

As for the international experts, their dependency on aid agencies varies. Some international experts have permanent appointments in universities or research centers and may appear—at least superficially—to be quite independent of the aid agencies' or the host governments' whims. Yet even this independence may be more apparent than real. The prestige of service on aid agency missions is a valued commodity. Probabilities of positive evaluation and advancement in universities or research centers are enhanced by international service. Many well-known professors have made a name for themselves by multiple international exposure.

Most other international experts are heavily dependent on aid agency service. Because they have specialized in international work, their only employment opportunities are with the agencies and they are at the mercy of agency hiring policies. Many international experts are known independent consultants who provide individual professional services to several aid agencies depending on needs and opportunities. Being blacklisted by one agency can result in the loss of income and even generalized blacklisting by other agencies. A reputation for being "difficult" spreads rapidly in the small international network of aid agencies.

The legitimation function of experts applies equally to planners, programmers, policy analysts, and evaluators. The reason experts are particularly useful in legitimating decisions is that they are expendable. The experts are called by their Prince: "We have decided to do this and this. Now, go and crank out some figures to justify this course of action." If the course of action is successful, the Prince is quick to claim credit; if it fails, he points a finger at the experts, and they can always be replaced.

If there is only one planning institution or one evaluation organization, the dependency of experts on the resources and other amenities provided by their Prince influences the possible extent of manipulation. Therefore, as we discuss American institutions of planning in chapter 5, we will want to contrast the advantages and penalties of a diffuse system of institutions with those of a more centralized planning system. The other important factor here, of course, is professional knowledge. Experts are not easily manipulated in areas where their knowledge is on well-established ground and a professional consensus exists about what is right and wrong. But as we all know, expert knowledge can vary widely in the gray areas of policy where there are options and room for interpretation. This is where the legitimation function flourishes and where the shrewd Prince can often select the advice he wants to hear.

Legitimation can have several dimensions. Sometimes it consists of providing the rationale for decisions that have already been made. Sometimes it may be a rationale for not taking any action. At times it might be used to test resistance to a contemplated action.

Experts are most useful to a Prince who is uncertain about what course of action to follow. Any Prince who announces his intentions and is thwarted loses some of his own political assets and gains nothing. Therefore, a Prince seeks to use others to test new ideas and approaches.

The choice of decoy is relevant. If the outcome of the plan the Prince is testing is unknown, and he wants to be able to repudiate it completely if it fails, he needs a legitimate decoy who can be heard and seen but is nevertheless politically disposable. Policy experts are not only disposable, they can also be filed away for future use at more auspicious times. The expert who is shot down continues to support his proposals in the shelter of academe or elsewhere. He or she can always be brought back into action when political conditions have changed.

The political leader who loses on a new proposed course of

action acquires a reputation for losing, but the expert qua expert does not incur such costs. Moreover, the expert can more easily alter a proposal for technical reasons and present a modified version that takes into account the lessons of past failures. The expert can therefore help the Prince respond to political pressures without giving any overt impression of yielding.

Before the experts test the political reaction to a new program, informal political sanction will be given discreetly, allowing political friends to take their cues and indicate support. If the opposition is devastating and the cause is lost, the Prince will still be able to recoup losses, either by accusing the opposition of disregarding expert advice and thus gaining some modicum of advantage from his attempt at reform or by repudiating the first experts and bringing a second set into service.

This function is well understood in some circles. For example, Harold Wilensky records it in his mid-fifties study of the role of intellectuals in labor unions:

> "They [the union leadership] can use me for a fall guy. They can let me extend myself in a situation. Then if we find it means trouble, they can repudiate me—say that '————'s' statement was unauthorized, made without our knowledge. I'm a decoy. If subsequent judgment is that the line I'm pursuing is a tough one to stick with, they'll dump it. I understand, so it doesn't bother me." (Wilensky 1956, pp. 37–38)

At times the Prince uses experts to legitimate a new public policy and, at the same time, strengthen his own position against contending political forces within his own administration or in the larger political arena. By a judicious use of their talents, a chief executive may use his national planners to reinforce his position vis-à-vis the strong ministries he is not able to control.

The creation of a national planning agency usually reflects the conflict between the central executive and the powerful ministries that surround a president, particularly the finance ministry. When the finance ministry is well entrenched, the central executive is seldom able to pursue political or economic programs that run counter to fiscal dogma. Therefore, the national planning body is usually staffed by economists and other professionals with an intellectual orientation different from that of the ministry of finance.

Even though small, the planning staff acquires considerable prestige and attention and therefore provides a legitimate platform for a national discourse on alternatives to fiscal dogma. Moreover, since the conflict between these two bureaucracies (planning and finance) has to be resolved, it heightens the dependency of the conflicting parties on the arbitration of the chief executive, thus providing new degrees of freedom from the control of the finance ministry and its constituencies.

Similarly, planners serve to counteract pressures from well-organized political groups by becoming the vocal and visible expression of opposing public policies. The Prince encourages them to make highly visible statements and to argue publicly for their position; for example, they might call for more state intervention in the economy, more government spending, or strict measures to retard the perils of the deteriorating physical environment. The Prince uses the arguments of his technicians in negotiations, placing himself in the position of adjudicating between the well-entrenched political forces and the appeal of a legitimate, articulate, and vocal intellectual minority (Benveniste 1970, p. 89).

Public discussion of certain issues provides the experts with visibility. The Prince accentuates this visibility by appearing to listen to their ideas even if he has no intention of acting on them. For a while the Prince seems to be swayed by his advisors. The well-entrenched political forces no longer confront a recalcitrant politician but the logic of a battery of advisors. At that point the Prince is able to exact a high price for not following the advice of his experts. He chooses a course of action that suits him, thus reaffirming his independence from both parties.

But even the experts who provide legitimation for their Prince are not completely at his mercy, at least during the period when the various actors play this game. If the experts are conscious of their role and become aware of the ways they serve the Prince, they will be able to extract some modicum of influence as the small price for their service.

Experts as Private Staff of the Prince

COMING BACK TO the experience of planning in newly independent countries, we said that one factor bringing it
about was the uncertainty of the early days of independence.
The immediate crisis of independence was the departure of the
colonial power. As long as the colonial power was present, the
focus of the national movement for independence was easily
defined and cohesion of political action easily maintained. Once
the common enemy had left, modernization, social justice, and
formal planning combined ideological motives with an institutional framework to refocus national purpose.

Planning helped maintain centralization of direction; more
importantly, it provided a central location away from the existing bureaucratic apparatus and therefore separate from the
existing civil service which had been socialized during the colonial administration. It gave the new Prince his own private staff
and served as a substitute for nonexistent legislative bodies
while these bodies were created and acquired experience under
new constitutions. In short, it became the operational arm of the
elite that had brought about independence.

This function of expertise is most easily perceived in developing countries, but it takes place in any public administration.
Large government bureaucracies are headed by political appointees, but they are staffed by a permanent civil service.
Therefore, any new political appointee can change the bureaucracy if he can obtain the cooperation of the existing staff or
replace it.

The permanent staff of any government bureaucracy invents
its own defenses against the politicians periodically appointed to
head it. A natural defense is to limit sharply the number of
appointments the new appointee can make. The new Prince can
use these positions, which are not protected by civil service
regulations, to bring in a few trusted lieutenants. But outside of
this handful, his ability to fire or replace the existing service is
constrained by statutes and custom. He will therefore have to
attempt innovation in an indifferent if not hostile environment.

The new appointee does not have the luxury of time. The

power he acquires is not expected to last forever. In fact, his own time on the public scene will be short unless he is able to bring about visible results. He needs to be seen, and for this he needs to achieve rapid changes. In contrast, the civil servants under him pursue their own long-term career objectives, which usually do not coincide with his; they are familiar with the terrain and problems and are rarely in a hurry. Their own experience within the civil service has taught them that caution and a long-term perspective are more useful to their career ambitions than risking new ventures.

Systems experts, evaluators, programmers, and planners are an effective personal staff for a Prince in this predicament. First, they help their Prince acquire facts about his bureaucracy. A protective practice in any bureaucracy consists of maintaining high levels of secrecy; what the secretary or minister does not know will not hurt. The civil service is aware that there is no need to inform the hierarchy unless you have to and nothing to gain if you do so. Knowledge is a source of power, and the resulting visibility a source of trouble. Systems analysis, planning, and evaluation provide both the legitimacy and the staff to find out what goes on within the bureaucracy.

In my study of planning in Mexico, I was often struck by the importance of the fact-gathering function. As a top Mexican administrator pointed out:

> "I will tell you why I favor the idea of planning. When governors come to my office to ask for more funds for education for this or that project, I am able to tell them: 'Mr. Governor, did you know that in your state there are already x number of schools of the type you wish to build; the federal government is already spending so much for these schools; did you know these schools satisfy the needs of such and such a percentage of the school-age population, and the project you propose is too large and would take care of a population that does not exist!' . . . In short, planners give me the facts and in this job one needs to have facts. . . . The times have changed, you know; we cannot keep asking for more money without asking ourselves how we spend that money. Those union leaders just have to understand this, the politics of education today are not the politics of education of the past. Today you need facts, you need to have a basis for your arguments and planning gives us those facts." (Benveniste 1970, p. 69)

The direct staff function of the experts is not limited to intelligence gathering. A Prince in search of additional means of control over his bureaucracy will create new operational programs and staffs of his own. The experts provide the infrastructure for these new staffs. Pilot projects and temporary operations are initiated with outside people. This is particularly true in developing countries where international expert assistance is used. The new programs are expanded by forcing the bureaucracy to reorganize. The reorganization itself provides legitimacy for bringing in other outside experts. As pilot projects become operational, the bureaucracy is shuffled around. In that process, undesirable elements are pigeonholed where their influence is lessened.

Most United States government departments go through these periodic reorganizations. Experts on short-term task forces or commissions carry out the work—for example, the various presidential task forces that have, at one time or another, been charged with reorganizing the United States foreign aid program. Outside experts provide the new rationale and design, but a main preoccupation is the elimination of those bureaucrats whose power and control make it difficult or even impossible for the political appointee to act.

The experts who serve their Prince in his efforts to acquire control of his bureaucracy are not without their own sources of influence and power. The Prince depends on them. They can easily sabotage his efforts, and the Prince knows it.

Sometimes a Prince does not or cannot rule directly and he finds it easier to rule through the intervention of experts he controls. For example, when there is a sharp, well-defined, and roughly equal cleavage around a political issue, the Prince may be unable to reduce this cleavage by conventional trade-offs. Any course of action he pursues will result in strong opposition.

In such situations, experts are called to help their Prince justify courses of action that are bound, one way or another, to result in high political costs. They are an additional political resource, and the Prince who faces a divided house brings them in and justifies his choice by turning to "reason" or to the "right" solution. Therefore the sharper the cleavage and the more equally balanced the contending forces, the greater the political vacuum and the more we expect systems experts to be called in and technocratic solutions to emerge.

An example of this was the debate about American involvement in the war in Southeast Asia. In the late sixties, sharp internal political division about American involvement explains the emergence and influence of military and systems experts during this period. Conflict among experts existed, but it was hidden as some experts succeeded in influencing the Prince and dominating the discussion.

A political vacuum also exists when a strong political figure initiates his own succession around the time of elections or in the declining years of his charismatic leadership. Any strong Prince who remains in power for a long time maintains contending and aspiring political forces at a stalemate, i.e., he keeps all those who wish to take his place at each other's throats. The dilemma consists of allowing a favored successor to come close to the Prince, thus letting the successor acquire influence while the Prince retains his own options and his own power.

To limit the influence of the successor during the grooming process, the Prince uses his technicians to create a "non-political" administration. He gives them the appearance or even the reality of influence in the affairs of state. The Prince is careful to keep the technocrats as much under his control as possible while at the same time he gives his successor more power. As a result, a new stalemate exists, although the succession has been initiated.

This modern balancing act was illustrated in Spain by the increase in the influence of technocrats when General Franco began to relinquish control of the apparatus of state. In the late sixties and early seventies, General Franco simultaneously chose his successor and relied on a new government staffed by younger professionals. He encouraged these technocrats to be more concerned with modernizing the Spanish economy and bringing Spain closer to its European neighbors than with the issues and ideology of his regime. They made important changes in Spanish social structures: the entire educational system was reformed to provide access to social classes that had not been favored before. Just before his death, the political tension became excessive and the balancing act was no longer possible. Thus, the technocrats lost some of their influence, though they regained it somewhat after his death as Spain began to democratize its political institutions.

As Jean Meynaud points out in his study of the technocratic order, technocrats have often played political roles, and have even gone as far as joining other forces to topple regimes that did not seem to fit their needs. But even where regimes were toppled, new political forces emerged, and the technicians who had been instrumental in the action did not benefit and did not accrue any further influence (Meynaud 1964, p. 106).

There exists another type of succession that might more correctly be called a retreating maneuver: a political group, which held power and is now losing out to an emergent force, seeks an intervening alternative before yielding power. Experts and planners provide a temporary or even a permanent shield while the offensive of the enemy is contained. For example, the early widespread demand for planning in the war on poverty was less a genuine need for rationalization than a retreating maneuver by existing political forces. The new and well-meaning planners discovered they had been invited into a political arena for purposes quite different from those they had imagined for themselves. They were often unprepared when they discovered that they were strategically placed between two or more rival political factions: usually between the traditional power groups and the emerging forces of the poor and minorities.

Even when the ideology of the programs called for the participation of the poor, the experts provided the first effective mechanism to delay such participation. Peter Marris and Martin Rein illustrate this in their study of the Ford Foundation "grey area" projects:

> A policy of institutional reform clearly could not depend for its mandate only on the support of the institutions to be reformed, however powerful their influence. Mayors, school superintendents, public-spirited bankers, representatives of organized labor, pastors of churches, were not the accredited spokesmen of the poor. They stood rather for the established power.... The Ford Foundation and the President's Committee had already

devised safeguards against the abuse of their aims through . . .
the requirement of rigorous preliminary planning. . . . The grey
area projects were to "plan with people, not for people" [but]
the leaderless, ill-educated, dispirited people of a city slum, if
they could find their voice, would hardly speak to the brief of a
nationally-minded elite of university professors and foundation
executives. Research, planning, coordination, must seem remote
answers to a rat-infested tenement, the inquisitorial harassment
of a welfare inspector, debts and the weary futility of killing time
on the streets. (Marris and Rein 1969, pp. 164–65)

The experts and planners come from one social milieu, while
their clientele includes different ethnic and social backgrounds.
The planners do not have access to the communities they think
they serve. In contrast, they find that they have excellent access
to, and communications with, their social counterparts in the
wealthier parts of town.

The old elites find the planners more accommodating than
the emerging groups; they seek planners on decision-making
bodies to talk for or replace the emerging groups. The *New York
Times* reported on 5 November 1965:

The Budget Bureau has told the Office of Economic Opportunity that it would prefer less emphasis on policy making by the
poor in planning community projects. . . . Those individuals believe that pressure for this policy was coming from the mayors of
big cities, most of whom are Democrats. The mayors have
openly protested demands of the poor for policy-planning positions. The mayors see a threat to their patterns of governing and
to their political security, if the poor develop into articulate,
militant lobbies at city hall.

But the substitution has to be legitimated, and expertise provides the basis for this. Decisions have to be made, the reasoning goes, and the poor are not capable of dealing with the problems at hand. There are too many of them anyhow, so that consultation would take too long and make little sense since those
who have the remedy are not among them. As a staff planner
wrote in a position paper:

"There can be an exaggerated 'democratic' bias which lies behind
the concern for participation in planning by the poor. The
Founders of the American Republic did not suffer from this
bias: they believed that 'pure democracy' was an impossibility,

especially in a country of this size; and they further believed in the wisdom of representation. So, too, in a complex urban context (given the limitations on full participation by any citizens— not only the poor), I personally do not see any substitute for the planner." (Quoted in Marris and Rein 1969, p. 176)

Secrecy and Buying Time

MOST PRINCES HAVE a penchant for secrecy. When they ask experts to study a problem, they usually keep the process under wraps. Secrecy has evident advantages to a Prince. Policy research and planning can be used to hide his intentions until it is too late to change the course of events.

Moreover, the process of planning itself takes time and resources and often needs some protection while it gets under way. If the research and the advice that might result from it are perceived beforehand to favor certain policies and deter others, opposition may be rapidly organized. The sooner the reseach is stopped the better for the opposition, since the facts and figures may speak for themselves.

Therefore it is not unusual that in the early days of any planning and research exercise, every effort is made to stress the noncontroversial nature of the research or to keep it secret. If it is described, it is described in terms as nonpolitical as possible. Once the results are in, political consequences will take place, but by then it is too late to organize the opposition.

The experts help the Prince gain time while the facts are gathered. Once the facts are available, the Prince can move swiftly on the basis of his facts while the opposition is still unprepared. The need for secrecy to protect the experts is also a way for the Prince to gain a lead-time advantage.

Experts help their Prince gain time when political action is contemplated. Conversely, they gain time and give the impression that something is being done when, in fact, no action is contemplated. Examples of this game abound in political life. Take, for example, President Nixon's announcement when he first came to power that he had adopted a "secret plan" to disengage American forces from South Vietnam. Knowledge of the existence of the secret plan served to reassure the general public that the president and his advisors knew what they were up to: the ship of state had purpose and direction. The fact that the plan was secret made it unassailable; it did not provide any opportunity for criticism. Legitimation for secrecy was conveniently provided by the realities of war. The existence of a secret plan meant that a course of action was under way. Since it was under way, it could not be altered readily, and since no one outside a limited circle could be certain of the course of action, the administration could always reject proposals on the grounds that they did not fit the plan. Yet when it suited the administration, the content of the plan could be altered without any loss of face or appearance of yielding to external pressures. Thus the magic of expertise and planning suited the needs of a Prince, at least for a while. In this case, several years were to elapse before disengagement was achieved in Vietnam.

Defining What Is Relevant in Policy

G RIEVANCES ARISE when people become conscious of the nature of their problems. If no facts are available, the participants in a social situation may be dimly aware that something is wrong, that the social situation is not what it might be. Yet they are not able to be precise about their grievance. Facts define the grievance and also the terrain of negotiation between conflicting parties.

The availability of facts and figures determines the choice and mobilization of relevant political actors in the formulation of policies and plans. By relying on experts, the Prince can confer legitimacy on one set of facts rather than another.

In the long and tortured process of formulating American policy on Vietnam, it was the greater availability and understanding of facts about military and economic matters that seemed to predominate. Facts about local attitudes, political commitments, and culture were not as easily understood and often seemed to bend to fit military or economic facts. It is the experts who had the more "hard-nosed" facts who found access to the president and to the inner councils where decisions were made. Yet the evidence indicates that the hard-nosed facts were in error, that the expected reactions of the "enemy" were systematically downgraded, although these facts were available to American intelligence and efforts were made to make them known in Washington. In the search for solutions, the decision-maker tends to eliminate, to simplify. Poorly defined "soft" knowledge is displaced by quantitative information that appears to be more precise. Yet the policy errors of Vietnam suggest that soft is no less important than hard-nosed knowledge.

Since facts imply measurements of one kind or another, and since measurements deal with aspects of the world that are better understood than others, it follows that this process of displacement tends to favor policies based on the experience of the past and to make innovation more difficult. Quantification downgrades feelings, desires, and dreams. Hard facts start with dollars and cents and include everything else that can be counted with some precision. What can be counted is usually what is understood. Emergent problems are often tied to emergent feelings and values for which indicators do not yet exist.

In education, policy experts, planners, and evaluators focus on those educational issues that are well understood and can be quantified; they pay lip service to issues that are not yet well understood and are therefore not measurable. It is the actors in the forefront of educational institutions who tend to be concerned with the qualitative and philosophical issues.

Quantity deals with numbers of students, numbers of teachers, teacher-training needs, locations of schools, sizes of buildings, use of facilities, fees, dollars and cents, and construction norms, and it means testing and test measurements. It necessarily avoids the nature of the relations between teachers and pupils, since it is not practical to deal with feelings and attitudes.

To be sure, educational experts are the first to admit the significance of "soft" issues and to stress the relevance of what goes on inside the schools. But in the final analysis, the unavailability of facts and the ignorance of experts predominate. Some authors recognize this, but they have no answer:

> Educational planning... must be concerned not simply with expanding the old educational system but also with changing it.... It inevitably leads educational planners to inquire about the validity of the underlying premises of various conventional

pedagogical practices; for these lie at the heart of educational outcomes. Yet they also lie beyond the professional competence of most planners. (Coombs 1967, p. 60)

Knowledge of well-understood relationships eliminates consideration of less-well-understood relationships, particularly new innovations and new ways of thinking about emerging problems. For example, the emphasis today is toward accountability, which means testing and measures of behavioral results that are visible but not necessarily important. But this emphasis also stultifies innovations that do not correspond to the domain of measurement. You can measure reading ability more easily than intellectual curiosity. Therefore the teachers who are evaluated on this basis emphasize reading ability and downgrade their own attempts to develop the intellectual curiosity of their students. The schools gear themselves to assure the parents that children know how to read. If in the same process they kill curiosity and interest in reading, this is not measured.

There is a natural lag in the ability of the systems analyst to deal with emerging issues. As long as the GNP was not quantified, the experts could not defend economic growth policies the way they can at present. Similarly, as long as other social measurements are not available, the experts cannot be very helpful in attacking the problems these measures would illustrate. Yet these problems may already exist and be perceived as such. They may be talked about in vague ways, yet the vagueness does not eliminate the fact that they represent genuine concerns. Since the systems analysts can do no more than discuss them in the same vague ways, they add little to the discussion.

Moreover, the experts' dependency on measurements is very real. Measurements and quantitative analysis are the basis of the knowledge which differentiates them and are, therefore, a basis of their social power. They cannot spend too much time talking in vague ways. Sooner or later they need to concentrate on the issues on which they can exercise their skills. But in so doing they may appear to be out of touch with the times.

Even if expertise serves an intellectually conservative function of narrowing the terrain of negotiation, it is erroneous to qualify this function as favoring either the left or the right or any other political position. Clearly, policy issues that can be quantified can have either conservative or liberal political implications. Measurements of access and performance in the education of children from different ethnic and social classes have had an important role in shaping policies for the democratization of education in Europe and in reducing some of the racial barriers in American education. Accountability and planning in education and other sectors have important political repercussions for both the left and the right. The point is that they are limited and, in certain domains, inadequate instruments.

Summary

L EGITIMATION AND STAFF roles are secondary functions of experts. Why are they important?

Any expert who provides a service is needed in some way or other. The Prince is dependent on his expert, and the extent of this dependency is a basis of the expert's power. Sometimes the expert seems to be controlled by the Prince, and there is little room to maneuver. But in social life, power is never absolute. No one is totally controlled by anyone else. To know how or when to move, the expert needs to understand how and why some people need his or her services.

four

Analysis
and Politics

THIS CHAPTER EXAMINES the relationship between politics and impartial, objective analysis. At first this may seem incongruous, since politics are not supposed to be impartial and objective and analysis is not supposed to be politically oriented. Our argument is simple: analysis has to be or at least appear to be impartial and objective but the uses of analysis are political. Therefore, there exist direct relationships between analysis and politics which we discuss in this chapter. These relationships are not well understood and are considered controversial among social scientists (Frankel 1976, pp. 3–7). The reason they are not well understood is due in part to the fact that the roles of experts—planners, programmers, policy analysts, or evaluators—are still so new that we confuse these new roles with the older and better understood roles of social scientists.

Moreover, playing these new roles still requires trappings that are made necessary by existing role expectations. For example, it would be a serious mistake to assume that since planning or policy analysis is revealed to be both political and technical, the expert is allowed to drop the mask and play the new role overtly, i.e., be less an expert and more a politician. The expert's own understanding of the hidden purposes of certain patterns of behavior does not eliminate the need for these patterns. As long as the new role is not universally understood and accepted, the politically conscious expert has to appear in the narrow or old definition of the role. But now the expert recognizes the difference between the two sets of expectations and uses time and resources accordingly. Experts do not undermine the reality and legitimacy of being experts but manage time and resources so that they can attend to politics.

Nothing here suggests that concern with process implies that the objectivity and quality of analysis should be downgraded or disregarded. It is essential to distinguish between the actual research and the way experts participate in policy formation and planning. The point is that experts have to be concerned both with the content of research and with the political dimension.

Research in the social sciences is oriented toward the development of a discipline within the social sciences. It uses data from the empirical world and concepts from the social sciences to arrive at a better understanding of what is happening. Research in planning, evaluation, and policy analysis uses data from the empirical world and concepts from the social sciences to help make better policy choices. Therefore, a principal difference between the role of policy analyst and that of social scientist is the way each uses knowledge.

This means that the strategy adopted for selecting problems and data is different; policy research has the additional mission of interpreting the results of discipline research for policymakers. It also means that the timing of policy research is determined by a client; therefore, the research strategy has to reflect the fact that the work has to be completed within definite constraints of a time and money budget. But experts cannot allow their analysis to be less precise or careful than that of their peers working on discipline concerns for two reasons: first, their academic peers will be the first to criticize shoddy research and undermine the credibility of experts; second, experts are in many cases also bona fide social scientists. Since they play both roles, they cannot allow themselves in the role of expert to undermine their credibility in the role of social scientist.

Experts cannot avoid the consequences of their statements and actions. They cannot assume that clients, implementers, and beneficiaries talk their language; understand the assumptions that underlie the research; do not confuse scientific explanations with deterministic cause-and-effect statements; or comprehend the probabilities inherent in forecasts. Therefore, at a first level of conceptualization, the experts recognize that to transmit their own professional message in the least distorted fashion requires a careful modification of technical language: a translation that results in the layman responding correctly to the message, although the layman may not be able to understand it.

Experts recognize that if they are political actors, they need to transmit not only technical information, but also political messages. They must be able to do this within one formal channel of communication; this means they must play one role formally and the other informally, using the informal opportunities and social circumstances of the first to play the second.

"Planning" the process of expertise is therefore adapted to existing role expectations in terms of the way time is spent, how political action is organized, how the definition of policy research can be used to gain access to political consultations, how professional consensus is obtained, and so on.

In this chapter, we examine how selected aspects of policy analysis, programming, evaluation, and planning have political implications. We show how the problem consists in using one role to play another without spoiling the act. The political actors pretending to be experts cannot show their hands too clearly lest they undermine what faith there is in expertise. Nevertheless, since they are sensitive to the fact that some actors perceive their role as a political one, they also show, as delicately as talent allows, that they have acquired political sophistication. Other political actors have to be reassured that they are dealing with experts who are not fanatic in the domain of expertise and are, therefore, pragmatic in approach, aware of their own political commitments, and able to organize political support for their recommendations.

We discuss how the apolitical stance of experts—their concern with the future, coherence, optimization, and feedback—provides them with assets in their initial dealings with their Prince.

Apolitical Politics

THE APOLITICAL DEFINITION is explicit in the normative literature on policy analysis, evaluation, and planning. Years ago, Harold Lasswell defined the policy sciences in these terms:

> The expression "policy sciences" is not in general use in the United States, although it is occurring more frequently now than before. . . . It is not another way of talking about the "social sciences" as a whole, nor of the "social and psychological sciences." Nor are the "policy sciences" identical with "applied social science" or "applied social and psychological sciences.". . . The policy orientation . . . includes the results of the social, psychological and natural sciences insofar as they have a bearing on the policy needs of a given period for adequate intelligence. (Lasswell 1951, p. 4)

Lasswell and other policy experts and planners are always careful to minimize the threat they might pose to politicians. Therefore their role definitions always stress that political chores will remain political. The purpose of any rational calculus in any policy science is to relate means to ends, not to alter the ends in themselves. A typical analysis of the role of systematic analysis in government defines expert knowledge as the knowledge required to link desirable outputs (i.e., values and goals as determined in the political process) with needed inputs (i.e., specific government programs):

> In the case of federal social programs, the analysis of production functions provides the crucial link between program specifications on the one hand and values or objectives on the other. The link is fashioned by relating inputs to outputs. Outputs can, in turn, be evaluated in terms of social values. The advocacy process of reconciling divergent values through consideration of particular program measures cannot proceed meaningfully without some knowledge of this link. (Schultze 1968, p. 63)

The author goes on to suggest that the political process will be enhanced when the relationships between the inputs and outputs of federal and state programs are exposed by systematic analysis so that the political process of reconciling divergent desirable outputs can take place in full awareness of the implications in terms of inputs.

The choices will be made by politicians. The experts will not alter the political process; they will only enhance it:

> In one sense PPB [Program Planning and Budgeting] can be viewed as introducing a new set of participants into the decision process which, for want of a better term, I have labeled partisan efficiency advocates. At each level of the decision process these participants become particular champions of efficiency and effectiveness as criteria in decision making. (Schultze, p. 101)

But the author is aware of some of the functions we have described in the preceding chapters, and in his book he recognizes one of them: the experts help a Prince control his empire:

> PPB also tends to modify the political process in another way: It improves the capability of the agency head to shape the program of his agency, and increases his power relative to his operating subordinates. Theoretically, this shift in power could go too far, but at present I feel that some movement in this direction is needed. (Schultze, pp. 101–2)

Finally, as Harvey Brooks points out, the expert also serves to depoliticize issues:

> Perhaps nowhere outside the United States is the appeal to value-free knowledge relied upon so extensively as an instrument to achieve political consensus for government actions. . . . There is constant pressure to convert political questions into technical questions, so that they can be referred to experts without actually confronting the value differences that frequently are the real origins of conflict. (Brooks 1976, p. 244)

This apolitical stance has political utility for the expert: it downgrades the visible influence the technocrat has on the political system, particularly when this influence is contrary to the prevailing ideology. The expert in high circles is sensitive to potential attacks from all quarters. The image of a small group manipulating the social system has to be avoided, partly because the experts rarely feel they have that much influence, but more importantly because widespread awareness of this dimension of their role could place their jobs in jeopardy: the influential advisors appointed to office are subject to the wrath of the electorate because, in contrast to elected officials, they do not represent anyone.

Moreover, the experts' apolitical stance serves to distinguish policy experts and planners from other political actors. Without this differentiation the experts would have no access to social power, since they do not represent or have the support of political groups. Therefore, a principal function of the apolitical definition of the policy expert's role is the exact opposite of the definition: it provides access to social power without political election.

Orientation to the Future

EXPERTS SUCH AS planners, programmers, or policy analysts are concerned with future time horizons. Even evaluators are concerned with assessing past performances to recommend future programs. This is the main difference between the policy sciences and the social sciences. There usually exist different agencies for different future time horizons: short-term planning (usually three, four, or six months); medium-term planning (one to five years); long-term planning (five, ten, in some cases even twenty years); and futurism (beyond ten or twenty years, usually the year 2000 and thereafter). Forecasting and setting targets are two distinct ways of thinking about the future.

Forecasting is making probability statements about the future. On the basis of knowledge of the past relations between social, economic, or technical variables, the analyst is able to provide a range of probability that certain events will take place in the future. For example, an expert in demography can make fairly reliable predictions of the future population of a country if he or she knows something about the birth and death rates, migration patterns, and other factors. The analyst will make a range of predictions depending on the way the key variables behave in the future.

Setting targets is the selection of desirable policy choices that lead to outcomes that can be attained if a set of actions is implemented. For example, an educational planner in a developing country may be told that universal primary education should be achieved by 1980. From knowledge of the future size of the school-age population, the numbers enrolled, the available number of teachers, the needs for new facilities, and the costs of education, the analyst is able to translate this target in terms of a program of investment for education that provides for new schools and an adequate teacher corps.

Both forecasting and setting targets involve scanning. Scanning is the systematic search for emergent problems that have policy implications, the study of the lead times required to provide solutions, and the introduction of new policy options as these problems and their lead times are identified. It is therefore concerned with developments and their future interconnections, which may not yet be significant. As one pioneer of Program Planning and Budgeting put it:

> When the sub-systems of society were less interdependent, policies could be more discrete and separate agencies could administer their own programmes with minimum reference to each other. The greater degree of interdependence has changed this situation. Diffuse problems now arise affecting several sections or indeed the whole of a society and these problems tend themselves to be interconnected. Examples would be poverty, obsolescence, urban decay, pollution, overpopulation, regional disparity, water and other natural resource management, intergenerational conflict, etc. (Held 1968, p. 15)

Thinking about the future provides an entrée into closed policy circles. It is always difficult or at least embarrassing to a politician to hide undesirable facts, and this explains why a political leader cannot completely disregard experts. Of course, the facts can be questioned, but it is sometimes politically expensive to try to suppress them.

Usually experts alter the time horizon being considered, and the analysis reveals dimensions of the future that have not been taken into account—the experts reveal the longer-term consequences of proposed actions. They suggest unforeseen effects, and they raise the issue of making choices that favor the present at the expense of the future or vice versa. The analysis of policy issues raises difficult questions—so difficult that experts have to explain how to think about them and how alternative options can be compared and choices made.

Scanning gives experts the right to pay attention to any and all problems. Even when they have a very limited domain of responsibility, concern for emergent problems allows them to look around, to leave the confines of their authority and enter those of other government agencies and private institutions. They establish contact with other experts and develop informational networks of information exchange. Their own work becomes data for others, and the work of others becomes their source of data. Having broken the provincialism of their own organizations, they inform the Prince about the wider environment, and the Prince will listen, though not always with pleasure.

The Prince's attention may be somewhat grudging because experts devalue political commodities when they make overt statements about the future. For example, if a Prince issues a plan stipulating that five years from today, sixteen schools, six hospitals, and two roads will be built in Governor X's state, the ultimate political value of building these schools, hospitals, and roads is devalued. Any political commodity that can be exchanged is most valuable at the time it is offered. If our Prince calls Governor X and offers her the same schools, hospitals, and roads right now in exchange for some active grassroots work for the party, the value of his resources in the bargain is at its highest. If he offers the same package, but to be delivered five years from now, it is worth much less.

Moreover, after the plan is made public and Governor X already knows that her state is expected to receive the schools, hospitals, and roads, she expects the central government to make the investments and she will only be willing to repay the Prince with a much smaller political favor. Thus, as future events are made more explicit and less uncertain, fewer political assets are left for the Prince to give or exchange. Therefore, any Prince seeks to reduce or alter this political cost of making decisions ahead of time. He prefers to keep the exact location of the facilities in doubt, sharpen potential interest in them, cultivate their political value with all potentially interested parties, and postpone his decision until he can maximize their political utility.

Our modern Princes usually belong to political parties that necessarily view policies and plans from the perspective of their impact on the electoral process. Even in a one-party system, the ability of any faction to hold power will depend on relatively short-term considerations. The Prince will therefore be pressured by his own political apparatus to insist on courses of action that bring immediate and visible benefits. In contrast the experts may be concerned with long-term policies and plans that require postponing immediate benefits to safeguard the future. The experts find that they are the advocates of a politically unpopular course of action and have to lobby for it around and against the Prince:

> The head of a national planning organization has the obligation to engage in a certain type of politics. His job as a public servant is to lead a lobby for long-term economic growth inside the government; this may conflict with the party politicians' short-range imperatives. Like the governor of the central bank, he is ultimately subject to the orders of the government of the day; but it is expected of both governor and head planner that they will urge the policies which they judge to be right in their fields of expertise, on the country at large as well as on the government, and to do so with clarity. Plainly this does not give either of them a license for unrestrained feuding. But it does make them politicians of a discreet variety. (Schonfield 1965, p. 234)

The perceptive experts attempt to limit the devaluation of political commodities by keeping options open or by maintaining choices within the outlines of the plans they elaborate. They select issues where the future is more important than present expediency with an eye to the ways they can be argued and defended politically. But they also know the Prince has to listen because the Prince fears uncertainty. The experts balance the cost of uncertainty against that of certainty.

Goals

EXPERTS ARE CONCERNED with goals, or, more exactly, with intended outcomes and functions. "If I ask you to describe an automobile," states C. West Churchman (1968, p. 12), "you may immediately switch off your thinking process and simply blurt out the things you recall about your own automobile—its wheels, engine and shape. . . ." The systems approach, however, orients thinking toward functions—for example, the function of a system that transports a few people from one place to another at a certain prescribed cost—"as soon as you begin to think in this manner, then your 'description' of the automobile begins to take on new and often quite radical aspects" (Churchman, p. 13). A floating machine on blown-air cushions, he suggests, might ultimately replace the system we call the automobile.

The concern for outcomes, functions, and goals is logical: since experts are supposed to help politicians choose between various courses of action, and since experts are not supposed to be political actors, they need to know where the politicians want to go. Once they know the destination, they can specify the road to follow. If the goals are not specified, this does not mean that they do not exist. Any decision or absence of decision has outcomes that affect goals. The analyst argues that if the goals are not specified and priorities among goals spelled out, the politician is nevertheless pursuing some without knowing what they are:

> The central issue is, of course, nothing less than the definition of the ultimate objectives of the federal government as they are realized through operational decisions. Set in this framework, the designation of a schedule of programs may be described as building a bridge between a matter of political philosophy (what is government for?) and the administrative function of assigning scarce resources among alternative governmental objectives. The unique function of a program budget is to implement the conclusions of a political philosophy through the assignment of resources to their accomplishment. . . . In a number of areas no clear objectives have ever been laid down. This undesirable condition has prevailed in the field of international aid and investments, but it can also be found in many domestic areas including,

among others, agriculture, transportation, education, and unemployment. (Trist 1970, p. 303)

Insistence on goal specification is so logical and self-evident that one may not notice the ways it influences the relationship between the experts and their Prince.

Goal specification requires a high level of political consensus. When such consensus exists, goal specificity does not create political costs. When many divergent views exist, however, the possibility of establishing well-defined goals that satisfy everyone becomes much more difficult. Even the process of spelling out goals may result in considerable conflict as each contending faction struggles to place its own preferences high on the list of objectives. Vague and ill-defined goals are an equivalent to having secret goals. As long as goals are secret, it is possible for competing groups to pursue their own ends without necessarily appearing to encroach on each other.

This uneasy coexistence is shattered when the analyst asks for a detailed specification of priorities among objectives. The Prince may not be able to deny the request. Since all decisions on resource allocations have an impact on future outcomes, not specifying priorities looks like manipulation and secrecy. The experts ask the politicians to show their cards. If the politicians hesitate, they must be hiding something.

Wise experts know that they may go too far and be too threatening, so they focus their attention on policy areas where widely shared consensus exists and treat delicate issues cautiously, leaving some of them outside their recommendations. But the call for goal specification still catches the politicians unprepared. The experts force the political actors to identify themselves and state their positions as explicitly as possible. Yet, while the politicians do this, the experts remain uncommitted. They do not attempt to provide advice since the goals are not yet clear, and it would be inappropriate for them to define goals. They can attend policy meetings and remain silent while the air clears, waiting to speak until the strongest factions emerge. Meanwhile, the various contending forces begin to show their colors and conflicts erupt. As the Prince and his entourage discover their own confusion, the experts consolidate their position in the policy-setting arena. They have identified the relevant political actors in the immediate entourage of the Prince.

Coherence and Optimization

ONCE GOALS ARE specified, the question is how to reach them. To select among options, experts have to eliminate courses of action that will be costly, overlapping, or not feasible. Therefore, they will conceptualize the problem so that they can specify the relevant systems to achieve the desired goals. Coherence is achieved by taking account of the relationships between the relevant components of the systems. For example, if 600 new primary schools are to be built in the next five years, it will be necessary to locate these schools in populated areas so that students will actually fill them; teachers have to be trained and hired; and orders for equipment and materials have to be placed. Moreover, all the components have to be accounted for at the right time. It is incoherent to plan the expansion of automobile production without a necessary articulation in the production of steel, rubber, glass, and so on, and without examining the future demand for automobiles.

Coherence maintenance does not suggest a single best approach or solution. It simply categorizes processes and outcomes in two distinct classes: what is possible and what is not. The analysts are interested in finding out how the systems will change over time. They identify the components of the relevant systems so that they can take them into account and not forget any of them as they prescribe a future course of action. They may even spell out a series of alternative courses of action, and select one as the most desirable, if they can find a rationale and a method to do so.

The analysis for coherence maintenance allows experts to demonstrate technical skills. But it also has repercussions on their relations with politicians.

Coherence maintenance requires integration. Within the analysis undertaken by the experts, it is the integration of subsystems within systems and of systems within other systems. But politically it is the integration of political arrangements.

Policy research and planning forces the integration of many political arrangements that fall within the scope of the analysis.

In the past, political give-and-take affecting decisions could take place all over the organization and at any convenient time, but policy planning centralizes and limits the place and time when policies are set. For the politician, it is a "packaged" deal. Therefore, it unsettles past styles of governance, and this, of itself, is an initial advantage for the experts in their relations with politicians. Furthermore, since much information is needed in one place at one time, it accentuates the Prince's dependency on his experts and their knowledge.

Experts also benefit from popular beliefs that there exists a best way to solve problems. To be sure, in some instances there is sufficient knowledge about the characteristics of the systems to allow for what is called optimization, i.e, finding a "best" solution to the problem. But optimization is only possible if the analyst can define an objective function specifying the relations between a desirable outcome and a whole set of variables that are necessary to achieve this outcome. It is not possible to optimize if more than one desirable outcome is specified. In other words, if the system has several goals, optimization can be achieved in relation to any one of them. The other goals can be treated as constraints that have to be met, but the "best" solution optimizes only the principal goal.

For example, take an electric system providing power to various load centers. The probable expansion of these load centers in a definite time span can be determined. The future characteristics of the load can be estimated (i.e, peak demand at certain times of the day and for certain days of the year, total energy demand during the year, etc.). The constraints on the system can be specified: maximum peak load must be met within a given tolerance of voltage variation, and total annual generating demand must be met with existing energy inputs. Let us say that the goal for optimization is to minimize annual costs. Knowledge of the costs of different possible additions to the system (hydroelectric, coal, gas, or nuclear thermal plants) is available. The systems analyst selects an optimal plan for timing the construction of generating, transmission, and distribution facilities.

But this plan is optimal only in terms of achieving the lowest possible annual operating costs.

If the analyst is told that it is important to keep visible transmission facilities as short as possible so as not to spoil the beauty of the landscape with towers and cables, and if he is given a cost constraint—e.g., the cost is not to rise by more than three percent—he will crank up the data and provide a new answer that keeps towers and cables as short as possible without raising costs beyond the imposed limit. If the constraint is too severe, he will answer that he cannot find a solution without a bigger increase in the cost.

It is important to distinguish between coherence maintenance and optimization. National planning, such as that in the Soviet Union, is highly dependent on coherence maintenance. The various state and all-Union planning agencies are continually articulating the different targets of the components of the systems they plan for. But optimization can only take place in subsystems where, in the language of the analyst, an objective function has been identified for optimization purposes. Optimization is possible when the problem is defined in such a way that the analyst has enough information to find the mathematical solution. In most social planning, the goals are vague and numerous and the relations between the systems' components are less well known. In such situations it is foolish to think of a "best" solution. For example, no experts can specify the "best" education for a community on the basis of their professional knowledge. In the first place, they cannot easily define the operational goals; and secondly, they cannot know how the various components of the educational system have to be arranged to arrive at desirable outcomes.

Notwithstanding all these limitations, general popular belief in the possibility of a best plan often means that the work of systems analysts is perceived as an optimal solution, even if the analysts make no such claims. Thus, optimization has become a potent myth of systems analysis, and is an important asset for the experts in their confrontation with politicians. The Prince may have power, but the experts appear to have access to a new kind of truth, a new approach that allows them to define what is best. They disclaim this, but their humility only serves to re-affirm the popular conviction that they do, in fact, know best. As experts circulate in an administration, particularly at the lower levels, they find consistent support for planning. When I studied Mexican educational planning, for example, I was often told by people I met who were not involved and were unfamiliar with the process that planning would somehow help Mexico find *that best solution* which is out there somewhere, but which Mexicans have so often failed to reach because politicians are such crooks (Benveniste 1970, pp. 107–8).

Feedback

FEEDBACK IN SYSTEMS analysis is finding out how the system responds to the policy changes that have been introduced. Suppose the new goal is to reduce a balance-of-payments deficit and a new import tax is enacted. The analysts want to evaluate the impact of this tax on all relevant aspects of the problem: Is it sufficient? Need it be modified? Are other policies needed? Feedback involves obtaining the information, evaluating it, and reorienting action. It is a continuing process, i.e., continued analysis correcting and refining the specification of means and goals.

Because of the importance of feedback, the systems approach to policy research stresses continued and sustained efforts over long periods of time. This is best illustrated by continued planning in certain capitalist and socialist countries. Planning agencies do not elaborate a single plan, but continually evaluate data and set targets for one, five, or more years ahead. This is called a rolling plan, i.e., a statement about a desirable future, which is always one or more years ahead and is continually being redescribed and modified.

Not all policy analysis, programming, planning, or evaluation is practiced in continued efforts. Many exercises are one-shot affairs and come to an end. But experts decry such lack of continuity and call for permanent and sustained efforts.

Sustained efforts imply the institutionalization of policy expertise: the creation of organizations within which and from which policy experts can operate. The experts obviously realize that the nature of these organizations—their resources, the composition of their staffs, the knowledge they can store and have available, and their relationship with government and the rest of society—has a direct bearing on the scope and strength of expertise.

Like all professions, that of the expert must have bases of operation. If permanent organizations exist, it becomes possible to consolidate one's position. If policy research and planning are ephemeral, the actors constantly have to start anew and the Prince can keep them at bay with greater ease. The establishment of permanent analytical institutions with career paths for experts, the creation of positions in universities to train policy analysts and planners, and the establishment of a literature are all means of strengthening a new profession. They also provide necessary communications among members of the profession and, to a limited extent, provide a forum for setting normative definitions of what is proper professional behavior and what is considered adequate research.

The ability to acquire, store, handle, and analyze large volumes of data sharply distinguishes the new policy experts from their predecessors and, at the same time, makes the policy-maker much more dependent on their services. It is not irrelevant that control of facts can often be translated into social power. Analysis is a differentiated and specialized activity relying on large staffs who are brought together because of the nature of the problem and the contribution each can make to the whole. In such staffs a well-earned reputation from many years of exposure to policy situations is no longer as important as specialized expertise in a particular discipline or data-handling skill. This process of specialization and professionalization of policy expertise has introduced the large research team in government and other organizations.

Another result of the professionalization process is that experts tend to be closer to other experts than they are to field people. They feel more allegiance to professionals who share their approach and philosophy of policy formulation than toward the permanent staffs of the bureaucracy. But this has distinct costs. Foremost is the natural tendency of experts to disregard or have little direct interest in the implementation of their plans. Since experts tend to socialize with other experts, they also tend to lack access to the circles of bureaucracy where the implementation of their scheme will stand or fall. Quite often the analysts do not know or have little practical experience with the programs they elaborate. They deal at levels of aggregation and simplification that place them at some distance from the implementers, and the implementers naturally tend to distrust them.

This is a weakness of the new profession and one of the reasons experts fails to play the political dimension of their role. They have an entrée among their peers, but they do not perceive the issues as they are perceived in the bureaucracy or the community they expect to serve.

Implications for Those Who Aspire to Become Experts

THE FIRST TASK of the young analyst who aspires to work on policy and planning is to get into the act. He or she cannot expect to start at the top of the ladder and must be prepared to serve a lengthy apprenticeship on a policy expert team before one is invited to take a leading advisory position in Washington or elsewhere. The aspiring analyst will spend several years doing research for others, cranking out the facts and figures and drafting policy reports, before he or she can hope to acquire a reputation.

Clearly, the acquisition of an advanced degree in any policy science is not sufficient to open the doors to great decisions and influence. In fact, to get a foot in the door at all, the aspiring systems experts need to possess a specific commodity to sell to a team of experts. They might be the most inventive generalists or have the most genuine concern for human betterment, but they might not be hired if they do not also have access to a specific body of knowledge that they know inside out and can use better than almost anyone else. In other words, they must be specialists.

Analytical skills are the basis of specialization. They provide the ability to (1) discover relevant data, (2) gather this data, (3) analyze it, and (4) on the basis of the analysis, reach policy conclusions. These abilities in turn are based on established and well-developed disciplines. In this respect, it is erroneous, even disastrous, to assume that since academic disciplines are narrow, policy problems wide, and policy sciences multidisciplinary, the aspiring policy expert should receive a multidisciplinary training. No single mind can take graduate courses for two or three years in economics, anthropology, sociology, political science, history, philosophy, and systems analysis, not to mention statistics, computer languages, and so on, without wasting time. Smorgasbord programs of this type produce well-meaning and well-read but superficial analysts who have no differentiated analytical ability. If you try to hire them and ask them what they can do, they tell you they want to learn and cannot really do anything. If you do hire them, you waste your time helping them do their work. In due time you get rid of them because the only job they think they can do is your own.

The title of this book, *The Politics of Expertise,* does not imply that policy research can be disregarded and rigorous analysis forgotten because experts play a political role where other considerations prevail. There is no quicker way for any policy expert to fail than undertaking dubious research projects that ultimately are subject to severe criticisms.

The aspiring policy experts need to have at least one set of analytical skills they know thoroughly. If they have learned how to create programs and use computers, they know how to do it "by heart," and can work and invent more rapidly than most. If they specialize in cost-benefit analysis and budget programming, they are familiar with all the established techniques and are also inventing new ones. If they are economists, they are well-trained economists who understand the policy implications underlying their own disciplines. If they are sociologists interested in survey research, they know research design and questionnaire work and are impeccable methodologists. In short, they have skills they can use, and can therefore become contributing members of the policy research team, and they are aware that the methodologies of policy analysis, evaluation, programming, and planning are constantly being improved upon and they are contributing to this development.

But analytical skills are not sufficient. Policies are set in a complex environment within which many different persons and groups have ideas, opinions, or theories about the situation. They know or discuss what has to be done, what could be done, what should be done. Practitioners in the field have written books about practical issues that are read by other practitioners, so the environment includes a history of ideas, philosophy, and practices, sometimes going far back in time. There is also a history of past attempts at reform and experimentation, some of which succeeded, many of which failed. At any time there is a flux of issues that are being discussed, and there are issues that should be discussed.

The policy environment also includes a history of both good and bad relations among political actors who espouse various aspects of the existing conventional wisdom. The past and present politics of the field—whether it be public health, transportation, education, communication, foreign aid, community development, urban renewal, or social welfare—have characteristics of their own. Moreover, there also exists a legal basis that constrains or defines political responsibilities.

The would-be experts cannot expect to draft policies without knowing a considerable amount about the policy environment. They must be able to recognize the arguments of practitioners, to realize their strengths and weaknesses, and to temper their own narrow field of expertise with the kind of generalized folklore and knowledge that prevails in the environment. In most social situations the folklore and conventional wisdom have been acquired over time by trial and error. The would-be experts trained in an analytical discipline can question aspects of this conventional wisdom. But they should not be so foolish as to assume that it is all rubbish. Parts are dysfunctional and should be changed, but parts are needed.

Superficial treatment of policy problems takes place all the time, and in the policy world the hardest customers to please are the implementers who know their domain inside out. It is not enough to be a narrow specialist with a set of skills. The would-be planners need to be generalists in their domain of interest. They need to understand the issues, because this is where skills count, and they need both skills and understanding to make a difference.

Finally, the aspiring policy expert will need to understand the political dimension. To be effective, he or she will need at least some political savoir-faire. There is no guaranteed way to acquire this skill. Maybe it can be gained in practice by watching incomparable bureaucratic infighters and statesmen and learning from close exposure and experience. Theoretical knowledge is helpful, but it is no guarantee of political sensitivity. Some very good political scientists or political sociologists are terrible politicians and vice versa.

Even if the art cannot be taught, some skills related to the art can be acquired or improved; for example, the ability to work under pressure and time constraints, the ability to communicate and acquire trust, and the ability to work on a team and present results. We can say that to realize the political dimension exists is half the battle.

five

The Institutions of United States Planning

IN CONTRAST TO the centralized planning in socialist countries, in Western non-socialist nations such as France, and in most developing countries, planning in the United States is decentralized and diffuse. Policy analysts, programmers, planners, and evaluators are employed in many different organizations to think about the future. It should also be stated at the outset that while Soviet and French planning were highly centralized in the earlier days of their development, these systems have evolved considerably since then and have also become far more complex and far more dependent on a more diffuse and decentralized form of planning than was the case earlier. Nevertheless the United States still remains the country where policy analysis, programming, evaluation, and planning remain the most diffuse and therefore more difficult to describe or influence in their totality.

American planning takes place in many different industrial firms, foundations, banks, marketing unions, voluntary groups, and think tanks, and it also takes place in government agencies at all levels, in the executive, and to a limited extent in the legislative and judicial branches of government. This fact alone would make United States planning decentralized. But since it arises when needed, and there is no overall policy for the allocation of resources, it is also diffuse. Moreover, it is subject to the provincial interests of existing organizational structures. Some organizations are more sophisticated than others and use experts to their advantage, while the others have not found out how to benefit from expert help.

Planning in the United States has its own history, starting with early examples of government intervention, such as the creation of the Interstate Commerce Commission in 1887, the passage of the Sherman Antitrust Act of 1890, the establishment of the Federal Trade Commission, and the development of the conservation program under President Theodore Roosevelt. It has roots in the planning for national resources and production undertaken during the First World War in such institutions as the War Industries Board, the War Trade Board, the Shipping Board, the War Labor Board, and many other organizations of that time. It developed further during the years of the Depression, when city, county, and regional planning agencies began to spring up. The Tennessee Valley Authority is the best-known regional experiment, but there were many less well known efforts undertaken by such agencies as the National Forest Service, the Bureau of Reclamation, the Army Corps of Engineers, and the U.S. Geological Survey. A number of state planning boards were set up to study pressing state problems.

The closest to a national planning body that is usually mentioned in histories of American planning is the National Resources Planning Board created by President Franklin Roosevelt in 1934. It was an advisory body under the executive, yet it undertook diversified studies and made recommendations on resource use, population trends, the social effects of inventions, the structure of the economy, and consumer income and expenditures. The board operated in part through technical committees bringing together various personnel from interested government and private institutions. It also acquired consultants and developed its own research staff. It sponsored such work as Gardiner Means' classic *The Structure of the American Economy*

and a study of public works by John Kenneth Galbraith. As it
acquired influence, it acquired enemies, particularly in Congress, where its survival was often debated. It was finally abolished in 1943, and Congress ruled that its functions were not to
be transferred to any other agency—a piece of legislation that
has been termed "a vindictive prescription without historical
precedent" (Lepawsky 1971, p. 298).

As we defined it in chapter 1, planning includes policy analysis, programming, and evaluation, and has to be concerned with
implementation. If we apply this definition to the National Resources Planning Board, we see that the work of that board was
policy-oriented but was not planning. The specifics of deciding
how policy would be implemented were left to the implementing agencies (Millett 1947, pp. 14–15). Therefore, even during
the New Deal, there was no tradition of peacetime comprehensive centralized planning in the United States.

The Council of Economic Advisors was created in 1946 and
took on some of the responsibilities of the National Resources
Planning Board. But as the crises of war and depression were
replaced by the so-called crisis of affluence (Galbraith 1969),
the planning needs and responses of the public administration
and the private sector took place at many levels, in piecemeal
fashion, and in small incremental steps. In contrast to developments in other societies (e.g., France) where totally new national
organizational arrangements were invented, in the United States
the process evolved within existing structures. The major planning invention of this more recent period is the ebullient growth
of institutions known as think tanks. Some of these already
existed in the thirties, but they mushroomed in the fifties. Yet
even the think tanks are simply extensions of existing structures
in the sense that they generally work on contract for clients.

To be sure, in the United States, and in some countries that
have been heavily influenced by the United States in the immediate postwar years, there have been some attempts to create
new institutional mechanisms of national planning to bridge
existing organizational limitations. For example, in West Germany semi-independent policy research and planning bodies
have been established separate from the existing and powerful

Bonn ministries. The Advisory Council on Social Policy and the Expert Council for Giving Opinions on Overall Economic Development have a mandate beyond the narrow interests and preoccupations of the traditional bureaucracy (Arndt 1966, p. 64).

Similarly, the short-lived National Goals Research Staff, which President Nixon established in July 1969, was an attempt to have a research staff with a broad mandate on policy issues going beyond the organizational parochialism of the existing administration. But it was probably not accidental that this staff was abolished exactly a year later on the day its first and only report was issued. In his introductory statement to that report, Daniel Moynihan delicately alluded to the potential conflicts between such a staff and the existing administrative structures:

> The National Goals Research Staff was not to be a planning agency, nor was it in any way to usurp or replace the process of decision making within the executive branch of government. Much less was it to assume the functions of any other branch or level of government. Rather, it was to provide information and analysis so that those making decisions might have a better idea of the direction in which events are moving, the seeming pace of those movements, and alternative directions and speeds that possibly could be achieved were policies to be shifted in one direction or another. (National Goals Research Staff 1970, p. 5)

One is reminded of the earlier problems of the National Resources Planning Board. As Congress debated its abolition on April 12, 1940, Congressman Dirksen of Illinois had this to say:

> [The NRPB] has one value. It has the supreme value of coordinating with state planning agencies and encouraging them to spend money for everything under the sun from the study of the genealogy of the safety pin to the creation of a park along the C. & O. Canal.... The President's fourth reorganization plan seeks to effect greater efficiency and economy and to eliminate duplication of activities. Would this not be an excellent place to apply those very principles?... Here is an excellent opportunity to plan the conservation of a few of our fiscal resources by permitting the Planning Board to plan its way out of existence by June 30 of this year. (Galloway 1971, pp. 75–76)

Mott of Oregon went further. The board, he charged, was not only "extravagant and useless" but "harmful and even vicious. ... It has interfered with the regular established functions and agencies of this Government, and with legislative jurisdiction by Congress at every opportunity. . . . It has interfered without any authority whatever with the orderly consideration of legislation by committees of Congress." The board, it seems, had vetoed one of Mr. Mott's pet projects in his home state (Galloway, p. 76).

The piecemeal approach to American planning is revealed by the proliferation of new government regulatory and development agencies whose policy mandate seeks to bridge the parochial limits of organizational interests: for example, the Energy Research and Development Administration, the Nuclear Regulatory Commission, and the Federal Energy Administration, all of which have responsibility in policy and planning of the future energy situation. The Employee Retirement Income Security Act of 1974 created a new agency, ERSIA, which regulated the future of workers' and employees' pensions. Other regulatory agencies created in the seventies include OSHA (the Occupational Safety and Health Agency), EPA (the Environmental Protection Agency), and CPSC (the Consumer Product and Safety Commission). These, together with the older Food and Drug Administration and other agencies with regulatory powers such as the Federal Reserve Board, impinge heavily on both the public and private sectors. As a result, there has been considerable opposition to the spiraling legal and bureaucratic costs of the interventions of many different agencies with policy-making mandates, some of which even conflict among themselves:

> Indeed the health and safety regulations have grown so rapidly that OSHA not infrequently collides with the equally industrious and controversial EPA.
> For example, OSHA decided that construction vehicles should have back-up warning beepers, but the demanded beepers exceeded EPA noise standards. (*New York Times,* 9 January 1977, p. F15)

WHY HAS AMERICAN planning been diffuse? In the United States, the constitutional prerogatives of both Congress and the executive pre-empt the creation of formal national planning bodies. Both institutions would have to control a national plan and this is not feasible. Therefore analytical capability resides in the executive agencies such as the Department of Defense, the State Department, etc., and most of the analysis tends to pursue the parochial interests of these agencies. Even if much social invention has taken place in the last two decades, and even if congressional or presidential commissions, White House conferences, and task forces seem to be much in evidence, the fact is that most of the day-to-day affairs of the government requiring coordination are routinely negotiated in interagency committees. These are staffed directly by representatives or consultants of the involved agencies. They rarely undertake research of their own. They depend on the data, research, and position papers prepared within the agencies.

Concern with wider social issues beyond the parochial interests of these agencies might reside more in Contress than within the executive. But the executive has access to far more resources for policy analysis and planning. Of course there are the Library of Congress, congressional advisory bodies, and some congressional policy research. The Congressional Budget Act of 1974 created the Congressional Budget Office (CBO), which provides a new policy analysis capability in Congress. CBO can obtain budget data from executive agencies and can provide Congress with alternatives to the budget proposed by the executive. The act also set up Senate and House Budget Committees, which were established in 1975. These new committees are concerned with the total level of appropriations and with allocations to major budget functions so that Congress now has to establish some priorities among such areas as defense, welfare, health, education, etc. But the level of effort is nowhere comparable to that of the executive. Moreover, the work of other congressional committees still follows the lines of parochial interests within the executive branch, since congressional committees are structured along departmental and agency lines. Nevertheless, these reforms have enhanced congressional ability to deal with the executive, including the Office of Management and Budget (OMB) in the White House.

Even the OMB is not the only source of executive analytical strength dealing with budgets. In recent years, the OMB has been given primary responsibility for implementation and program management studies as well as for the preparation of budget requests, but the OMB has not been where new presidential initiatives usually come from. New ideas, new programs, and new appropriation requests are still generated by bureaucratic entrepreneurs who have the ear of the president or some of his assistants and who know how to bring together policy analysis, agency interests, pressure groups, and the necessary congressional support (Pious 1975).

Given the complexity of policy-making in Washington and elsewhere in the country, there is a tendency to use ephemeral planning bodies. From time to time, a mandate is given to a public commission, task force, ad hoc body, or staff, such as the National Goals Research Staff, to undertake an overview of a society-wide policy problem. The scope of discussion may be as broad as the goals of the nation, or as specific as the problems of violence, urban survival, education, land use, pollution, pornography, or any other subject of general and multi-organizational interest.

When such overviews are undertaken they focus on specific policy problems, which usually fall in the purview of different organizations and for which no single organization is responsible. As a rule, these planning bodies are small in comparison to the organizations they are supposed to deal with. They are composed of a small number of individuals, usually recognized public figures in their fields of expertise and public service. These are assisted by a professional research staff. In the course of their work, they consult with numbers of other experts and interested parties and have some contact with the bureaucracies they are supposed to influence. They search out the nature of the problems, identify solutions, and make recommendations, and, at some point, they furnish findings and receive some attention in the press.

Their life span is limited, generally ending with the publication of a set of recommendations. The principal reason for their transience is that they encroach on the prerogatives of existing organizations and institutions, and this encroachment can only be tolerated for a finite period. Moreover, if they were not abolished they would want to continue to influence policy, and, as Mr. Mott's tirade indicates, they might acquire more power than Congress or other agencies of the executive want them to have.

There are advantages to these ephemeral commissions and task forces. They can be created on short notice in response to policy needs. Since they are ephemeral, they are perceived as a minor threat by the existing bureaucracies, and they tend, therefore, to receive mandates allowing them to take a bold look at policy issues. Moreover, since the principal staff members serve for prestige reasons and have other career positions to turn to, they are emboldened to make courageous recommendations. The sum of all this is, at the least, a report that is an enlightened and even refreshing perspective on the national scene. Indeed, it is often so enlightened or refreshing that it is disowned by its sponsors in the administration.

While these proposals are imaginative or courageous, they also tend to have little hold on the immediate reality. Most reports of this type do not influence their authors' contemporaries for the obvious reason that it is the large bureaucracies that carry the day-to-day routine, and the level of effort needed to influence them has to be sustained over long periods of time. Once a task force or presidential commission is abolished, there remains no advocate for the suggested policies. The absence of a continued hold on reality means that another report is added to the dreams of desirable alternatives while the daily machinery grinds on unchanged. As Nathan Glazer puts it:

> The truly valuable policy research of the future, I am convinced, must be undertaken in agencies with a long-range commitment to some problem areas, and with a close relation to government. ... The point is more long-range, sustained, committed research on government programs in a given area—and specifically, on their effects—by a body of researchers committed to that task. (Glazer 1969, p. 45)

Yet when more permanent overall planning agencies are created, as is the case in city and regional planning, from the experts' point of view the experience is not much more successful. City and regional planning literature decries the lack of power granted to planning bodies. Their influence on implementing agencies is resisted by the jealous desire of the implementers to maintain their own prerogatives. The story is always the same: no one in the department of public works minds city planners as long as they do not meddle in the affairs of the department, and this situation is repeated in all departments:

> Most city officials looked with disfavor on planners' assertions that their view was comprehensive. The heads of other agencies generally said without hesitation that they had no quarrel with planners so long as the planners did not try to tell them how to run their own depatments. To planners this qualifier seemed extremely serious. The Minneapolis planners felt, for example, that they could not possibly develop a downtown plan without considering the handling of traffic control, much to the annoyance of the city engineer. He took the position that street planning was none of their business. (Altshuler 1965, p. 369)

One can argue that all these problems are to be expected, because any Prince seeks to maintain his experts under control. He always defines the experts' domain of responsibility narrowly enough that no single expert can claim to be the only relevant one in his entourage. He establishes various competing sources of expertise with sufficient overlap to limit the domination of any single group. He encourages conflicting advice because conflicting advice calls for adjudication, and he can adjudicate in directions he believes to be beneficial.

The Prince's relationship with the experts is always complicated by the experts' difficult relationship with the Prince's lieutenants, i.e., the various departments heads working directly for him. The experts want to influence the programs and actions of the bureaucracy. But portions of the bureaucracy are controlled by the Prince's lieutenants, who see the actions of the experts as attempts to meddle in their own affairs. They naturally resist encroachments on their perceived domains. The cries for more power come from experts who fail to perceive the nature of their role and thus oversimplify the problem. In fact, planners never lack a mandate to look at problems; what they often lack is adequate support to undertake the necessary research. If nobody listens to their advice, it is usually because they are ahead of their time and neither they nor their Prince can educate a recalcitrant or apathetic public to the issues.

On the other hand, it must be said that since many public issues involve the various government administrations at all three levels, namely federal, state, and local, the American system of public administration is deficient in its integrative capability. Federal agencies and even bureaus within these agencies operate directly at state and local levels. There is no equivalent at the state or local level of the United States ambassador to a foreign country who has a mandate to integrate and plan the activities of many of his government's agencies in that country. Therefore planning of federal action at the local level requires coordination in Washington, which is expensive, time-consuming, and often frustrating. Ad hoc bodies often attempt to serve this function, but they rarely replace or displace the existing structures. They tend to be marginal, do not influence the large bureaucracies, and therefore do not solve this type of problem.

Another aspect of this problem is that the implementation of innovative programs involving federal, state, and local agencies requires considerable political sophistication because many independent agencies have to be induced to work together. We are back to discussing the multiplier effect. The failure of many federal programs can be traced to a lack of grassroots support or to the existence of local centers of power that are not going to be swayed by Washington. A good example of this is the well-documented study of President Johnson's attempt to use federally owned lands in cities for housing. A vast nationwide program was initiated with much fanfare in 1967. But four years later only 120 new units of housing had been built (Derthick 1972, p. 83). There were many reasons for this failure; the principal reason was the very limited supply of incentives the federal government could offer local communities. The planners were unable to create support. The multiplier effect did not take place.

The call for planning in the United States is therefore also a call for coordinating institutions at the grassroots level to facilitate federal, state, and local cooperation in joint projects. For example, the Comprehensive Employment and Training Act of 1973 called for the creation of local planning councils, and the proposed "Equal Opportunity and Full Employment Act of 1975" (Senate Bill 50, submitted January 15, 1975, by Senator

Hubert Humphrey) calls for strengthening local planning councils because "the President, the Secretary of Labor, and other officials and agencies of the Federal Government need the continuing input of ideas, proposals, advice, and criticism from local governments, communities, and individuals" (U.S. Senate Bill 50, 94th Congress, 1st Session, 15 January 1975, p. 7).

But it would be quite wrong to conclude from this brief discussion that no overall planning takes place in the United States. As we said, much integrative planning takes place, but it takes place within many different institutional frameworks. The equivalent of the planning function of formalized national or regional planning bodies in Europe and elsewhere is carried out by the research staffs in a variety of institutions, such as the Office of Management and Budget or the Council of Economic Advisors, and the various councils to deal with the economy, all in the executive offices of the president; in many government agencies and departments; in ad hoc bodies; and in independent or semi-independent organizations. In short, the bulk of American thinking about the future depends very much on informal professional cooperation among experts in many organizations. The fact that formal interorganizational systems planning is limited does not mean that mutual adjustment does not take place (Lindblom 1965). Decision-makers are continually adjusting their choices to the decisions made elsewhere. Informational interorganizational planning, therefore, does take place; indeed, without it the social system would not be articulated.

The marketplace is part of this. In the marketplace, price information arising from supply and demand provides the bulk of the planning information for the United States economic system. But prices in the marketplace are only one component of the information and knowledge used to articulate the system. The systems planners generate another component.

Information is spread and shared through informal links between experts and through exchanges of information. Within any planning sector the experts know each other, planners working for large corporations know their colleagues in the think tanks, and periodic visits to Washington ensure contacts with systems analysts working for relevant agencies of government. Internal information is shared, and research reports issued for limited circulation are exchanged. The experts who know what is going on outside their own organizations acquire knowledge and give out information. The think tanks act as information brokers by working for large numbers of clients; even when they protect the confidentiality of their sources, they often use their information to improve the level of articulation among their clients.

One advantage of the informal professional networks of information gathering and distribution is that the United States experts are less at the mercy of their Prince than their counterparts in centralized systems, because the Prince cannot control the experts' informal sources of information. Another advantage is that the system provides many alternative employment opportunities for experts. Therefore, they have more opportunities to take stands on issues and defend their professional values, and they can more easily avoid situations in which they serve the Prince only to legitimate his pet project. American experts have often taken public stands against the current dogma of their time, sometimes by resigning publicly, sometimes by making public secret information that embarrassed the administration, sometimes by organizing into pressure groups to counteract trends they objected to.

American policy-making typically involves considerable expert participation in skirmishes, both in and out of the relevant agencies. As John Newhouse points out in the introduction to his study of the Strategic Arms Limitations Talks (SALT) with the Soviet Union, to understand the process, it is necessary to understand the issues, "the grist of the talks; a recognition that the skirmishing between interest groups in Washington, and doubtless Moscow, too, dominates the enterprise . . ." (Newhouse 1973, p. 13). It is probable that experts qua experts play a more important role in American skirmishes, whereas conflicts in Moscow are more typically generated by different viewpoints within the affected bureaucracies.

It is typical of the American system of planning that a disenchanted expert, Dr. Daniel Ellsberg, could continue to teach at a major university after he had announced publicly that he had leaked the secret Pentagon study of the causes of the

Vietnam war to the press (*New York Times,* 29 June 1971).

While it is difficult to describe, and difficult to influence over-all, a complex set of planning functions and agencies is easier to penetrate and influence in piecemeal fashion. While it clearly reflects the distribution of power in society (i.e., the rich can pay for planning, the poor cannot), it is also true that such a system is more amenable to divergent points of view and to advocacy planning, i.e., having experts help specific groups elaborate plans that suit them. Since it is not a unitary monopolistic system, it may sometimes be less able to reduce uncertainty, but on the other hand it may be less erosive of democratic institutions.

To conclude, there is no intrinsic reason why planning should be either centralized or decentralized. These forms differ to fit the administrative culture and distribution of power in each country or organization. The evils that arise from planning need correction in both centralized and decentralized systems, not by altering the planning structure, but by recognizing both the political and technical dimensions of planning.

Planning in the Private Sector

DURING THE LAST two decades management in the American private sector has adopted the notion of organized and formalized policy-planning within the firm. In the past, conventional board-room wisdom tended to associate planning with threats to the free play of the market. But crisis and rapid changes forced the private sector to reconsider. As John Kenneth Galbraith reports in his study of the industrial state:

> For understanding the economy and polity of the United States and other advanced industrial countries, this reaction against the word planning could hardly have been worse timed. It occurred when the increased use of technology and the accompanying commitment of time and capital were forcing extensive planning on all industrial communities. This has now been sensed. And, in many quarters, the word planning is again acquiring a measure of respectability. (Galbraith 1968, p. 34)

Today many corporations employ large, full-time staffs of experts and researchers who advise top management on long-term planning. The scope of their work is varied, going all the way from analyzing new trends in the corporate environment and studying new market opportunities, product diversification, technological innovations, corporate acquisitions, and wage and financial trends, to studying lead time for management decisions and digesting planning information from other private and public sources. The systems approach to planning is typical not only in giant corporations, but also in small firms that can afford to hire consultants.

The trend has reached not only industrial corporations, but also many other sectors of the economy where the future is uncertain and lead time is important in decision-making. This approach is commonplace in insurance companies, banks, hospitals, and even complex educational institutions, where long-range planning staffs are now commonplace.

It is difficult to estimate the level of research effort going into private-sector planning within the United States. But we can get a clue from an estimate of the amount of money that corporations spend for the specialized long-range planning services they buy from think tanks. Since most of their planning is internal, this is only a small fraction of the total. Erich Jantsch, in a study of forecasting conducted for the Organization for Economic Cooperation and Development in Paris, estimates that United States, Canadian, and European firms spent about fifteen million dollars for outside services, nine-tenths of which is accounted for by United States and Canadian firms (Jantsch 1967, p. 252). Assuming that this is one percent of the total (a guess but not an unreasonable one), more than a billion dollars a year may go into policy-planning research in the United States private sector alone.

Planning within Government Agencies

IN AUGUST 1965 the major agencies of the federal government began to adopt Program Planning and Budgeting (PPB), and established formal planning staffs for this purpose. This innovation with federal agencies was part of a conscious attempt to initiate medium-term, i.e., five-year, planning of government activities and to reinforce short-term, i.e., quarterly, planning under the Bureau of the Budget. As we saw, the purpose of PPB is to make visible the goals of government agencies, to provide for systematic comparisons and trade-offs between alternative decisions, to expand the time horizon within which the purposes of government agencies are re-examined and refocused, and to provide analytical tools to evaluate alternative means of reaching future objectives. The introduction of PPB in public administration increased the level of effort devoted to policy-making by forcing the administration to analyze goals and alternatives and to justify budget requests on that basis.

PPB was first introduced in the public administration, at the federal and then at the state and local levels. Difficulty with its application in complex multi-goal administrations led to some disenchantment, and in 1971, the Office of Management and Budget (OMB) separated program planning in federal agencies from budget preparation, thus weakening the integrative function these offices were supposed to serve (OMB Revised Circular No. A-11, 21 June 1971). In so doing, the OMB removed power planners acquired from their proximity to budget decisions (Schick 1973, Worthley 1974).

Nevertheless, the availability of analytical talent in the public administration and the management style introduced by PPB has continued if not always in content, at least in form. The PPB format is often used to justify decisions and to provide the appearance of rationality in situations where there does not exist any rational basis for policy choices. Programs, each of which has political implications and each of which can only be selected on political grounds, are sometimes subjected to spurious analysis. On the other hand, analysis—particularly cost-benefit analysis—is often used to highlight advantages or disadvantages of competing programs, thus eliminating arbitrariness and increasing the rationality of decisions. Ida Hoos has provided the best and most definitive critique of the use of systems analysis in public policy (Hoos 1972). Our argument is not whether PPB or any other analytical technique should or should not be used or whether its use does or does not increase the level of rationality in public administration. Our argument is that these techniques are used; analysts are employed, and therefore they have organizational and political importance.

A distinction should be made between the PPB approach in the United States and the centralized national planning in some European market economies. Notwithstanding rhetoric to the effect that PPB and the five-year horizon provide the White House with a means of interagency comparisons, the focus for experts' intervention and influence in the United States remains within the agencies. The analysis and the experts have more influence within each agency in justifying various possible sub-goals and in presenting the agency's case for budget allocations. But the adjudication of the total budget among all the large bureaucracies has not been changed by PPB. It is principally influenced by broader political considerations, which are well described in Aaron Wildavsky's classic study of the American budgetary process (Wildavsky 1964).

In contrast, formal national planning bodies have direct access to, and sometimes even control of, formal mechanisms for con-sultation (and therefore influence) outside the structure of tradi-tional ministries and influence groups. This means that experts in countries that practice formal national planning are closer to the political process of adjudication between conflicting de-mands. They may, as a result, have more opportunities to influ-ence decisions. But we should keep in mind that influence is a knife with two edges. Experts who acquire too much influence also acquire many enemies and tend to lose their power. The trend throughout the world is increasingly away from central-ized comprehensive planning and more toward piecemeal multi-institution planning. This may well be due, in part, to a growing realization by government agencies, by legislative bodies, and by influence groups that they can learn the language of planning, that they can use this language for their own narrower purposes, and since they are close to the sources of data, they can control their own planning and ultimately displace centralized planning.

There does not exist any danger of centralized planning in the United States. The fragmentation of the planning apparatus is nowhere more evident than within the executive office of the president. A strong centralized planning capability would tend to be unitary in character. But the competition between jealously independent departments and agencies, supported by their respective congressional committees and the presidency itself, and the natural reluctance of any president to let his advisors dominate the presidency, results in a multi-functional apparatus within his office. There we found, in the mid-seventies, the Council of Economic Advisors, the Council on Environmental Quality, the Office of Economic Opportunity, the Domestic Council, the National Security Council, and the Office of Management and Budget, among several score lesser bodies, all reporting to the president. The reforms of the Carter administration attempted to consolidate the bureaucracy, but they did not alter the fact that in a pluralistic society, there exist many centers of power and, therefore, more than one channel of influence to the White House or to the Congress.

E XPERTS WITHIN government agencies can be more closely controlled by their Prince than outside experts. Their tasks tend, therefore, to be set by the administrators or political appointees they serve. The reason this is so important is that inside experts can so easily be controlled by their Prince that the relationship may be distorted: experts have to say whatever it is their Prince wants to hear. In such situations, they can only provide legitimation for ideas or schemes the Prince pursues and are unable to transmit any information the Prince does not wish to hear.

To avoid this, experts pursue several strategies. The first and necessary prerequisite consists in acquiring the right to look at each and every problem that may impinge on the organization. Scanning news, information, and analysis of future development in the outside world provides experts with the kinds of knowledge the Prince tends to be avid for. A first strategy consists in expanding the scope of responsibility of the analytical group, which may be simply achieved by redefining tasks or even changing the name of the office:

> When an analyst took over the Evaluation Branch of the OEO's Office of Planning, Research, and Evaluation, she added "analysis" to the name so that the staff would be empowered to make program recommendations beyond the scope of existing field operations. (Meltsner 1976), p. 185)

The second strategy consists in obtaining information the Prince cannot afford not to listen to. This means that the experts want to focus on alternative options for the actions the Prince can undertake: What would happen if this were done? What would happen if we increased these programs and phased out these? The ability to provide succinct and reasoned statements about the consequences of possible actions of a Prince is a talent the Prince values. He wants to listen to his experts when they show him where he might burn his fingers.

The third strategy consists in forming alliances, both inside and outside the organization, with other analysts. The point is to be informed, and experts need to have access to the work of other analysts in government, industry, the think tanks, and universities. Work is commissioned to scan ongoing research to find out what is happening that may affect the agency; experts circulate, attend conferences, exchange papers with their colleagues. They compare notes on the kinds of analysis undertaken, the way work is perceived, who wants what in the executive, the legislative, and among pressure groups. Research is organized across department units, bringing outside experts to participate and bringing the interests of many units. Ad hoc groups within the agency or interagency task forces undertake the brunt of analysis. The Prince has less control on his experts when these are united and present a common interagency position.

The Think Tanks

THE THINK TANKS emerged in the last three decades, although some date back to the thirties. These institutions provide a supportive environment with all the necessary facilities for large, multidisciplinary professional staffs who devote most or all of their time to policy research. The absence of teaching functions provides flexibility in the use of staff time. The research is under contract or supported by grants, and may be done for government agencies, foundations, or private institutions.

Since most think tanks do not have large endowments, there

is always considerable competition for staff, research ideas, and contracts. Expertise is bought and sold in a competitive market and therefore generates new ideas, approaches, and methodologies on a basis of professional differentiation and advancement. In contrast to the universities, where tenure protects the researcher, the think tanks have often eliminated large research groups when a particular problem was no longer receiving external support. They have to be more flexible than the universities, but at the same time their dependence on contracts and grants does not always guarantee high-quality research. Yet when the researcher can obtain external support, new approaches and innovative research find immediate acceptance from think-tank management.

For example, pioneering research on very long range planning has been initiated in think tanks. Several studies of the year 2000 are under way in the United States and Western Europe. The Hudson Institute specializes in scenario writing and the evaluation of future environments for policy. Similar research is carried on by the Institute for the Future; TEMPO (Center for Advanced Studies, General Electric, Santa Barbara); and SEDEIS (Société d'Études et de Documentation Économiques Industrielles et Sociales), a think tank in Paris that publishes *Futuribles.*

Other inventions include subscription services, such as the National Planning Association's national economic projections and the Stanford Research Institute's "Long Range Planning Service," which provides a continuous stream of brief and informative reports on new developments and trends affecting corporate growth possibilities.

Institutions such as RAND and the Institute for Defense Analysis (IDA) were, at least originally, sponsored by Defense Department agencies, but were given some freedom in the choice of problems. More recently RAND, the System Development Corporation, Abt Associates, and other organizations have been diversifying and entering the emerging research market related to social problems.

Some of the think tanks specialize in the social sciences; for example, the Brookings Institution and the National Planning Association. Others, such as Arthur D. Little, Battelle Memorial

Institute, and Stanford Research Institute, are large conglom-
erates spanning both the natural and the social sciences. These
large think tanks have professional staffs running into the thou-
sands and annual budgets in the hundreds of millions of dollars.

Many think tanks are nonprofit organizations. Some are affiliated with universities. For example, the Institute for Defense
Analysis was created mostly for reasons of legitimation under a
consortium of universities, but it is quite independent from the
universities and carries on classified policy research for the military. During its formative years, Stanford Research Institute was
affiliated with Stanford University, although the staffs of the
institutions were different. Today, the two institutions are independent, one from the other. Other think tanks are profit
organizations similar in structure to management consulting
firms. Yet some profit organizations, such as the Battelle Memorial Institute and Arthur D. Little, are similar to nonprofit
organizations and, like them, work under contract for many different government and private agencies. In the early days of the
think tanks, nonprofit status had advantages in seeking foundation or agency support and in financing growth by avoiding
some corporate taxes. But these differences do not seem to have
affected the nature of the research being undertaken in either
kind of institution.

Think tanks often serve many different sponsors. Therefore,
they have access to large amounts of information and to many
research areas, which in turn places them in a unique position to
assist other clients. For example, think tanks with staffs doing
research and development work for government and industry
have in-house access to direct information about market growth.
Think tanks undertake classified research and are not under
pressure to release their reports to the general public. But even
general knowledge about the nature and scope of classified research can be helpful to nonclassified work without in any way
breaching security regulations. Government agencies or private
corporations with large planning staffs of their own turn to the
think tanks for access to their sources of information. In this
way, a considerable amount of interorganizational planning and
coordination takes place at the research level.

The think tanks provide career locations for policy-oriented scientists away from the immediate government bureaucracy, and offer some of the intellectual advantages of universities. Moreover, they are free from civil service regulations, thus permitting salary schedules that are competitive with those in the private sector.

To be sure, think tanks are not independent of their sponsors, but they do provide a limited form of professional protection for their staffs. If their financial structure includes an endowment and they are able to create sufficient reserves, they can determine their own research policies independently of the more immediate demands of their sponsors.

Since the professional talent of the staff is the principal asset of the think tank, and since the talent market requires career security, the think tanks are often obliged to adopt aggressive promotional policies to obtain policy research contracts so that they can keep their staffs. Most think tanks begin at some level of financial insecurity. Therefore the tendency of their research administrators in a competitive situation is to seek or bid on more contracts than they can handle on the assumption that some research proposals will not be accepted. When the rate of proposal acceptance goes beyond the capacity of the existing think-tank staff, additions to the staff are made. These additions create higher levels of insecurity, and more aggressive promotional campaigns are initiated.

As a result, think tanks have had considerable impact, both on the private and on the public sector, in promoting the use of policy analysis, programming, evaluation, and long-range planning. Many ideas for policy research are initiated in think tanks. Periodic visits to Washington or to state capitals provide opportunities to discuss possible research projects with potential sponsors. A mutual process of education takes place. The think-tank staff finds out the preoccupations of the bureaucracy. What programs are they contemplating? What kind of research might shed light on the problem? What is the assistant secretary thinking about? Has the agency considered a program of research? What studies are being discussed? What about the work being done elsewhere? Would an analysis of results be helpful?

After some time, research ideas fed into the bureaucracy become an agency decision to undertake a research project. At that point, the agency staff spells out the nature of the contract and issues an RFP—an official request for a proposal which allows any qualified consultant to bid on it. All think tanks and other consultants interested in the project work feverishly preparing their proposals. The think-tank group that initiated the idea and managed to induce agency thinking on the research topic has an advantage on its competitors—it knows what is wanted and it is known to the agency. But this does not mean it automatically obtains the contract. Another group may suggest a more interesting approach, have access to better talent, and offer to do the work for less money. After the due date for proposals, the agency selects a contractor. An award is made. The think tank that receives the contract has a policy research task at hand.

The proposal and the contract spell out the objectives of the work, the kind of talent to be employed, the time to be taken, and the general nature of the work. A project manager is assigned, staff selected, consultants hired. The work has to be completed by a definite date. The project is under way.

The think tanks are always close to the clients. That is, the Prince also controls outside experts because of their dependence on future contracts. If a client needs or wants a report with certain kinds of recommendations, there will be considerable pressure to write a report that justifies the recommendations. This is one aspect of doing research in think tanks. But the more prestigious and diversified think tanks can better resist these pressures, and have to resist them to maintain their prestige. Therefore, most think tanks have pursued conscious policies to diversify themselves. For example, the RAND Corporation gradually built a clientele among several separate government agencies to resist the potential limitations that one agency might impose. But diversification does not reduce overall dependence, nor does it reduce the dependence of small groups within the think tank. The research capabilities of subgroups are built to respond to agency needs. Over a period of time they will become closely tied to the agency's domain of interest and responsibility. A well-diversified think tank working for both public and private agencies is only a conglomerate of smaller research groups with limited domains of expertise and limited sources of sponsorship. Transfer from one research area to another is hampered by specialization within domains of expertise. Therefore, dependence on expanding contracts remains a characteristic of this type of research institution.

Policy Research within Universities

THE TRADITIONS OF individual research and the compartmentalized structure of universities do not facilitate the conduct of large-scale interdisciplinary research, particularly when the research has to be carried out for a sponsor under definite time constraints. But from World War II through the present, the availability of external funding from foundations and certain government agencies with a broad research mandate, the external demand and even pressure from other government agencies and the private sector, and the interest or curiosity of scholars have resulted in a mushrooming of policy research centers within the universities. These centers tend to be action-oriented and interdisciplinary and, while some teaching functions may still be provided for, many of them provide their faculties with new opportunities for uninterrupted research.

Location within the university permits direct access to the university talent pool: not only the faculty, but also large numbers of graduate students who may be available on short notice for short-term urgent research or may undertake long-term research in conjunction with their program of studies. It also provides access to university facilities: libraries, computers, and laboratories. It assures a linkage between the research accumulated in departments and that undertaken for policy purposes. For example, in the last few years, the computerized data banks established for empirical research results were recognized as a valuable resource for both policy- and discipline-oriented social scientists. Just as independent think tanks acquire access to information by working for many sponsors, university think tanks accumulate stores of secondary information that are available for further research. This also places them in a competitive position; as institutions differentiate themselves, some of these universities become increasingly better able to carry out policy work and attract new talent and additional external resources.

University think tanks have some advantage in recruiting staff, even if the appointment does not involve a joint appointment with a department and is not a permanent faculty position. One reason is that the university has more prestige in academic circles than independent think tanks. To be sure, this status difference disappears when the think tanks acquire professional reputations of their own. But it is easier to initiate a new research facility close to a university. It appears that when totally new think tanks have been created away from universities, it has been necessary to provide considerable discretion to the staff and more than adequate resources to make the move attractive to talented researchers.

To some extent the university think tank provides a more stable professional environment for policy research since general support for universities is available. Quite often policy research is carried on by faculty on permanent appointments. They transfer from a teaching function to full-time research and part of the contract money is used to hire a substitute professor to cover the teaching function. When the contract ends, the professor reverts to his or her normal functions.

University think tanks are subject to the politics of university governance. At times these can limit research capability, particularly if the research implies restrictions that are incompatible with the norms of academic research. Secrecy, for example, is incompatible with the university mandate of advancing and transmitting knowledge, and secret projects are usually handled by think tanks with no university affiliation.

Universities are often attacked for taking policy research contracts with government or private agencies, because this is interpreted as overt external control on the generation of new knowledge, which, while not necessarily threatening to the overall intellectual balance of the university, is at least a threat to balance in the selection of policy problems the university considers important. These attacks on the university have often led university administrators away from involvement in policy research. This is unfortunate, because the attack on the universities is an oversimplification of the issues involved.

The university is only one component in the wider national system of policy expertise. Reducing the involvement of the university in policy research simply reduces the level of independence of experts vis-à-vis their Prince. It does not correct any real or imaginary imbalances in policy research. Reducing university involvement in policy research results in increased investment of government and private resources for policy research in less-independent think tanks outside the universities. It is highly debatable whether such resource transfers strengthen or weaken the universities. But they certainly weaken the quality of the policy research undertaken, since they place the burden on organizations that are, in the aggregate, more dependent, less secure, and less well established than the universities.

In some universities, policy research is not considered at a par with academic or discipline research. Faculty promotions can be delayed or rejected because policy work is considered to be applied research which is not fitting for a prestigious academic department. While it is understandable that academic social science departments should encourage their faculty to contribute to the development of a discipline, it does not follow that the rest of a university, particularly the professional schools, should be penalized for undertaking perfectly legitimate professional work for government or private sponsors. These problems emerge—as we suggested earlier—from the confusion that still surrounds the role of experts.

Implications of a Laissez-Faire System of Planning

POLICY RESEARCH and planning require resources. Therefore planning takes place within organizations and depends on the availability of resources that are obtained from other organizations. The nature of the institutions created to think about the future and the nature of their dependence on external resources dictate the nature of the problems that are studied.

Firms in the private sector as well as government departments and agencies make decisions to use resources for policy research and planning on the basis of their own goals. The selection of policy problems for research and for the generation of new expert knowledge depends on the nature of those goals.

Emergent problems are significant to existing organizations only if they impinge on their goals. Broad social problems, as perceived by large numbers of individuals in the society, may still fall outside existing organizational jurisdictions. Therefore, they do not impinge on any organization's goals and may be left unattended.

The availability of expertise for policy research is related to the development of the social sciences and to the extent to which insights from the social sciences can be usefully applied. Therefore, the availability of social theories together with facts and measurements limits the development of policy expertise. Where policy research and planning can rely on large bodies of existing knowledge, expertise influences policy-making and systems planning may be instituted. But if explanations are lacking, if uncovering facts and figures is expensive and time-consuming and existing statistics unreliable, expertise will be too sterile or expensive and will not be used. If an organization has widespread access to resources, it can buy expertise and use it to make policies or plans or to influence the policies and plans made by others. But if an organization has few resources, it may find it difficult to afford policy expertise and planning. Therefore, the future about which thinking takes place tends to be the future of those organizations that have access to resources and can use systems expertise to influence centers of decision.

At present the federal government research budget goes mostly for non–social science research. In 1975, an estimate of federal government expenditures showed that only five percent of research funds went to the social sciences; the rest went to the life sciences, engineering, the physical sciences, and the environmental sciences.

Moreover, most of these funds are distributed by agencies with specific mandates: the Department of Defense dispensed

24 percent of the total; Health, Education, and Welfare, 23 percent; National Aeronautics and Space Administration, 19 percent; National Science Foundation, 8 percent; Atomic Energy Commission, 7 percent; and Agriculture, 5 percent (Haviland 1976, pp. 222–23).

Resources available for research and development are indicative of the available resource base for policy and planning research. Therefore, in the United States, the allocation and control of resources for planning the future are not set by the citizens, they are not set by the nature of probable future problems, but they are set by the present strength of agencies that use research and allocate budgets for this purpose. This is a reality the aspiring analyst cannot underestimate. There are many interesting and challenging social problems that cannot be studied because these problems fall between stools. No agency can justify financing the research or there are too few discretionary funds to finance it. This is why it is said that allocations of resources for planning the future are distorted. This is a fundamental problem of our system—it suffers from its laissez-faire planning policy. Given this policy, the influence of departments, agencies, and private institutions, and the peculiar nature of their research needs, mold the pattern of United States planning.

This has two consequences: it affects the choice of social problems that are studied, and it affects the distribution of influence in society. The first consequence has attracted some attention, but the second may be more important.

A number of studies conducted in the late sixties and early seventies have focused on the first dimension of the problem. These include *The Behavioral Sciences and the Federal Government* (National Academy of Science, 1969); *The Behavioral and Social Sciences: Outlook and Needs* (The Behavioral and Social Sciences Survey Committee, 1969); *Towards a Social Report* (U.S. Department of Health, Education, and Welfare, 1969); *Knowledge into Action: Improving the Nation's Use of Social Sciences* (Special Commission on the Social Sciences of the National Science Board, 1969); and *Systematic Thinking for Social Action* (Rivlin 1971). More recent authors have also dwelt on this topic (Cooper 1973, Goodwin 1975, Lyons 1975, Orlans 1973, Rivlin and Timpane 1975, William 1975).

But all these reports and books have not altered the situation appreciably, and one reason is the way laissez-faire planning affects the distribution of influence in society. With laissez-faire planning, citizens and their elected representatives rarely have the time or the ability to influence policy. Instead, influence shifts to those corporate bodies, both public and private, which muster sufficient resources to use experts. These corporate groups speak the language of expertise and therefore displace other political actors. The distribution of influence shifts from legislative bodies toward the executive, and shifts from school boards, county boards, state legislatures, and even Congress toward the bureaucracies they administer and toward well-organized pressure groups. This shift of influence tends to create a corporate state, i.e, a state where political choices are more influenced by the needs of organized special-interest groups than by political judgment evolving from the electoral process.

It is in this perspective that laissez-faire planning has to be evaluated. There is some similarity to laissez-faire economics. Just as government intervention is needed to correct imbalances of the free market, government intervention is needed to re-distribute planning resources. But whether this is possible and how this is to be done requires a longer discussion. We shall return to this question in the last chapter.

six

Trivial, Utopian, Imperative, and Indicative

IN CHAPTER 3 we discussed the various functions experts serve. We discussed the way experts provide legitimation for decisions that have already been made, serve as private staff of the Prince, and help define how to think about policy issues. In chapter 2 we discussed the importance of experts in reducing uncertainty and elaborated from this social need a notion of how implementation is tied to the reduction of uncertainty. We mentioned two principles of implementation: altering the system of reward and punishment and the creation of the multiplier effect.

In this chapter we bring together these various elements to describe four ideal-type exercises illustrating the way experts intervene in the political arena. These ideal types apply equally well to policy analysis, programing, planning, and evaluation. The cast of actors includes the Prince, the experts, the implementers, and the beneficiaries (see chapter 1).

The four ideal-type exercises are labeled trivial, utopian, imperative, and indicative. The main difference between the first two and the others is that the former are not intended to, or do not, affect the course of events beyond legitimating what is happening anyway. The latter are intended to shift the course of events (i.e., reduce uncertainty) but rely on different sources of power to bring about implementation. Imperative exercises rely on existing channels of authority and power. Indicative exercises rely on various sources of power, including the multiplier effect discussed at the end of chapter 2. The specification of future events (i.e., the policy, evaluation, recommendation, or plan), associated with the belief that these will be implemented, reduces uncertainty. Therefore, the resources of social power that create this belief are a central consideration.

Trivial Exercises

A TRIVIAL POLICY, program, plan, or evaluation, does not alter uncertainty; it does not alter anything except through its legitimation function. It is a statement about future events that will take place whether the policy, program, plan, or evaluation is issued or not. A trivial exercise is used for show, for packaging and presenting decisions made in response to other considerations.

A common example of this is the introduction of program planning budgets in administrations that are more interested in the form of the approach than the substance. Take a school system that used to submit a line budget to its school board. The administration shifts to a program budget and submits it. Instead of providing a discussion of desirable goals and how resources might be variously allocated to reach these, however, the new program budget is simply a reshuffling of the old line items classified according to an artificial set of programs. These programs have less to do with goals than they do with existing bureaucratic structures within the school system.

Yet the new budget has been prepared by an expert in program analysis, and there is much talk about it being "a complete break with the traditional concept of line-item budgeting." Of course, it is difficult for anyone familiar with budgets and the rationale of program budgeting to find anything new or special about it. Yet the board is impressed with it: "After all it is a program budget," they say, as if this were sufficient to explain why it should be approved. In fact, the program budget may have been useful instrument for the superintendent in negotiating with his troops, but it is a mystery for the school board. They do not have the expertise to question it.

Moreover, the new presentation gives the impression that considerable analysis has been given to alternatives. In fact, nothing of the sort took place. The young analyst who prepared it was given a line budget and simply told to "translate it and make it a program budget." But the new program budget with its impressive sets of objectives and behavioral tests will survive board scrutiny. "It's so well thought through, we would find it difficult to criticize. After all we have to trust our superintendent."

Boards and legislatures are not the only ones to be confused by trivial plans. The public is deceived as well. The administration calls the planners; fanfare, ceremonies, press conferences, consultations, international experts, and announcements follow. But what is obtained? Only a laundry-list budget request from the various ministries. The allocations are the same as last year with minor modifications reflecting new trade-offs. The press release is nevertheless filled with hope: "The Planning Commission has submitted the new plan. It is a complete departure," etc.

Trivial exercises have several characteristics: There is a tendency to use past trends to predict future developments, i.e., to predict "more of the same." The research report may even include long discussions on various other methodologies that might be used to study the problems. But in the final analysis, it will appear that the authors have simply extended past trends into the future: essentially no changes are anticipated except those any administration can already foresee.

More important, the experts are not asking any difficult questions. They take the status quo for granted. They raise no policy options. They do not seriously suggest alternative courses of action. When you read a trivial plan, there is always much that is implied and not stated. Sometimes it has only one solution, for the obvious reason that suggesting alternatives might be misinterpreted as intent. If it does explore alternatives, it does so with a vengeance. The alternatives are exposed, the better to shoot them down. Since the trivial plan is always a vehicle for presenting a set of decisions, it uses its arguments to present political choices as favorably as possible.

If the trivial exercise is an evaluation of a program, the Prince tells his experts what he wants: "We want that program to look good." This means that the experts must figure out how to make it look good. How can the statistics be presented to give the impression that results are being achieved? What might be done to compare this program with others that are less successful? At one extreme we can expect that some experts are obliged to participate in the falsification of data.

Trivial exercises are well publicized. When policy analysis or planning influences policy, it requires protection and therefore some secrecy. Trivial exercises are public relations–oriented, and the last thing their designers want is secrecy. The experts do not threaten anyone; on the contrary, they are harmless pets to be exhibited to all. There is much opportunity to consult, advise, and express opinions. Everyone is encouraged to participate and have his or her say. The policy design is beautifully printed, and the less content it has, the longer it becomes.

The Prince who hires evaluators and knows ahead of time that the evaluation will be positive is anxious to create suspense: "Yes, we will have a major evaluation. Whatever the outcome, we will act accordingly. If the program has to be abolished, it will be abolished." But that Prince is well aware that the program is secure and that his evaluators are bound to write a strong report in favor of the activity.

Trivial exercises are sequential. A trivial exercise gives the appearance that something is being done about a problem when little or nothing is intended, but the problem remains. Therefore, new experts, new reviews, re-examinations, and re-appraisals are needed. No sooner has one set of experts made its bland recommendations than another set is studying the same problem or some appropriate variant. This set is followed by others, and all their reports gradually furnish a small library.

Most trivial exercises are undertaken by ephemeral bodies,

task forces, presidential commissions, and the like. These bodies have the dual advantage of relying on prestigious outsiders, thus adding to the bodies' visibility, and providing these experts with insufficient time to find out how they might effect changes. Meanwhile, a few conscientious civil servants lent to the commission do the actual drafting. (On the other hand, the outsiders sometimes get rid of the planted insiders and issue a resounding cry of innovation. Usually this unintended utopian planning is quickly rejected by the Prince who has lost control of his experts.)

Trivial exercises tend to be used by conservatives, since, by definition, they protect the status quo. But conservatives or liberals can use experts to their ends. Sometimes it is a conservative Prince who hires experts, and sometimes it is conservative experts who work for a not-so-conservative Prince. Several sociologists have called attention to conservative tendencies among experts:

> If technocratic approaches begin in crisis, they often terminate in fear—in the belief that only the engineering of the soul can stave off the march of the masses to the seizure of power through violence. In this way the manifest *anti-politique* of technocracy often disguises a latent reinforcement of the social order as it is presently constituted. (Horowitz 1969, p. 550)

Most experts tend to espouse a mild reformist ideology; they are oriented in their professional training toward making things better, contributing to improving the lot of mankind by finding new, more efficient, or more effective approaches. They are, therefore, quite unprepared emotionally, not to mention professionally, to find themselves in a situation where they are told to write what is expected or be fired. The experience can be devastating and lead to professional anomie. Experts become cynical, they feel that "anything goes" as long as a Prince is willing to pay, they are willing to write what he wants in their reports. In time, such experts do lose credibility—but while they survive in politics, they tend to undermine the profession. This is why it is important for experts to recognize the limits of the power of their Prince.

Utopian Exercises

A UTOPIAN POLICY or plan is a description of a future set of events that no one inside or outside the administration expects to see happen, at least while they are around. For example, the administration of a poor country announces it has a plan to abolish poverty or illiteracy, a mayor announces his plan to end city corruption, or the president assures us that a plan to end a war will also end all wars.

A utopian evaluation tells us that a program that is a well-known failure is going to solve a social problem, that a program that cannot be initiated will be initiated, or that a program that does not even exist is a flourishing enterprise.

Utopian exercises, by our definition, do not affect anyone's immediate behavior or decisions because the concerned implementers or beneficiaries are well aware that experts are being used as a smokescreen by the Prince, or they are aware that what is being proposed will not happen within the relevant time horizon. A utopian exercise does not reduce uncertainty: those in the know continue to behave as if nothing had happened.

Utopian exercises have much in common with trivial exercises. They, too, are well publicized. The experts are used to give the appearance that something new is being done when there is really no intent to alter existing policies. The elaboration of the plan or of the evaluation is announced with fanfare, hopes are voiced and slogans made, and speeches frequently refer to these activities. The utopian statement highlights the good intentions of the Prince.

The utopian plan provides an opportunity to please all political groups. Since it does not have to be coherent, there can be something in it for everyone. It can also be imaginative and flamboyant, because no one seriously believes it will be implemented. Instead of a dull laundry list, we can have a bold plan that leaps ahead of the times.

Utopian planning tends to attract a more creative, if limited, type of talent: people with "large vision," who are convinced that they happen to know what is best and that it will be sufficient to reveal their version of the truth for its spontaneous adoption. These experts become deeply frustrated when their plans are not implemented, and spend subsequent years decrying the futility of planning in a democracy and emphasizing the need for strong governments where planners can have their way.

As in the case of trivial planning, the staffs of utopian exercises come and go. The wise Prince is always careful that utopian planners do not stay in office too long. They may acquire too much influence; the utopian ideas might appear so desirable that people consider them seriously. It is useful to have conflicting utopian plans or to have anti-utopian statements that explain why the desirable is not feasible.

A Prince alternates utopian exercises with trivial ones. This provides a change of pace. He tells us what he will do, and he makes it sound good. Then he tells us about all kinds of imaginary future achievements, which we all know will not happen. Then he tells us what he is doing and makes it sound good, and so on.

A basic distinction between utopian and trivial exercises is that representations of desirable yet utopian futures accentuate the discrepancy between ideology and reality. If the utopian plan reaffirms the existing political ideology, the contradiction accentuates disillusionment and allows for unfortunate comparisons. Even if a utopian plan is first perceived as such, these perceptions may not be sustained as time passes. Continued exposure to the unsatisfactory reality may result in changes of values and ultimately changes of attitude and behavior. Therefore, many experts who find themselves in impossible situations (i.e., the Prince has no intention of listening to advice and recommendations) prefer to issue utopian statements, if only to accustom outside audiences to new ideas, to build receptivity for future interventions.

Utopian planning helps change predominant values. Many social scientists are aware of this and are interested in the process. Wilbert Moore once argued that sociology had a scientific stake in forecasting or describing future states of affairs that might be preferable to the present (Moore 1969). This function of utopian planning is usually well understood by participants in ephemeral planning commissions: "We knew we were ahead of our time and that the government would not want to move as fast as we suggested. But we wanted to be at the cutting edge." This kind of statement is often made in expert circles.

Sometimes utopian planning is very close to the edge of the possible. The Prince may even encourage the experts to stick their necks out: take the example of economists recommending further government spending or tax cuts in times of recession. The myth of the balanced budget is ingrained in the American mind, and any move away from balance still has high political costs, particularly if it fails. President Kennedy moved cautiously on this front (i.e., not as fast as his Council of Economic Advisors wanted him to), keeping some distance from his experts as long as the ideas were still utopian to some. In time the policies were enacted. But for a while the experts in the council were very much on their own:

> President Kennedy, in particular, encouraged the Council to get out a bit ahead of him in the battle to gain acceptance of modern economics and its policy precepts. He would say to us "I can't say that yet, but you can." In the television "Westerns" they would say we were "riding points." Both the pleasures and the dangers of that position are obvious. (Heller 1967, p. 42)

A utopian plan or policy evaluation that cuts the edge of the possible is no longer utopian. It is either imperative or indicative.

WE NOW TURN to the last two exercises: imperative and indicative. The major difference between these and utopian and trivial exercises is that these make a difference. Experts alter the course of events: implementers behave differently. Social power is exercised. Implementation takes place.

Imperative Exercises

THE TERM "IMPERATIVE" is used in the literature on planning to refer to situations where the government has the commitment and the power to bring about the implementation of a plan. It usually refers to socialist planning where the plan provides the norms for administrative decisions. Presumably the government controls the relevant means of production, and the norms in the plan are directives of implementation. Uncertainty is reduced because it is known that the government can perform as stated.

We use the term to refer to situations where the Prince who hires experts has the power to have a policy, a program, a plan, or the conclusions of an evaluation implemented. It therefore refers to situations where experts work (1) within a well integrated organizational structure, usually a single organization where the Prince is the top management that instructs the implementers; (2) for one organization that controls another organization—for example, experts hired by a funding agency to evaluate the performance of one of their grantees; (3) for a political body that controls a set of organizations (e.g., socialist planning).

The power used to bring about implementation is provided by (1) the existing administrative structure—top management can use its authority and the existing organizational system of reward and punishment to incite implementers within the organization to adopt a new policy, program, or plan: (2) the existing dependencies between organizations—a funding agency can exercise power on one of its grantees to the extent that the grantee is dependent on the continuation of the grant for reaching its own goals; and (3) the creation of specific incentives and punishments designed to bring about the implementation of the recommendation of experts—for example, when continued funding by a federal agency is tied to specific outputs to be determined by experts hired to evaluate a project.

Although administrative or political power is used, we must keep in mind that no state or organization ever has absolute control of the future behavior of all its members. Subunits of government or of organizations, as well as individuals, act in response to various factors. The bureaucracy can always resist the center. But in its ideal form, imperative planning refers to the situations of absolute control in which the expert has no political influence of his own. The Prince sets the goals because he controls the implementation of the plan. His ideology and the political structure have to be taken for granted.

Imperative exercises imply that experts serve the Prince and are not politically differentiated from him. The Prince may depend on experts because he has no ideas of his own or cannot conceptualize goals or cannot interpret or invent an ideology, but the experts are only an appendage of the Prince, an extension of his role. They are not independent, because all their acts are channeled through the Prince, who controls the means of implementing decisions, policies, and plans. Nevertheless, although the Prince controls the experts, they are able to influence him by providing data, information, or knowledge he does not have.

The notion of imperative planning is very important because it fits the conventional definition of the expert's role. Although it is rarely exemplified in its pure form, it is the model that tells us that the expert serves a client and pursues only the client's goals. This is the origin of the notion that experts serve in a staff function and do not exercise political power; of course, the notion fits certain situations, but not many.

Imperative exercises have the following characteristics:

—They require high levels of communication between the Prince and the expert. The Prince spells out clear and precise objectives and the expert knows them. Similarly, the expert knows exactly what resources the Prince can command. Information about resources and objectives flows freely between them. Secrecy does not prevail in the relationship. For example, if a firm has a single, well-defined goal—e.g., to furnish electrical energy in a given region—the expert works directly for the management, and it is the authority of management that matters. As long as the goal is clear, the expert's influence is purely technical.

—The scope of the expert's intervention is limited by the boundaries of the Prince's resources. The evaluation, policy, or plan cannot mandate where the Prince is not obeyed. Moreover, as already mentioned, if a Prince has many resources and his influence is felt in many quarters, he does not fear uncertainty since he can handle most eventualities. Therefore, important and powerful Princes do not need the help of experts as much as small and weak ones unless, of course, they attempt adventurous tasks. Furthermore, the scope of real imperative exercises is sharply constrained because Princes have only finite resources under direct control. Imperative plans deal with limited aspects of social reality: for example, expanding the sales of new products of a single corporation, or reaching the moon. Secondary consequences of these plans are irrelevant to the agency and are not included.

—The experts best serve the Prince by providing information about conditions outside his domain (when he already knows a fair amount about his own operations) or by helping him think more systematically about ways to use his resources (when his domain is complex). To the extent that the surrounding environment matters, imperative exercises also rely on communications between experts working in separate yet related planning endeavors for separate units. Imperative planning within a single unit or corporation is the best example of this.

—The experts can also serve this Prince when he has power and authority to act but does not have information on how to act and fears the repercussions of not acting. The funding agency is always fearful that the organizations it funds will not use the money properly and that the resulting political scandal will affect the funding agency adversely. Therefore, the Prince is highly dependent on the information the evaluation experts provide.

S INCE IMPERATIVE EXERCISES have a limited scope adapted to the Prince's political or administrative resources, they do not resolve uncertainty that is a result of collective action. Therefore, even when many subunits are able to keep their own houses in order and rationalize their operations, the need for adjudication of direction and resources among all subunits is still present. In socialist countries, this process of adjudication is formalized within the national planning apparatus in light of ideological commitments. In market economies, on the other hand, this function is filled partly by the market and increasingly by informal communication networks of professionals.

Therefore, it is erroneous to refer to overall socialist planning as imperative. It is imperative after the fact, that is, after the effect of ideological commitments and after formal processes where negotiations and political give-and-take provide the basis for establishing overall national policies. But these formal processes are not necessarily so different from those that take place in a market economy. The difference lies in the quality and volume of information that can be processed, and in the ideological values that dominate the formulation of policy. It is also erroneous to refer to national (or intraorganizational) planning in market economies as imperative. In all of these instances, planning is both political and technical in nature and depends on the legitimacy of the political and technical apparatus for its implementation.

Indicative Exercises

THE TERM "INDICATIVE" is used in the literature to refer to expert interventions where the existing means of control available to the Prince are insufficient or unrelated to the implementation of the policy, program, or evaluation. The politicians who hire experts may control a few means of implementation, but unless the plan is trivial or utopian, implementation is brought about because of inherent characteristics of the process. Implementation depends on the agreements that are reached, the way the plan is perceived, and the way it orients individual and collective action. (See discussion of the multiplier effect in chapter 2.)

In contrast to imperative exercises, indicative exercises do not fit the conventional definition of the expert's role. Yet, they are the reality in which most experts find themselves unless they are concerned with the needs of an organization having a single well-defined goal or are involved in the evaluation of a very specific program where the Prince can spell out very precisely what goals are to be achieved.

The central difference between imperative and indicative planning is scope. As we have seen, the imperative plan is as comprehensive as the grasp of the Prince. As long as his authority or his power is present, the plan mandates the course of events. In contrast, the indicative plan reaches people outside the Prince's authority. It is the way the experts combine technical arguments with political support that matters. The multiplier effect functions when a minimum coalition of supporters emerges behind a rational argument and when this support is generally perceived to be sufficient to assure implementation. An indicative plan, therefore, is only as comprehensive as the ability of experts to create the multiplier effect. Beyond this, it necessarily fails. Nevertheless, since coalitions of supporters can be created both inside and outside the Prince's domain, indicative planning is better suited to reduce uncertainty in complex situations involving many organizations pursuing diverse and even conflicting goals.

An indicative evaluation takes place in a situation where the Prince (say the funding agency) is quite unclear about what the goals of the activity should be, the managers of the funded program and the beneficiaries of the program have different views about what should be done, and the evaluators find themselves in a situation of high uncertainty where the decisions, if any, taken by the funding agency may or may not be listened to. Again, the success of the evaluators will depend on their ability to bring about a consensus about the goals of the program and to evaluate performance accordingly.

Indicative exercises have the following characteristics:

—Communications between the Prince and his experts are less significant than communications between the experts and the members of a potential coalition of supporters. This potential coalition of supporters may or may not include the Prince.

—The scope of the intervention (say a policy, plan, or evaluation) is not limited by the domain of the Prince, but it is nevertheless limited by the ability of the experts to generate a consensus around an issue. This means that notions of "comprehensive" planning are meaningless. It has been fashionable to assume that everything could and should be planned, or, at least, that the more comprehensive the plan the better. This was based on a notion that planning is all benefit and no costs. But there are evident costs to articulation and rationalization, not only the money costs of research and planning but also the non-money costs, such as the impact of the perceptions of those who

believe in a plan's reality and the impact of planning on the
political process. Since planning can never be completely comprehensive, how comprehensive it becomes is a matter of judgment. Experts have to weigh the costs and possibility of articulation with the benefits. They have to keep in mind the way
planning depends on and affects participation in policy-making.

—Indicative interventions depend on partial secrecy. In contrast to the three other scenarios, indicative interventions cannot be successful if everything is out and open. This fact may be
distasteful to aspiring experts who associate secrecy with evil
motives. In fact, secrecy is a necessity to build up consensus and
a potential coalition of supporters. For example, indicative planning is always selective about publicity. Portions of the plan may
be kept partially secret. Since the plan depends on negotiations,
excessive publicity can be damaging, and, as we shall see later,
there are strategies for disclosing the plan when political consensus emerges.

Summary

MOST EXPERTS ARE involved in situations that combine
elements of the four scenarios. Their interventions can
be slightly trivial and somewhat utopian. Their Prince will exercise power and their intervention will be slightly imperative. To
the extent that they manage their affairs well, they will influence
the course of events on their own and might also be mildly
indicative.

In a typical situation, the Prince may be more concerned with
uncertainty than with legitimation, but both aspects are meaningful to him. Moreover, he may control a few implementers,
but most of the significant actors, whose behavior is important
for the implementation of the policy or plan, are independent.
They are free to adopt or reject the content of the policy or plan
or, at least, to obstruct the implementation.

Existing lines of authority, incentives, legal constraints, and
other control resources do not assure behavioral compliance.
The policy or plan covers the work and prerogatives of many
independent private and public agencies that do not respond to

the instructions of the Prince. Within complex government or private bureaucratic organizations, the lines of control between the leadership and the bureaucratic apparatus are tenuous. Even when a policy or plan takes the form of a set of instructions, compliance is not necessarily assured.

In these cases, it is the combined power of the Prince and the experts or of other participants in a coalition that matters. For example, it would be quite misleading to attempt to describe the process of "jawboning," which various United States presidents have practiced to maintain price levels, as a form of planning where the experts exert influence without regard to the influence of the president. It is the combination of expert knowledge and presidential influence that matters. In most planning, it is the potential combination of expert, client, implementer, and beneficiary power that is relevant.

Therefore, policy experts and planners are concerned with identifying significant implementers and beneficiaries. These will become the target of their recommendations and exhortations. But the significant implementers may espouse goals and values that are different from those of the political leadership who hired the planners. Moreover, they may not agree among themselves. Therefore policy experts and planners may write policies and plans they know will please the Prince but will have little chance of being implemented, thus failing to fulfill their role of reducing uncertainty, or they can write policies and plans that have a chance of being implemented, thus playing a political role that may not please the Prince.

Since policies and plans deal with events in the future, the beneficiaries are not always identifiable when a policy or plan is established. They may be actors who do not yet exist—for example, future generations of students. Moreover the potential implications of policies and plans may not be clear. For example, it will take a while for the membership of trade unions to become aware that inflationary policies are being pursued, and by that time inflation will have nullified past wage improvements.

Some beneficiaries exist and are organized in the form of pressure groups. These organizations are able to exercise influence on implementers or even directly on the Prince. Policy experts cannot disregard organized beneficiaries, just as they cannot disregard implementers.

Therefore, most planning, programming, policy analysis, or evaluation that is not utopian or trivial reduces uncertainty by searching for a consensus among selected clients, implementers, and beneficiaries. The experts invent a coherent and rational outcome or solution that has a high probability of implementation. Coherence is a constraint that limits the range of political alternatives. But within this constraint, the experts' dilemma is not to find the best solution under a set of rational assumptions. It is to find a solution that has a high chance of (1) being adopted (i.e., voted upon or approved by official bodies charged with receiving the plan), (2) being actually implemented, and (3) being desirable in terms of the experts' professional knowledge and values.

In this book we are more interested in indicative exercises than in any of the other three varieties. In the next chapter we will explore the sources of experts' power and the tactics they use to create the beliefs that make such exercises possible.

seven

How Experts Acquire Power

WHEN A PRINCE invites experts to give him advice, he takes care to keep them under close control. For example, when Robert McNamara took over the Department of Defense in January 1961, he placed his analysts in the newly created Office of System Analysis directly in the Office of the Secretary of Defense reporting to the Secretary and the Deputy Secretary. Even when there exist several analytical groups. the Prince will attempt to keep close control of them. For example, the White House often receives conflicting advice from different experts in many agencies. The natural tendency in such situations is to leave the experts to fight among themselves and hold back the power of decision for as long as possible. Thus, the Prince often rules over a divided house.

The Prince's concern for controlling his experts increases the more experts are close to important decisions. This is particularly true of major policy-planning exercises. For example, I once studied a major planning effort to modernize education in

Mexico. When the Mexican government created the National Commission for the Overall Planning of Education in 1965, the minister of education did not name a planner to head it. Instead, he assumed the chairmanship himself. The minister staffed the commission with economists and analysts from the Bank of Mexico, but he left little doubt who was in charge (Benveniste 1970, p. 75). This practice is common and has a simple reason: the Prince must not allow his planners to become an embarrassment.

The chairmanship of any important planning exercise is kept in trusted and friendly hands. The chief technician or chief professional planner is rarely the titular head of planning groups. Usually a national planning commission is chaired by the prime minister, or the minister of planning may be a political appointment with the vice-minister as real technical head.

Sometimes a Prince is not just one agency or the head of a government but a potential coalition of implementers. For example, when the English Labour Government set up the National Economic Development Council (NEDC) in 1962 and entrusted it with the task of planning, it asked the chancellor of the exchequer (the English finance minister) to chair it and invited six industrialists, six representatives of the Trades Union Congress (representing labor), two independent academics, two other ministries, and the director of the National Development Office to join it. Thus, NEDC was "a tripartite forum" in which unions, employers, and government would collectively participate in setting medium- and long-term economic policy (Smith 1975, p. 55). The Council had its own staff of experts, but the Council itself was composed of implementers whose interests could be protected from the start and who could, by the fact that they were on the planning body, first control the experts and second facilitate the creation of a coalition of implementers and, therefore, the multiplier effect.

In many other countries, the planning agencies are under the chief executive or under the control of the finance ministry. This is particularly true in socialist countries, where the central planning agencies are always close to and under the source of executive power which is controlled by the Communist Party.

The planning agency reports to a council of ministers or, as in Yugoslavia, to its equivalent, the federal executive council (Waterston 1965, p. 471).

Notwithstanding all these precautions, in all societies and situations, experts acquire social power of their own. We have already mentioned some reasons for this, including the multiplier effect. Five additional sources of power are discussed in this chapter: (1) the ready access of experts to existing power centers, (2) the political value of information, (3) the possibility of coalition formation both inside and outside the government, (4) the expert's monopolistic position, and (5) the cost of external intervention.

Access to the Powerful

WHETHER THE PRINCE is the president of the United States, a prime minister, a minister of education, or a city council, the experts have access to him. To be sure, the doors to the Prince's office are not always open. Any Prince wants to keep some distance from his experts. Even when he trusts their ideas, he prefers to rely on the proven paths of the past. He wants to be known for new courses of action if they succeed, but he also wants to be able to save face if they fail. He may call on the experts because the conventional wisdom is not working and a radical new approach is needed; but he hides his own boldness until proven right. His own time pressures legitimate his aloofness, and his doors will certainly be closed if the experts acquire an exaggerated opinion of their own influence. He evaluates the potential political costs of their recommendations by keeping attuned to complaints and recriminations. He jealously defends his own political resources and bails his experts out of trouble only if he pleases:

> Not only are the State Department and other agencies often kept in the dark, but the expert staff toiling under Henry Kissinger's direction in the Executive Office Building next door to the White House is sometimes no better informed. This celebrated bureaucracy, erected by Nixon and Kissinger to strengthen their hold on national-security matters, works at an exhausting pace to

prepare and hold open options for presidential decision. But it is
not often consulted on what the President and his chief advisor
ultimately decide to do. It has no access to the President himself
and must rely for guidance on what Kissinger tells it, which may
be much, little, or nothing—depending on the issue and the
moment. (Newhouse 1973, p. 7)

But though the Prince seeks to control his experts, he has a
dominant weakness. The Prince cannot afford not to pay attention to what his experts think and write. Even if he decides to
reject their advice, he wants to know what it is. Therefore, the
Prince is always curious to know what the experts know, and
almost in spite of himself, he calls them from time to time. The
astute experts use these occasions wisely. To educate the Prince
requires special skills. Since access time is a precious commodity, a half-hour presentation may have to accomplish what a
graduate student takes months to achieve. Clarity of presentation and condensation is essential. The learning process cannot
be overt, because the Prince may be impatient if lectured at.
The presentation has to be practical, and the technical dimension and political context cannot be dismissed. If the policy has
to be explained to relevant publics, the experts suggest how this
might be achieved. They know the Prince cares less about why
than he does about how to bring about the new venture.

This skill is highly developed at high echelons of decision-
making, and the reader will appreciate the quality of talent involved from the following description of the National Security
Council meeting of Saturday, October 20, 1962, when President Kennedy, confronted by the deployment of Soviet missiles
on Cuba, decided to blockade the island instead of bombing it:

The National Security Council meeting resembled a Greek
drama in which the players maneuvered according to the plot,
which moved inexorably toward the predetermined outcome.
McCone began with the latest photographic intelligence, a daily
ritual of such solemnity that it was referred to by some as "saying
grace." Then the two basic tracks were presented in considerable
detail. McNamara, in a "brilliant architectonic presentation,"
argued for the blockade; it would "maintain the options": it
would be a first step, leaving open the alternatives of destroying
the missiles or even invading Cuba. . . . Bundy outlined the case
for the airstrike: it was the most direct and efficient means of

eliminating the problem.... Deputy Secretary of Defense Gil-
patric broke the silence with the remark: "Essentially, Mr. President, this is a choice between limited action and unlimited action; and most of us think that it's better to start with limited
action." The President "nodded his agreement to limited action."
(Allison 1971, p. 208)

But to have the ear of a Prince, however briefly, requires per-
severance and access. When direct access to the Prince is unavailable, experts have to develop informal channels of communication. Opportunities to present the case anew or to present it
under different circumstances can sometimes make the difference. Walter Heller's account of the slow conversion of President Kennedy to Keynesian economics includes some low moments during the summer of 1961 when Kennedy was considering a tax increase, which ran against the recommendations for a
tax cut of his Council of Economic Advisors. The tenuous quality of communications between the council and the president is
highlighted by Heller:

> The Council, though ably represented by Sorensen in meetings
> of the National Security Council (which we did not attend),
> fought a lonely and losing battle against this decision until a
> narrow corridor of power, the small corridor leading into the
> oval office of the President, was opened by O'Donnell. His sym-
> pathetic intercession provided access to the President on this
> issue and enabled us to set forces in motion that brought a re-
> versal of his tentative decision. Another strategically placed ally,
> Paul Samuelson, helped the cause with a timely visit to Hyannis
> Port on the weekend just before the final decision. (Heller 1967,
> p. 32)

The process was long and the effort deliberate, and, ultimately,
the tax cut was enacted.

Access to existing power centers is a source not only of direct
influence, but also of indirect influence in dealings with other
components of the administration. Pierre Massé, who headed the
French Plan Organization for many years, wrote: "While weak in
terms of its own resources, the Plan Organization owes some of
its power to its location in the administration ... placed, as it is
again, under the authority of the Prime Minister, while keeping
close ties with the Finance Ministry (Massé 1962, p. 4).

The Prince's immediate lieutenants will not be impressed by the experts' limited access to the ear of the powerful. But at lower levels of the bureaucracy, the glamour and potential power of the policy experts and planners are much more impressive, and they open doors that are closed to ordinary scientists and researchers.

For the medium-level bureaucrat, the planners' access to high levels of decision-making means that they can be used as a bridge over department heads to recognition at the top. In my study of education planning in Mexico, I found that some department directors in the Ministry of Education were clearly cooperating with the planners, because, as one informant told me,

> some directors, like X, have a broad vision of their career in the Mexican administration. They are banking on the President's interest in planning to move upward. Keep in mind that a previous director in X's position stepped from that position to become governor of his state [a Presidential appointment in Mexico]. (Benveniste 1970, p. 104)

It is not only single individuals who decide to support the planners; informal groups within the bureaucracy perceive the usefulness of joining them. These supporters find advantages in the new style of administration, which they understand and can use to their own benefit. These spontaneous alliances are illustrated in a little-known French sociological study of the relations between the French Plan Organization and the ministries of labor and transport. Some of the respondents in the Ministry of Transport indicate the informal nature of their support: "We suddenly found we were interested in the [planners'] games.... We have created in the Ministry our own external informal study group; we have decided to make the transport plan our business" (Lautman and Thoenig 1966, p. 125).

These natural alliances are the beginnings of coalitions of implementers and are the basis of the planners' ability to erode the influence of the Prince's present lieutenants. He will listen more attentively when the planners demonstrate that his lieutenants are not always well informed, and do not know everything that goes on in their own houses. He will always pay more attention if a suggested course of action has support from those below who are familiar with the day-to-day operations of the administration.

Access to the powerful is a political commodity that can be exchanged for other favors. Those in the bureaucracy who do not frequent the centers of power sometimes need to. The experts facilitate such communications. Thus they acquire friends and allies. But like all political commodities, access to the powerful is a finite asset. The experts cannot abuse it; they must cultivate it.

Access to the powerful includes access to important functions. If the planners are charged with elaborating a development budget or if they draft position papers for the Prince, this very fact provides them with power. The choice of issues, the choice of language and argument, and even the examples used in their drafts provide opportunities to please some and bring their interests to the attention of the Prince. Of course, no experts ever please everyone, but they attempt to give the impression that they are concerned; they visit the key administrators, listen to their points of view, and appear to support them. Later they can always blame the Prince or some other faction if the administrators' demands are not met. Meanwhile, if they do not acquire permanent friends, they acquire enemies as slowly as possible.

The Political Value of Information

EXPERTS DEAL IN a scarce commodity: knowledge, which includes not only the knowledge to which they have access, i.e., their expertise, but, more importantly, the information they obtain and generate. Even if a Prince defines his experts' mandate very narrowly and delegates no authority to them, he still allows them to gather facts. Experts always have the right to seek information that is relevant to the problems they study.

This right does not mean that other sectors of the administration will readily volunteer to give information. Since information and knowledge bring power, all bureaucracies are anxious to conserve theirs. But having the right to acquire data means that knowing of its existence may be sufficient to obtain it.

Since it is a political commodity, information can be exchanged. The second source of allies for experts is other professionals and experts already in the public administration or in the private sector who have access to information, research results, and other relevant data, who identify on professional grounds with all experts, and seek to influence public policy along lines that reflect particularly professional points of view or perspectives.

A potential informal professional network of information exchange is created each time a particular school of professional thought finds itself close to a seat of power. Information flows to the experts, bypassing normal hierarchies of command. These informal networks are supplemented by the experts' official right to seek information and their ability to exchange it, which results in their acquiring facts and figures no one else has access to.

Access to information is facilitated by providing status to those who have information. For example, the Mexican planners were careful to include the heads of the various statistical units of the Ministry of Education in one of the subcommissions of the planning commission. By propelling these minor officials into the limelight, the planners obtained access to information in their possession (Benveniste 1970, p. 96).

Contrary to conventional wisdom, the secrecy that prevails in any bureaucracy, instead of being a deterrent, is an asset of planning. Given enough time, planners acquire information which they can exchange for different kinds of favors. Moreover, their access to facts and figures differentiates them politically from the other contenders surrounding the Prince.

Experts use facts and figures to exert pressure. Unfavorable facts about government operations have their value. Delicate allusion to such facts helps keep a lieutenant in his place and may even assure his support. But the experts are careful not to go too far in threatening or blackmailing the Prince's lieutenants. If they acquire devastating facts and make them known, they also acquire bitter enemies who will pay back at the first opportunity. Some facts are best stored and forgotten.

Other facts are leaked. This is easiest when expertise is

located, as it is in the United States, in many different organizations. The expert who cannot influence a recalcitrant Prince sometimes goes directly to the general public. Thus, research results may find their way into the hands of friends in the press.

But information is a limited political asset. The Prince and his lieutenants cannot absorb knowledge beyond their own capability or desire to listen. A minister, not to mention a head of state, operates under severe time constraints. It is not feasible to read everything. Moreover, many a pompous Prince is so convinced he knows best that he deliberately disregards advice or selects what he wants to hear. Lieutenants may become aware of the political ploys of the experts and make it their business to sidetrack unwelcome recommendations. Any complex organization provides mechanisms for this purpose in the form of review committees or clearance procedures that can easily be used to delay or lose a report. If they cannot disregard it, they can at least question it. It is often possible to generate counter-expertise, which provides different facts and interpretations and causes doubt and confusion. This is particularly easy when there is a multitude of expert organizations. If the experts can be shown to disagree, the Prince and his lieutenants can disregard them, and in any case the competition will keep them on their toes.

Courses of action are initiated and continued against expert advice because the advice is too late, the alternatives are not convincing, the considerations or assumptions of the experts are not those of the Prince, the political costs of taking any decision are too high, or the experts are so heavily against the prevailing ideology that the facts cannot be accepted, at least not until the ideology can be altered.

Access to the powerful and the political value of information combine to provide another dimension of expert power. Quite often experts are feared because it is known that they have certain facts, data, or analysis, and either the Prince or the implementers fear what might happen when, and if, these are disclosed. This is particularly true when experts participate in evaluation exercises. Sometimes, the Prince who hires evaluators does not really care what the outcome of the evaluation will be. The federal agency which is obliged under the enacting legislation to conduct evaluations of old programs is just as happy whether the evaluation is positive or negative. If it is positive, it will be used as a success story in negotiating future appropriations. If it is negative, the program can be terminated and the funding used for other ventures. As a result, the implementers in the field are aware that the evaluation can mean life or death for their activity. Therefore, the experts have considerable power over them: any suggestion to improve the activity will be readily accepted. This sometimes confuses evaluation experts. They assume that the reason their advice is listened to is due to the superiority of their expertise. In fact, it is due to their power.

Coalition Formation

NOT ALL EXPERTS are politically oriented. As mentioned earlier, many experts disregard implementers and beneficiaries; they pay attention to the Prince. Those experts who do not understand their political role disregard implementation. They simply assume that the content of their analysis will be sufficient to motivate its adoption.

Those who are concerned with implementation go a step beyond. They want to know who will support their recommendations. Implementation analysis means that the analysis also examines the possibility of coalition formation. That is, for each option, and each recommendation, there will be supporters and opponents. These can be identified ahead of time, and the knowledge of their existence can be used to shape the kind of research which is undertaken.

The nature of the language of expertise, i.e., the fact that certain kinds of problems, measurements, and concerns are highlighted by technical language, favors some implementers and beneficiaries and does not affect others. Those it favors can become aware of this and take advantage of the planning exercise. The politically oriented expert makes it his business to arouse this awareness and seeks allies who are independent of the Prince.

Given very limited time and resources, even the politically

oriented expert is able to organize coalitions only with selected political actors who are accessible to him. In contrast to the search for information, which is legitimated by the conventional definition of the expert's role, the search for supporters must take place sub rosa, disguised by other professional activities.

Given two target groups—implementers and beneficiaries—experts tend to disregard beneficiaries and seek support among the implementers. These experts are not necessarily elitists, but there are real time and resource constraints. Implementers are easy to identify; they are usually located in close proximity; and if a significant number of them support the experts' recommendation, the probability of success is high.

Beneficiaries are important if they are vocal, well organized, and able to place much pressure on the implementers. For example, no educational planner is going to involve students in planning unless they organize and demand participation; this is not because students are ignorant of educational issues, but because they are irrelevant to implementation if they are not organized. In any case, it is assumed (a paternal assumption) that everyone knows what students want, so there is no need for them to say anything.

Because they have insufficient time to deal with all beneficiaries, experts often assess by other means what their demands might be. Need assessments and survey research with samples of target populations provide information which is used to convince implementers of the political desirability of programs.

The search for coalition involves trade-offs. But negotiations have to respect the constraints imposed by the technical framework introduced by the experts. Therefore the language of expertise will shut out the conventional politician if he cannot use it. As Lautman and Thoenig show, the political exchanges take place through a set of new intermediaries:

> Planning modifies the norms of competition or of coordination within the public administration: it makes it more intensive and more dependent on documentation ... politics takes a technical expression ... the Plan Organization ... introduced ... an economic language. (Lautman and Thoenig 1966, pp. 140–41)

If access to the language of expertise is a requirement for

participation in the coalition, the experts are hindered when potential allies cannot negotiate or play the necessary counter-role because they do not know the new language. If those beneficiaries whose support is needed cannot formulate meaningful demands in terms of the rationality and logic imposed by the experts, the possibility of creating a coalition is delayed. In such circumstances advocacy planning, i.e., having experts help the beneficiaries in formulating their needs, assists the planners. It allows additional and necessary participants to play the game. But advocacy planning is only beneficial when a consensus is reached and a single plan prevails. It is not true, as an early proponent of advocacy planning argues, that a "lively political dispute aided by plural plans could do much to improve the level of rationality in the process of preparing the public plan" (Davidoff 1965, p. 337).

Plural plans reduce the basis of monopolistic practices in planning, but they do not eliminate uncertainty. From some points of view this may be highly desirable, but if we limit ourselves to discussing the sources of the experts' influence, it is undesirable because it reduces the possibility that the multiplier effect will occur. Reducing the monopolistic character of planning reduces the degree of freedom that planners have in their dealings with the Prince or even the implementers. It tends to make the professional experts more subservient. Moreover, the rich and powerful are still able to hire many experts, the poor can afford fewer experts, and expertise qua expertise has less power of its own because its monopolistic position is weakened. Initially, therefore, advocacy planning appears to weaken the planner's political role.

On the other hand, beneficiaries may be totally unaware of a process that affects them decisively. Therefore, advocacy planning is highly pertinent to emerging political groups whose interests are neglected by the existing power structure. Even if the rich and powerful can hire their own experts, some expert concern for these groups can help establish a more just and politically desirable solution to their problems. Moreover, it permits different coalitions of supporters and provides new and direct support for planning.

But plural plans are not a necessary consequence of advocacy planning since there exists another alternative. Advocacy planning does not weaken monopolistic planning if a single plan is ultimately elaborated. Therefore, as long as a final single plan is negotiated and monopolistic conditions are preserved, advocacy planning makes possible political participation by beneficiaries. It serves not only to educate or defend the beneficiaries, but also to educate the planners. In such cases, advocacy planning strengthens overall planning, because it reinforces the participation of relevant actors.

The new language of negotiation alters the value of the political resources of the various contending parties. For example, those departments in the administration whose subgoals are easily quantifiable and whose task activities are clear components of the planning framework created by the experts, perceive that their own advantage lies in supporting the notion of planning and in encouraging planners.

When the language of economics is used in a growth exercise, it highlights those organizational activities that are understood to have immediate and relevant significance to economic growth. In the previously mentioned study of the impact of the French Plan Organization on two French ministries, the authors discovered that departments in the Ministry of Labor whose activities had clear and immediate economic implications (e.g., those concerned with manpower training) supported the work of the planners, while departments concerned with social problems without apparent or immediate relevance to economic growth (e.g., those dealing with administration of labor laws) tended to feel that the plan "was a lot of hot air" (Lautman and Thoenig 1966, p. 142). These natural allies of the planners are supplemented by others with the imagination and analytical skills to translate their programs into the new language.

In that perspective, the use of policy analysis in the political arena tends to break up old patterns of coalition formation. Whereas in the past, political affiliation, social class, religion, or school attendance may have been the normal channels of association, now political coalitions also center around a computer output. One can argue that analysis has the merit of orienting political thinking toward problems instead of individuals.

COALITIONS OF IMPLEMENTERS and beneficiaries are not created rapidly. Important implementers and beneficiaries are cautious in their initial relations with the experts, particularly when they already have their own political resources. High-level administrators play a little game of watch-and-see before committing themselves to supporting the planners. They do not want to be identified with the planners' recommendations until they have sensed which way the political winds will blow. They acknowledge the experts' initial attempts to organize formal consultations with reluctance. Potential allies do not even want to attend meetings. This was the case in Mexico:

> The solution adopted by some department heads appointed to the [Planning] Commission consisted in participating in the Commission to the extent of attending the inaugural ceremony of the Commission and sending low-level representatives to the working meetings: "Not only did they send representatives, but they did not send anyone of importance—younger people, young economists just out of school, whoever could attend without implying a commitment. The representative was only there to gather information, but he did not commit his principal. These would wait to see how the Plan shaped up. They want to keep their cards in the game as long as it does not seem too dangerous; but the moment they fear the risks are too high, they want to be able to get out unscathed." (Benveniste 1970, p. 102)

In contrast, those with little political influence have high expectations for participation. This is particularly true of some beneficiaries and the lower levels in the bureaucracy. They even seek out the planners or wait expectantly to be asked to participate in the planning exercise. If they are not invited they ultimately turn against planners and planning.

Therefore the creation of a coalition of supporters among implementers and beneficiaries requires adequate lead time: first, gradually to induce the powerful, who may be reluctant, to take the jump; and second, to control the aspiration of those of less significance whose alienation is detrimental. Lead time, as we shall see in the next chapter, is a central preoccupation of planners.

Monopolistic Planning and
Professional Consensus

E XPERTS ARE AWARE that they cannot disagree among themselves if they want the Prince and others to listen. Uncertainty is not reduced and the multiplier effect does not emerge
spontaneously. Herman Kahn points out that receiving conflicting advice is a way of life in government:

> Every senior man in Washington or other allied capital must
> have at least five people a day come into his office with *the* solu-
> tion to his problem, and since almost all of these solutions have
> incompatible premises, it is quite likely that four of the five
> people are wrong and possibly all five are. (Boguslaw 1965, p.
> 69)

Monopolistic institutions of planning (for example a national
planning commission that has no equivalent elsewhere in government) enhance the collective influence of the experts. But
even these institutions are subject to external attacks (for example from the private sector), and individuals within them
cannot achieve consensus if the Prince opposes their ideas.
They are always subject to dismissal: there may be only one
Council of Economic Advisors, but the president is free to hire
and fire its chairman, and the chairman has much to say about
the composition of the council and the hiring of staff.

Planners consolidate their monopolistic position by (1) acquiring widespread external professional consensus on policy
issues and (2) creating large integrated research teams whose
advice cannot be easily dismissed.

Widespread professional consensus may be impossible to
achieve. Professional divergences of opinion relate not only to
political stances but also to professional careers and theoretical
orientations. Economists and other social scientists are well
known for their divergent viewpoints. Yet a large portion of a
professional body may be organized to stand for a policy, and
when possible experts seek such support to defend their
positions.

For example, the experts on a planning team will select a

number of leaders in their professional fields to consult on short-term assignments. Then they will organize larger conferences to discuss policy options, inviting well-known authorities to bring together the nucleus of a professional coalition. Such approaches are practical in policy areas where the number of well-known experts is small; for example, experts on the balance of payments. In this area the total number of recognized American experts may not exceed fifty or sixty, and it is relatively easy to bring them together. Let me describe one of many such gatherings. An urgent meeting was organized in the spring of 1961 because the balance of payments had begun to show a serious deficit starting in 1957, and President Kennedy was examining various courses of action to deal with this new problem. The gathering of American experts was turbulent and there was much disagreement. But several of the best-known scholars in the field kept urging their colleagues from universities and government to disregard their individual professional stances and reach some consensus to avoid what most of them agreed were evils: excessive restrictions on world trade, foreign investments, and aid. With some pain and after much palaver and drafting, a common position was finally elaborated.

When widespread professional consensus is not feasible, planners limit possible outside interference by resorting to partial secrecy. Invitations to outside consultants are highly selective and excessive divergence is avoided. But secrecy has costs of its own. Scientists and academicians are typically opposed to secrecy, and the wider community of scholars resents overt attempts to keep them out of policy decisions where points of view are promoted without attention to widespread divergences of professional opinion. Yet the conditions under which much government policy is made provide opportunities for secrecy that can be extended to provide shields for particular professional viewpoints, even if they do not have widespread professional legitimacy.

Large integrated research teams provide several means of defense against disagreement among experts. Selection of team members with known intellectual commitments in various camps may deter potential attacking parties, and consultation with selected groups having divergent views provides enough prestige to assure support.

Some schools of thought are eliminated ahead of time by direct reference and rejection of their assumptions; others are omitted in the hope they will not choose to attack on an issue that might discredit them more than it discredits the planners. Some opponents are discredited ahead of time by exposing their political commitments or, if they happen to work for known political interests, by revealing the source of their support.

Reference to opposing points of view may be spelled out in a report to give the impression that they served as a basis for the final recommendation, even if they did not. In the ensuing debate, confusion will reign: meanwhile the planners gain time, and their opponents may never make their point.

Access to unique sources of secret intelligence provides opportunities to compile research data and other materials that may not be generally available to other scholars. Lead time advantages and data specialization allow the experts to produce a large body of research that cannot be disputed in the short time within which policy decisions have to be made or that can never be disputed by scholars outside of government. The careful programming of policy research programs to come up with recommendations when it is too late to mount a counterattack ensures that the insiders will get their say without appearing to depend on excessive secrecy.

Monopolistic institutions for planning provide intrinsic opportunities to force professional consensus because experts are dependent on them for appointments in policy work. The prestige of continued involvement cannot always be disregarded, and the most honest scholar is always tempted to bend, particularly when it can be done gracefully. Social scientists with academic career orientations are much less amenable in this respect than their colleagues in think tanks. Therefore monopolistic power tends to emerge more readily in policy areas where most of the relevant research is conducted outside universities, either within government or in think tanks. While the Council of Economic Advisors often finds ready and vocal critics in the academic community, defense analysts are more subject to the pressures of analysts in the employ of equipment manufacturers, who are too concerned with increasing the sale of their products to attack the substance of defense policies.

High Cost of External Intervention

FORMAL ARRANGEMENTS FOR the formulation of expert policy opinions and, more importantly, for the formulation of national or regional plans, are in themselves political assets in the hands of those who control the procedures of planning bodies. Complex, time-consuming procedures provide a shield against external intervention and a legitimate basis for resisting external demands for information exchanges. Procedures for large-scale formal consultations under definite time constraints sharply limit the possibility of bringing conflicting facts and figures to the attention of expert bodies. Definite limits on participation in formal consultation permit the creation of a selective consensus.

The general character of policy alternatives may be predetermind by the scope of these consultations or the way the policy research is oriented. Yet once the process is under way, it becomes difficult to alter or counter it. This is particularly evident in countries with formalized national planning bodies. The levels of information flow are such that a totally monopolistic planning situation is created. The national plan becomes an integrated document that cannot be altered, not so much because of its coherent structure as because an enormous apparatus of selective consultation and consensus already lies behind it.

For example, the success of French planning owes a great deal to the planning procedures that were established. By the late fifties and early sixties when the Fourth Plan (1962–1965) was elaborated, the Planning Commission had developed, through the experience of the previous plans, a set of formal consultative bodies called the Modernization Commissions. Each of these was charged with a sector of the Plan. By 1965, reforms of the public administration which were aimed at creating economic regions to integrate development work had also provided the Regional Economic Development Commissions, which were made up of local political, social, and economic leaders. The plans were elaborated by the Planning Commission, but the consultative commissions spent considerable time meeting and advising on their respective areas of concern. The Modernization Commissions were composed of individuals chosen for their experience, but they represented the major implementers concerned with each sector of the plan:

> Membership was not equally distributed. Business was always the most heavily represented group, followed by administration, then by the trade unions, and finally by the farmers. Real influence was even less equally apportioned. (Koch 1976, p. 375)

Each commission had a chairman and a *rapporteur*. The *rapporteur* had an important role because he or she did much of the drafting of the report. Each commission report was then integrated into the plan. For the Sixth Plan (1971–1975), more than two thousand people worked on twenty-five commissions and various associated groups and committees (Koch 1976, p. 376). The Modernization Commissions had considerable influence on the content of the plan because they were a de facto coalition of significant implementers and were staffed with influential members.

The point is that it is these procedures of consultation which made the plans highly resistant to counterattack. Once the plan was set, it was difficult to question because it was an integrated whole. No institution had the capability to question it in its totality. Even Parliament was quite unable to have much influence. One might therefore argue that the planners and their allies acquired excessive influence and that a reaction was bound to take place. It is no surprise, therefore, that the Seventh Plan (1976–1980) was reduced in scope. The Seventh Plan focused on selected areas for priority action (i.e., telephone, preschool education, energy, etc.); it was far less comprehensive and detailed than was the case previously. Some power and influence had been removed from the experts. Their domain had been restricted.

The situation in the United States is somewhat different, since no national planning institutions have been created. But American experts can defend themselves because the system is diffuse. Since American planning involves many experts, success in policy work requires knowledge of other research being done elsewhere in the country or in the world. Over time, experts build up informal channels of communication among themselves and with their clients. These make interventions by counter-experts more difficult because the Prince who hires experts also gives them lead time ahead of potential competition. This lead time can be used to hire relevant specialists so that there will not be an easy way to organize counter-expertise.

To be sure, large organizations are always able to organize their own internal counter-expertise to resist interventions of experts hired by a distant Prince. Evaluators sent by a federal agency may find in-house evaluators who already have the facts. Ministries in a country with national or regional planning agencies create in-house planning units to counteract the influence of outside planning agencies. But these attempts to reduce the power of outside experts can also be evaded. Large organizations, however large, have a limited domain of responsibility. The outside evaluator and the outside planner can raise policy issues that go beyond the scope of local or organizational responsibility. For example, the outside evaluators of a specific program find that a recent inside evaluation conducted by well-known experts shows that the program is being run correctly and the specific short-term results of the work are encouraging. But the inside evaluation did not pay much attention to wider or longer-term consequences of the program. The relevant policy issue for the outside evaluators is broader. The question is whether this program is having desired longer-term consequences for the target population. The second analysis turns out to be negative. The external experts hired by the distant Prince have eliminated the feeble organizational attempt to resist. They have altered the assumptions of the first analysis and the internal study, however prestigious its authors, becomes irrelevant.

Conclusion

SEVERAL IDEAS HAVE been presented in this chapter. First, experts are always controlled by a Prince. This is easily explained: the Prince does not want his experts to embarrass him. Second, experts acquire power of their own, either because the knowledge they have can be translated into power, because they can influence the Prince, because they can create a coalition of supporters, or because the scope and the procedures of the planning process are expensive enough to make it difficult for those who are left out to intervene and counterattack. As a result, experts can acquire considerable influence, and when they do, they should not be surprised when this influence is resented.

Experts are needed, but this need is not such that it means experts can displace too much of the political apparatus. At most, experts can be invited near the seat of power: they can participate in politics. But the final arbiters are those who are affected by the outcome of expert interventions: the final arbiters are the beneficiaries. The reason experts can never be too influential is simple. They cannot replace the existing political process. They are not elected. They cannot "represent" the beneficiaries. Some experts who have a broad vision of their role are aware of this. They realize that the logic of their role requires them to pay attention to the Prince and to the implementers. But they also know that in the long run it is the beneficiaries that matter.

eight

Tactics 1:
Time and Staff

THIS CHAPTER FOCUSES on aspects of the politics of expertise that are rarely mentioned in the literature; we deal with the time and resource budget for any expert intervention. Policy analysis, planning, and evaluation all take place in a given time span and require talent, access to data, office space, access to computers, etc. These elements are important to the success of the endeavor. There is no single rule for these tactics, nor is the style of the expert's intervention the same in all situations. In every policy-making environment there is a culture that affects the style of discussion and intervention. One of the tactics is to study the style and culture of the relevant environment, to find out how they can be used or altered to favor the expert's task.

But there exists a common set of tactics. Lead time to act is always a crucial element for any expert. Selection of core team members, addition of short-term staff, access to data, and organization of support facilities must receive attention. In the next chapter, we shall discuss the process of coalition formation. But to create a coalition, you need three ingredients: time, place, and staff.

The topics we discuss in this chapter apply equally well to policy analysis, programming, planning, and evaluation. But readers will have to interpret what is said to fit the peculiar circumstances of each expert intervention. In a policy planning exercise, it may be quite important for the experts to be quite visible and accessible. In an evaluation exercise, they may be more concerned with not appearing to be threatening. But all experts deal with similar situations: they are hired by a Prince, they work with implementers, and they affect the lives of beneficiaries. It is this common shared reality which provides the basis for the tactics we discuss. The topics for these tactics are past style of intervention, lead time, the core team, budget and proposal writing, data, documents and people, conflict within the team, short-term team members, staff size, location, and panache.

Past Styles of Intervention

THE STYLES AND RESULTS of past intervention by experts affect the way the Prince, the implementers, and the beneficiaries perceive the latest expert to appear on the scene. In some areas, there is no such history, but when experts have had occasion to provide advice that has been implemented and has proved useful, other experts have an easier time. There is a tendency to listen again, which spreads and is reinforced by general attitudes toward certain experts. Today, planners with close affiliation to the physical sciences have good credit in policy circles. In fact, this credit has more to do with their reputations in other areas than with the quality of their advice:

> The non-scientist often has an exaggerated faith in the exactness of physical science, and has great difficulty in distinguishing between what is known with a high degree of certainty and what is only a matter of reasonable probability or scientific hunch. Under pressure to make concrete recommendations, the scientist has often tended to exaggerate the validity of his data to permit the administrator to erect an elaborate superstructure of policy on a very flimsy technical base. Something of this sort happened twice in the nuclear test-ban negotiations when much too general conclusions were drawn from fragmentary data

obtained from one particular U.S. underground test. (Brooks 1969, pp. 49–50)

In contrast, the social-science advisor usually confronts a far less convinced audience. As we saw, this lack of trust is aggravated by conflicts within the various disciplines and schools of thought. The less-than-exact nature of the social sciences, combined with natural jealousies and the competition and rivalry of professionals, results in much conflicting advice.

Moreover, the social sciences provide opportunities for self-made experts and charlatans to seek the limelight. Distinguishing between good and bad advice is not always possible. When charlatans have given advice that has been taken and has proved erroneous, experts have a considerable backlog of mistrust to surmount. Past discredit requires correction. Experts must exercise caution, and must entrench themselves in those policy areas where they are knowledgeable. They need to provide advice that comes out right to rebuild their credit.

Policy experts are not always lucky in giving advice. They do not always predict correctly nor do they time predictions in a way that improves the layman's belief in their talents. Luck is important, and Walter Heller is correct when he recalls that:

> it was the Council's good luck—just when the skeptical, not to say hostile, spotlight was full upon it—to have the 1964 tax cut come when the economy was still moving forward. If the impact of the tax cut had instead offset an incipient downturn, holding the economy up but not moving it spectacularly ahead, we would have lost the force of the *post hoc, ergo propter hoc* reasoning that has undoubtedly played an important role in gaining popular acceptance for positive fiscal policy. (Heller 1969, p. 36)

All experts can consciously favor their own good luck. Giving advice that turns out to be correct more often than not depends on the probabilities they associate with their own advice. If the policy alternatives they select have solutions that are known to have high probabilities of occurring, the experts' advice will generally be proved right. If the probabilities are low, their batting average slumps correspondingly.

Since the choice of problem and the alternatives they select influence the way they are perceived in policy circles, the wise experts select problems that they have some reasonable hope of understanding. They avoid policy areas where they have no special contribution to make. They refuse to intervene when they do not believe they can come out better than anyone else. This is difficult because it is always pleasing to give advice and influence others. But the experts who dispense their advice indiscriminately erode personal and professional credibility.

Experts are rarely consulted in some policy areas, but the resistance is not caused by distrust. Communications between clients and experts are deficient. Administrators do not know how to formulate research problems, and analysts do not know how to ask questions that make practical sense. Even if this problem is resolved, administrators do not know how to use research results.

Experts have difficulty entering such policy areas. Funds for policy research are not readily available, and the experts are hampered if they cannot do research to improve their batting average. If they are wise, they shy away from intervention, but then the administrator may conclude that policy research is not useful. A continued cycle of poverty in agency policy research prevails. For example, the Department of State has for many years done some limited policy analysis, but never at any level approximating possible needs. The result is a "vicious circle whereby behavioral studies are not supported by the central foreign policy agencies because there is very little evidence of their usefulness, while little evidence of usefulness can be accumulated because of lack of support" (Davison 1967, p. 413).

This does not mean the experts do not intervene. If the agency does not sponsor its own research, the experts rely on agency encroachment. They locate in other agencies, and they invent legitimate reasons to scan the policy horizon. Scanning permits experts to transfer the research elsewhere. In due time, the agency that does not support policy research has other agencies pushing into its domain. This pressure ultimately forces it to hire its own experts. The competition between the Department of State, the executive office of the president, the Department of Defense, and the various intelligence agencies during the Johnson and Nixon administrations illustrates this process. We can safely assume that in due time, the Department of State will devote more of its resources to policy analysis.

A crucial choice all experts confront is how far they should extrapolate their knowledge. In most policy areas, it is customary to ask experts to make extrapolations from what is known to what may happen four or five years hence:

> On Skybolt there was the typical situation of all ambitious R & D proposals. When the project was being considered, there was general agreement that serious problems had to be solved before a weapon meeting the Air Force specifications could be developed. Nevertheless, the Air Force could produce experts who judged the task was a reasonable one, and outside reviewers could not *prove* they were wrong. Consequently, a fairly modest disagreement about what could be done within the existing state-of-the-art produced a wide disagreement about what could be reasonably expected with a few years' work. (Margolis 1973, p. 15)

If experts extrapolate into the future and are proved wrong too often, their credibility will rapidly decrease. On the other hand, extrapolation is what is wanted in policy circles. This is where expert advice counts. Therefore, experts confront real choices. To what extent do they risk credibility by plunging ahead in areas where expert opinion is bound to vary and the probability of making correct extrapolations is low? Obviously, they cannot afford to make too many such mistakes. They have to maintain—or even increase—their credibility. They therefore have to focus on implementation; they have to be concerned with the feasibility of their recommendations.

THE FIRST TACTIC, therefore, consists in finding out how and to what extent the Prince and his lieutenants trust experts. The experts to be hired seek out selected representatives before agreeing to intervene. They ask what might be expected from them and how they might be useful. They explore attitudes and history to diagnose the way the role is perceived and the kinds of expectations they will face at various levels of the bureaucracy and even outside it. To be sure, this has to be a very preliminary assessment, but it provides a basis for other tactical considerations: how much lead time the experts have to insist on before accepting the assignment, what talent is essential for the research team, and what kind of research budget is involved. During these initial forays into the policy areas, the experts build trust and communication with relevant political actors, and at the same time they survey the terrain.

Lead Time

TIME IS A SCARCE commodity in the world of policy and planning. Time constraints operate against the expert. If there is little time to work on a problem, the expert is less likely to come up with a solution, particularly if the problem requires a new solution that comprises both technical and political elements. Moreover, if time constraints are severe, it may not even be possible for the expert to channel enough information to begin looking for an acceptable solution. One way for the recalcitrant Prince to resist experts is to impose time pressures not only on his own experts, but also on those of his opponents. He plays the game so fast the experts are caught off balance. One can also think of situations where experts have too much time (people become wise to them), but this is a rare occurrence.

It is easy to underestimate the importance of lead time, but lead time is essential to coalition formation. A striking demonstration was given by General de Gaulle in the last days of May 1968, when the French student revolt was at its peak and the possibility of a new coalition government was emerging. All the political experts, middlemen, and other negotiators were feverishly attempting to build an alternative solution. But General de Gaulle did not give them time. Instead of staying visible, he upset the timetable by disappearing for twenty-four hours. (Later it was announced he had gone to Germany to consult with French military leaders and assure their support.) His action suddenly focused attention on the immediate dilemma of the succession. In those twenty-four hours, there was no time to create a solution; the politicians and the experts could not exchange the tremendous amount of information needed for this. A decision-making vacuum arose, and the general's return emphasized its existence. Within hours, he made a brief radio announcement of his refusal to withdraw and his decision to dissolve the National Assembly. The opposition was unable to continue, and the episode came to an abrupt halt.

When a Prince consults experts, he usually wants advice "yesterday." The new experts have to decide whether they should insist on enough time (in which case they would probably be told not to bother) or plunge ahead. First encounters are unsatisfactory in that the new technocrats have to move faster than they would like. But this is inevitable: there is always the problem of getting a foot in the door, and one cannot be too difficult in early days.

The young professor on her first visit to Washington is appalled by the dimensions of the policy problems she is asked to deal with; the absence of adequate facts; the incomplete and confused briefings she goes through in rapid succession; the endless difficulties in obtaining office space, telephones, and secretaries; the overwhelming urgency for final recommendations. Where to start, whom to consult, and how to organize a political coalition are questions that do not even begin to have reality. The professor has no time, no elbow room. She rushes from the airport, is sworn in, sees many people, gets confused, and finally takes refuge in a small office. There she quickly writes a technical report that has little to do with reality, fights again to obtain a secretary, and manages to get a typewriter. Late Sunday night she rushes back to her students.

In these initial encounters, the new experts play a limited, technical role. Their first purpose is to familiarize themselves with the Prince and his surroundings. Their first report is the opportunity to demonstrate technical knowledge and is politically innocuous. If they have any time during or after work, they begin to circulate and find out about the policy environment. Their first task is still to diagnose the opportunity for intervention.

Between the first encounter and the next, the experts think about doing the job correctly. How much lead time they will need depends on the problem itself and on the characteristics of the policy environment.

The experts are concerned with four dimensions of lead time: (1) the time constraints imposed by the Prince, implementers, and beneficiaries; (2) the time necessary to give the appearance that the policy is receiving thoughtful attention; (3) the actual time needed to undertake the technical dimension of the work; and (4) the actual (or minimum) time needed for the political dimension.

Take the second dimension first. Some policies and plans need lead time for purely psychological reasons; for example, a major new policy dealing with the implementation of welfare programs cannot be elaborated too quickly lest it appear to be merely an improvisation. This need is independent of the time required to conduct research or even to organize coalitions of supporters. There is an element of style in timing; lead time is needed to fit the problem, but not so much that it gives the impression of postponement or delaying tactics.

This need has to be considered in light of the constraints on active groups such as the Prince, his lieutenants, the implementers, and the beneficiaries. Asking for time must not be perceived as favoring one group rather than another. The expert may be accused of covering up, defending the status quo, and using research to deter action. Negotiating for time has to be done with the support of, or at least without opposition from, implementers or beneficiaries engaged in political action, even though they may fear their endeavor is going to lose momentum if it is delayed.

Lead time also depends on technical considerations. The experts have to design a time schedule that allows sufficient time for political action within the time required for technical work. Usually there is some flexibility in arguing for adequate technical underpinnings, but there are limits. The technical work cannot take years lest the experts give the impression they are incompetent. They have to build a rationale, such as, "We need ten months to conduct necessary background research on the effect of past policies, to undertake modeling and forecasting of alternatives, and to present the selected policy options; we need one month for consultation with the administration and experienced practitioners to test out and select among the options; we need three months to elaborate the final report; and we want an opportunity for oral presentations with top officials."

To be sure, the expert's estimate of lead time for political action is necessarily tentative. But even a guess is bound to be more realistic than complete disregard of the political dimension. As experience is acquired, more reliable estimates are used to determine sequences of work. Taking a date in the future when policy is to be made, the expert works backward, estimating the lead time involved: "We need two weeks to type it; therefore, we need to finalize the last draft in January. We need to plan those meetings in Congress two months before that. We need to let a contract for research six months in advance; therefore, nine months earlier we need to define the type of research required, identify the significant lobbies, and consult the administration. This means we start two weeks from now at the latest."

There are always uncertainties: policy research and drafting is a difficult business, and the talents involved are often mercurial, so the best-organized policy research exercise needs flexibility. There must be time to adjust to possible individual failures. Therefore, the time budget provides a safe period for the technical work, allowing for unforeseen technical and political eventualities. There is always the danger of having a fair amount of political support and not having a position paper to go with it. The opposite is also common: i.e., the technical work is completed, and there is no support for it.

Once set, the time budget must be followed. Postponing once or several times creates unfavorable consequences. The beneficiaries clamoring for action become convinced that the experts are being used to delay or avoid action. The Prince becomes suspicious. He hears rumors that his experts are giving him the runaround. It will be easier to dump them if they give him the opportunity. The implementers become edgy. The coalition is fragile, and the uncertainties of delay and postponement lead to its disintegration.

Yet while lead time is important, too much time is dangerous. The opposition will understand what is happening. This is particularly true when the experts come up with a new solution, the implications of which are not well understood. Potential opponents are not aware of what is going on and how they will be affected. The experts do not want to delay action while they find out. They move fast as soon as they have acquired enough support.

The Core Team

EXPERT GROUPS IN policy work require more than intellectual and professional capability and a great deal of practical and theoretical political know-how; they also need to be willing, even anxious, to devote their days and nights to processing and analyzing data, negotiating, drafting, renegotiating, and redrafting in order to produce not only a professional piece of work but also a shrewd political document.

The choice of membership for the core team rests on four considerations: (1) the content of the research and the kind of talent needed; (2) external perceptions of the political commitments of the team members; (3) external perceptions of the technical and professional competence of the group; and (4) the potential members' ability to work together.

The core team includes all those members of the group of experts who are to be identified with the final recommendations or are recognized as having intellectual responsibility for the work. In some cases it is limited to the senior members who sign the report. In other cases it includes a larger group; e.g., short-term consultants or staff members and lower-echelon staff.

Some problems are easier to staff than others. Margolis points out that some technical issues get studied just because they can be studied:

> Given a technical issue, experts can be called in, calculations can be done, schemes can be devised and rebutted, parameter estimates can be argued about. People can keep themselves busy, and to some degree, even entertained. (Margolis 1973, p. 30)

The choice of research strategy has to take account of the availability and desirability of existing talent. Conversely, since talent has to be employed and research has to be undertaken to provide credibility, the availability of talent and access to data may determine the research strategy. To formulate the research strategy, one does not necessarily ask, "What is the best way to achieve objective X?" but instead: "What data do we have? What questions could this data shed light on? Who can analyze it? What problem can it answer?"

This means that quantitative data and the ability to analyze it will be as important as qualitative data about which opinions can be made. Quantitative data means that several members of the team have to know how to obtain it, how to process it and analyze it and present results. This does not mean that qualitative issues are unimportant. It means that to do battle, experts have to be able to handle the quantitative dimension of policy.

SOME WELL-KNOWN EXPERTS have known political commitments. They have worked on other occasions with known political figures and are identified with their stances; they have expressed themselves publicly on related issues. It is doubtful that a minimum coalition of supporters can be organized if the political orientation of these potential supporters is different from the apparent political orientation of the team.

Trust is lacking in such situations. Creating a first coalition of supporters calls for risk-taking on the part of the early joiners. This requires trust. If experts do not know the political orientation of possible coalitions of implementers and beneficiaries, they must be careful not to limit their options. Therefore, they select a team with as few *apparent* political commitments as possible. Alternatively, if some team members are known to have a particular political orientation or strong views on particular issues, they are balanced by additional members with opposing views.

At a more mundane level, the team needs members who can circulate in and out of the administration among relevant groups of implementers and beneficiaries. These members must be able to identify with, obtain the trust of, and talk about the preoccupation of the potential members of coalitions.

It is useful to have experts who have served in the administration and who can talk in a language that allays the fears of civil servants. These members must understand the constraints and culture of the administration; the constitutional and other legal bases for its actions; the nature of its political constituencies;

and the existence of prevailing informal rules, including common illegal practices such as graft and other forms of corruption.

It cannot be assumed that talking the same language comes easily. Within the administration there is much distrust of experts, and the jargon of the social sciences is often more of a barrier than might be suspected. Writing about the problems of the Department of State, Philip Davison comments:

> A former foreign service officer recently showed the writer a letter he had received from a behavioral scientist at a leading American university. It requested his cooperation in a research project that, in the language of the letter, proposed to compare the judgments of several populations of experts with the results of simulation procedures on selected foreign policy issues. The foreign service man was baffled by the proposal. "What," he asked, "were 'populations of experts,' and what was meant by 'simulation'?" When the letter was translated into terms more familiar to him, he decided to cooperate. (Davison 1967, pp. 416–17)

But the problem is not always the jargon. Often it goes deeper: the planner conceptualizes problems differently:

> Initially, I tried to comb out jargon . . . but increasingly I began to suspect that it wasn't the jargon, but . . . simply that we were dealing with a conceptual framework which these people weren't familiar with. . . . It is a little like trying to explain navigation when everyone still thinks the world is flat. (Archibald 1970, p. 11)

Lastly, experts are too often completely unaware of the significant policy problems faced by their Prince. They fail to communicate because they talk about the wrong subject.

In any case, the academic expert, familiar with his own language, concepts, and frameworks, and accustomed to being understood by his peers and graduate students, often underestimates the communication problem. When he does not feel confident, he may use complex sentences to say that he does not really know, perhaps trying to justify the fee he collects and the travels he enjoys by the length of his report and the complexity of his discourse. But these tactics are counterproductive.

The administration is not the only relevant group. The team

needs members who can empathize and communicate with others, including their peers and relevant pressure groups, such as the private banking and industrial community, labor unions, Congress, rural interests, students, and minority groups. A complex policy issue involving different interested parties requires much diversification in the choice of team members. If the core team cannot meet all these needs, short-term experts and consultants are hired.

As we saw in the previous chapter, the team needs to be differentiated from competing groups of experts. One strategy is the multidisciplinary approach. A multidisciplinary team provides the resources of other disciplines to defend a position that runs counter to the prevailing school of thought in a single discipline. The multidisciplinary team protects its members by its unique intellectual conglomeration. Although it can be justifiably criticized and attacked by a similar intellectual conglomerate, it can reject the criticisms of a single profession as too narrow and too responsive to a well-defined but irrelevant domain of expertise.

A problem with multidisciplinary teams is integration, i.e., making them more than the sum of a number of individuals in separate disciplines whose separate reports can still be attacked separately by experts in their own fields. Since each discipline has its own theories, concepts, and ways of cutting and handling problems, synthesis is difficult; each profession feels that it needs to protect its own professional interests and autonomy. As a result, the sum of the parts of an interdisciplinary report often is no more than the sum of each of the parts taken separately.

William Alonso has coined the term "metadisciplinary" to distinguish the multidisciplinary team that achieves an intellectual communality among its members (Alonso 1968). They are not only well-versed in a particular discipline (e.g., economics, sociology, or political science), but are also able to bridge the gaps between their disciplines by their common policy interest. By learning to work together, over time they assimilate the assumptions and capabilities of their colleagues. Where the arguments or evidence from a single discipline might leave doubt about a particular course of action, the sum of arguments or evidence cutting across disciplines appears to add new dimensions. The metadisciplinary character protects the legitimacy of the recommendation. Of course, a policy that is substantiated from several intellectual points of view is not a priori more certain of success than one that depends on a single theory. As long as the various theories are not part of an integrated intellectual construct, the policy is no better than one substantiated by a single but stronger explanatory theory. That is not the argument. We are talking about appearances. The metadisciplinary report appears to be better, and this is not without relevance.

Budget and Proposal Writing

A NY LARGE-SCALE EXPERT intervention requires a budget. This means that at some point a proposal for research is elaborated, and the Prince is identified and cajoled into providing the necessary resources for the endeavor.

Proposals for policy or evaluation research are usually received by award committees representing several components of an administration. Quite often, the Prince who is going to hire experts needs a clearance from other departments or units of the administration before the proposal can be accepted. Outside experts may be hired by a federal or state agency to review its technical soundness. This is called peer review. In most of the administration, bidding procedures exist. Proposals have to be received by a due date and contract awards are made according to established procedures.

Vis-à-vis the Prince, the experts seek to maintain as much independence as possible. Therefore, the political art of proposal writing consists in saying the least, committing the experts minimally while managing to create the necessary credibility to obtain the award.

In contrast, the Prince is concerned with controlling his experts, and he will be demanding detailed specifications: what are the objectives of the research? what methodologies are to be used? how will the data be collected? how will it be analyzed? how many staff members will be hired? with what qualifications? what reports will be issued? how many copies will be given to the Prince? by what date?

The more experts are obliged to specify what they will do, the more difficult it will be to play a political role simultaneously with playing a technical one. That is, if all the money of the award has to be spent for technical work, the experts will be constrained in their ability to organize political support. Moreover, the more specific a proposal, the more it creates opportunity for opposition to the research within the Prince's administration. A very specific proposal is bound to alienate some members of the award committee who may find its scope too large or too narrow or the research topic poorly articulated. It is easier to create consensus in the award committee when everyone interprets the proposal in ways that fit his or her views of the research problem. This means that vagueness or, better still, indeterminateness is desirable. But too much vagueness, too many generalities, can also provide ammunition to the opposition: "How can you consider awarding one million to this outfit? They do not even seem to know what they will do with it!"

Proposals have to be specific enough to spell out what will be done, but must also provide opportunities to alter course, to consider new possibilities, to modify research strategy in the course of the research. They are specific but have built-in indeterminateness.

Similarly, experts attempt to present a flexible budget. Even if total expenditures are fixed, they will argue for the right to transfer resources from one sub-budget category to another. They not only want freedom from the Prince but also from his accountants. The Prince, his accountants, and contract officers argue for detailed budget specifications and want to be informed of or even approve all budget transfers. Now the experts need their own contract officers to advise them. They need to know what the contract or grant rules of the agency are: what is mandated and cannot be avoided and what proven ways exist to go around the rules. They maintain the greatest degree of freedom possible.

The total budget is set in part by the nature of the problem, in part by the overall budget of the agency, and in part by the capability of the experts to use resources. First, the budget needs to be sufficient for the performance of both the technical and political dimensions of the task. Second, the budget and the task have to fit the overall mission of the agency and its overall budget for research. You do not ask an agency with a five-million-dollar research budget for four and a half million to look at a problem that has low priority in its program. Third, the budget cannot be bigger than what the experts can spend: "They are asking one million, but it is clear they would never be able to spend that much. The talent is just not available."

Data: Documents and People

EXPERTS NEED INFORMATION: data and ideas. As Eugene Bardach points out, all of these fall into two general classes: documents and people (Bardach 1974, p. 121). Documents include files, reports, published and unpublished statistics, questionnaires, books, classified material, and the like. People include beneficiaries (all or samples of them), implementers, the Prince and his entourage, and everyone else who has studied them.

The choice of team members is made in light of their knowledge and access to documents and people, and the politics of expertise is also the politics of exchanging information about access to documents and people.

Since time is precious, the search for data must start immediately and end before the report is written. This means experts must immediately ask themselves: "What will our report say? How can we document what we will say?" The art of data gathering consists of acquiring only the data needed for the intervention: no more, no less. Gathering insufficient data, or unawareness of existing data, provides ammunition for the counter-experts: "How can they make this recommendation? Are they totally unaware of the result of the last study we conducted? Our data clearly shows that what they recommend is not feasible." Gathering too much data is time-consuming and removes available time from other activities: "I have no time to consult anyone in Congress—the report is due in one week. We have been delayed. We gathered all this data, but I do not know what we can do with it now."

Data is obtained (1) by asking and looking for data which is already available—Has anyone heard of a study that shows X? Do you have statistics on Y? Does the Z commission report say anything?—and (2) by generating it; that is, by gathering new data which is not available. The second approach will require more time to initiate data gathering and analysis. But when possible cost- and timewise, this is preferable, since the counter-experts movement does not have access to this data, at least not before our experts have completed their own work.

Data is bought and sold. The following anecdote will illustrate. I was doing a study on future energy requirements for a Prince and learned that an international agency had just completed a major two-year research effort which had immediate relevance to my study. My report was due a month hence. Unfortunately, the international agency would not release the report until it had been cleared by all member governments. "Could I have access to the statistics? —Nothing doing. Could I borrow the draft report? —No. When would it be available? —Probably in three months." What could I do? My own report would be out of date two months after I handed it in. A colleague came into town and heard my tale of woe. "Do not worry; in one week I'll get it for you." One week later this colleague came back and gave me a copy of the confidential and still uncleared report. "How did you get it?" I exclaimed. I was astonished. "Simple," the colleague announced, "very simple. I called Dr. Y who headed the study and told him that we were recruiting for an appointment in his field and that several persons had highly recommended him to our search committee. Could we have lunch? We had lunch at Prunier's [at the time, Paris's best fish restaurant]—we had a very good meal and wine, and he became quite interested in the possibility of the appointment. I asked if he had some recent writings and research we could consider. He mentioned a study he had been directing. We went to his office after lunch and he gave me a copy of the report. Here it is and here is the bill for the restaurant."

Conflict within the Team

THE ADVANTAGES OF expanding the team—making it "metadisciplinary"—have to be weighed against the propensity of experts to fight among themselves. Conflicts among team members are acceptable as long as they end rapidly. A little conflict shows that people are on their toes: all sorts of alternatives are being explored, and disagreement is to be expected. But too much conflict creates problems: the search for a coalition of implementers and beneficiaries is made more difficult. If it gets out of hand, some experts may decide to seek outside support for their position. As the conflict spreads outside, the team is fragmented into competing groups, and the monopolistic position is eroded. As news of the split spreads, implementers who joined the coalition regret their commitment and dissociate themselves. The externalization of the conflict provides opportunities for the opposition to organize. Unless the team regroups, the exercise fails.

To avoid this kind of confusion, the team attempts to limit the options it will consider at any one time. Since various proposals may have to be tested to find which gets sufficient support, these are tested one after the other rather than concurrently. At any time only one proposal is outstanding, and the opportunity for internal disagreement is limited. Of course, finding out the support for options in series instead of concurrently is more time-consuming, but the risks of division have to be weighed against losing time.

The search for support requires intellectual flexibility on the part of the team members. They must be able to respond rapidly to new evaluations of political reality, to alter the content and objectives of ongoing research projects on short notice, and to draft and redraft documents without feeling that their professional qualifications are questioned. This may overtax any expert's good humor. Well-known academicians are unprepared for such assaults on their pride and drafting talents. Most teams include at least one prima donna who comes to Washington expecting the attentions of a court. These personalities are amazed that neither their colleagues nor the Prince is immediately seduced by their ideas. When their drafts are left unused, tempers rise; when redrafting is called for, anger mounts; and when the final product is out, they swear never to come back.

It takes multiple exposure to policy work to develop a core team. Over a period of time groups of experts coming from different disciplines and different institutions work together in different policy situations. The groups are variously composed, but over time individuals learn to work together and informal contacts are established. Groups are created, dissolved, and re-created. Some members move back and forth between universities, think tanks, and public administration. In due time, informal networks of social scientists and other policy experts emerge and provide effective teams for policy work. This does not happen naturally. Organizing policy research teams requires entrepreneurs who understand the peculiarities of intellectuals—their motives and their pleasures—and keep tabs on who works well with whom.

Short-term Team Members

SHORT-TERM APPOINTMENTS of prestigious experts and leading citizens round out the team. In countries where international status has a high value, international experts provide access to external sources of professional legitimacy.

The choice of additional outside members is made in the same way members are selected, i.e., in response to: (1) the external perceptions of the professional qualifications of the core team; (2) the external perceptions of the political stance of the core team; (3) the ability of the team to operate as a unit.

A prestigious expert who joins the team for a short time can launch trial balloons without incurring costs for more permanent team members. His or her strongly voiced criticism can be used to assert a position that some implementers are finding difficult to accept. The prestigious expert can even be used to push such outrageous proposals that the implementers may become quite reconciled to an alternative plan submitted by their own experts. In brief, the prestigious expert on short-term appointment can fulfill many of the secondary functions the expert serves for the Prince. (Secondary functions are described in chapter 4.)

The problem, of course, is that such experts rarely conceive of themselves as decoys or trial balloons, much less as figureheads or decorations to improve the general appearance of a policy research team. Their own professional reputations have been established over time and are defended jealously.

But prestigious experts depend on participation in the policy process for prestige reasons. They are not quite as intransigent as they might like to appear. While their public image needs to be maintained, they can be moved within limits. For example, if they are well known, their politics are also well known. If they are foreign experts, their politics are associated with those of their governments. One cannot expect a United States foreign aid expert to urge policies that are opposed by Washington. Therefore, inviting the prestigious expert implies constraints that had better be understood beforehand. But even political constraints can be handled. For example, one can match the politics of prestigious experts; some government of the Third World are quite inventive in this respect, always inviting advisory missions from different countries or different international institutions to maximize their potential utility.

International organizations, such as the specialized agencies of the United Nations, and regional organizations, such as the Organization for Economic Cooperation and Development (OECD), provide an international and therefore apparently "politically homogenized" source of expertise. An international team of experts coming from different social systems reaffirms the technical dimension of the expert's role and downgrades politics. To be sure, the members of such teams may be oriented to political action. But international teams are very useful because they enhance the legitimacy of national experts. The United States has been very slow to avail itself of foreign or international sources of expert judgment, although it is noteworthy that foreign expertise is now playing a more influential role. Selected United States agencies participate increasingly in the activities of United Nations and regional specialized agencies, and there is a growing recognition of the usefulness of foreign experiences in solving problems in the United States.

International sources of expertise provide access to systematic comparative policy information across different countries. International example and comparisons are always a lever in the policy debate: "We must have one because they (the Russians or other relevant 'theys') already have it. If the Soviet Union has it, can we afford not to? If Paris does it, can London avoid doing it?" If the problem is confusing and it is hard to make choices, there is safety in doing what others do. International prestige has a subtle marginal influence. In addition to prestige, doing what others do rationalizes mistakes: "Sure we were wrong, but so were the French and the British. It was a common mistake."

Well-publicized confrontations of policy experts at international conferences provide opportunities to advance new approaches or defend eroding positions. An international forum can be used to vent internal policy squabbles and provides opportunities to advance ideas in countries that are lagging behind others or to defend approaches that are being eroded more rapidly in some countries than in others. This is particularly true when international agencies pioneer in new planning approaches. They initiate new work in a few enclaves in interested agencies of friendly governments. Later on, other agencies and other countries are induced to join. The ability of international agencies to carry on this creative work depends on the sophistication, imagination, and technical competence of their staffs. While all international agencies are not equal in this respect, some have been very successful; for example, the Scientific Directorate of the OECD, which pioneered in the early sixties in the establishment of national scientific policies in many of its member countries.

But there are costs in bringing short-term experts to the team, particularly international experts. They may be less committed to the work and its success than the core team. Agreement may be harder to achieve among many international experts coming from different countries and evaluated by different peer groups. The opportunities for mischief are increased when the short-term experts have too much leeway and too much influence on the work of the core team. Finally, the opportunities for time delays are multiplied when the report depends on contributions from many experts having different time schedules and traveling in response to multiple commitments and engagements in a world of market expertise; when cultural and language translations are required; when the experts turn out to be unfamiliar with local conditions and have to be educated; when the wrong expert is sent by mistake; when the outside experts generate problems of their own, such as making the wrong speech to the wrong group, making an international faux pas that the opposition can pick up, or even, as sometimes happens, failing to behave discreetly in their private lives.

Therefore, it is no surprise that international policy teams are difficult to organize. Existing links of communication between experts in different countries are more fragile and more difficult to maintain, and the tendency for individuals to play prima donna roles in foreign countries is somewhat accentuated. But whether from far away or close to home, the short-term addition to the core team deserves consideration as a potential resource.

In any case, the research budget must be large enough to provide opportunities for subcontracting with other existing expert groups, particularly potential critics of the work of the core team. Since any potential counterexpertise needs to rely on other experts hired for the purpose, it is useful when feasible to pre-empt the professional field. The idea is for the expert to be in a position to hire the best talent first. A short-term contract placing a few well-chosen experts on an advisory committee can keep many possible future opponents out of the game.

Staff Size, Location, and Panache

THE TEAM SHOULD remain small, by bureaucratic standards, because a large staff is too visible and therefore too vulnerable to attack on other than professional grounds. Any large, expensive staff of experts is easily accused of wasting resources and can be eliminated before it has a chance to defend itself. When necessary, a small staff can always be augmented with borrowed personnel from the public or private sector. The distinct advantage of such an approach is that it helps the core team resist the pressures of those who control their budget, and it allows potentially friendly groups inside or outside the bureaucracy to be involved in the exercise.

A number of other matters may seem trivial but should not be disregarded as unimportant. In countless situations they turn up as crucial. For example, the staff needs access to prime physical space. Space allocations are a visible indicator of social power, and coalitions are hard to create in basement offices. The experts want enough space to accommodate the core staff, visiting experts, and borrowed staff, and space or access to space where informal meetings can be held. The choice of location needs care. One possibility, of course, is the Prince's own facilities. But the Prince usually has space problems of his own and tends to provide low-status space to his experts. Therefore a location some distance away may be preferable as long as the locale has desirable characteristics. An older, small building, refurnished and refinished, may provide a distinctive location with facilities for meetings. The building should be fairly close to the principal government offices, permitting easy passage back and forth between the experts, the Prince, the implementers, and the offices of organized beneficiaries. If the expert group is temporary, it must rent space, and it will need a budget for this purpose. In certain cities, access to telephones and other communication facilities should not be forgotten, and negotiations for them should be initiated ahead of time.

Symbolic amenities must not be underestimated. If transportation is difficult, access to the official car pool is useful, particularly if the coalition has to be created with members of the civil service who do not have similar privileges. Where official clubs or dining rooms exist, access to these allows the expert to bring a potential supporter into a well known but restricted sanctum. Access to other amenities may be pursued: out-of-town transportation and official amusements may provide opportunities for small favors, and all these are both assets and channels of communication.

If possible and not totally irrelevant, the experts should have access to and use computer facilities, first because they may need them and second because of prestige considerations. This may mean subcontracting arrangements, and again budget implications need to be taken into account. The experts need to assure themselves of a sufficient and devoted secretarial pool that they do not share with others. Typing and other production pressures will be high. A production team with access to or control of reproduction facilities can make all the difference when meeting deadlines.

Last but not least, the experts need a talented administrative manager who keeps the accounts in order, supervises the rate of expenditures, bills the Prince, pays for services, and most important, keeps the activity within its budget limits and is able to account for all expenditures.

nine

Tactics 2:
Coalition
Formation

IN CHAPTER 2 we discussed implementation. Either experts work for a Prince who can alter rewards and punishments and the Prince can, if he wishes, implement their recommendations, or they work for a Prince who has limited control over implementers. The second case prevails any time experts are hired in a policy area involving many individuals and organizations. Implementation depends on the creation of a coalition of supporters. If the coalition is large enough, the multiplier effect operates.

The creation of a coalition of supporters is a delicate endeavor. The experts have to be careful not to give the appearance of bypassing the Prince; they must handle the Prince's lieutenants and present a policy or plan that is supported by a sufficient number of implementers and beneficiaries while they avoid the conflicting recommendations of other groups of experts.

They need legitimate reasons for circulating inside and outside the administration. Four technical functions provide this legitimacy and provide a screen for political activities: (1) gathering data, (2) evaluating past performance, (3) evaluating the future implementation capability of the administration, and (4) undertaking need assessments among beneficiaries. These provide opportunities for official consultation, sounding potential resistance, and establishing links of communication.

—Gathering data is the first logical route used by experts to seek out their allies among implementers and, to a more limited extent, to test out the attitudes and felt needs of beneficiaries. The Prince tries to control his experts—but as we saw, he does give them limited authority; he allows them to gather necessary data to conduct analysis. The search for data brings experts to the door of implementers. But the implementers in the bureaucracy are always fearful of outside interventions. They are not going to reveal everything they know just because experts ask for it. Theirs is not an open door. At first, they provide what data has to be provided and no more. They wait to see which way the experts move. When this becomes clearer, they decide to help or fight back. As a result, experts often need to fight their way past some implementers. That is, they may have to acquire data that (1) helps create the coalition of supporters, and (2) helps discredit the coalition of potential enemies. Unfortunately, the second set of data is usually in the hands of the implementers they seek to discredit. In such cases one of the other three routes to obtain information is used.

—Evaluation of past performances places experts in a position of authority vis-à-vis implementers. Whereas providing data to the experts for their analysis of future courses of action does not require full disclosure of ongoing activities, evaluation of past performance provides a direct mandate to examine the defensive bureaucratic structures erected by implementers: "What are you doing? How are you doing it? Why are you doing it?" Confronted by experts who have time to circulate and analyze, implementers are caught off balance; they fear the potential harm experts may inflict and seek to ally themselves with them. Evaluation is an important asset for experts involved in policy formation and planning.

But implementers are aware of this. They much prefer to keep evaluation of past performance separate from policy analysis and planning. Since the costs and lead time of evaluation are considerable, there is pressure to forgo evaluation, or even when it is undertaken, to have it take place simultaneously with the planning exercise. This means that different experts are hired by the Prince, and the ability of planners to use evaluation to bring pressure on the reluctant implementing bureaucracy is reduced.

—Evaluation of implementing capability differs from evaluation of past performance. Instead of asking, "What are you doing, how are you doing it, why are you doing it?" experts ask, "Can you do it?"

"Can you do it?" is important for two reasons. First, it provides experts with an assessment of the strength and weakness of their allies. There is no point in forming an alliance with implementers who cannot deliver. Second, it provides a basis for eroding the strength of the counteroffensive of potential enemies: "It is too bad department Y is opposed to this policy, but it is clear from our analysis that they do not have the capability of implementing the alternatives they propose. Therefore, there is no choice but to pursue our proposal."

Since evaluation of implementing capability is directly tied to implementation, it is harder for the bureaucracy to resist it. In contrast to evaluation of past performance, which is often made to appear irrelevant to future policy—"Why bother with an evaluation? That's not the point. We want to do something totally new"—evaluation of implementing capability is a requisite—"We have to look at implementing capability. How can the board ask us to advise on policy options if we do not know which policies can be implemented and which cannot?"

Concern with the technical dimensions of implementation capability (concern with the actual human and technical resources and with the administrative, financial, and legal dimensions of implementation) provides a convenient way for experts to assess the political dimension of the problem: Who is going to support this approach? Who is going to oppose it? What arguments will the opposition muster? How can we counter them? The experts get to know the implementers.

—Need assessments focus on the beneficiaries and provide a way to bypass implementers. They provide an important source of ammunition: "We have interviewed a random sample of those habitants who would be affected by the new policies and found that an overwhelming majority, 82 percent of the sample, favored the new course of action." Need assessment can provide the justification for a change of policies: "How can department X be opposed to this approach when we find that 88 percent of the affected population would be able to reach the minimum accepted standard in this area instead of 33 percent as is the case today?"

Usually, experts cannot reach beneficiaries directly. They are obliged to obtain their information through the implementing bureaucracy, which deals with its clients on a daily basis. This means experts need to have their own budget for need assessment research if they are to bypass the implementers. The existence of independent survey research capabilities (for example, independent opinion survey centers that conduct opinion surveys independently from the government or other bureaucracy) provides an alternative for using need assessment.

CREATING A COALITION of supporters requires time for learning. No one adopts new ideas immediately. It also requires time to select among ideas. Some ideas may appear most promising at first, until their drawback becomes apparent. Experts do not really want to reveal their own hands too quickly.

In any public administration there are informal communications networks that can be used to provide a basis for creating a coalition. But when testing and searching for initial potential support, experts are careful to keep their distance from immediate would-be supporters lest they become prisoners of their narrower interests. Experts do not embrace their friends too quickly. The exploration must reveal the nature of various possible political configurations before they embrace their supporters and reveal their enemies.

Fortunately, the Prince provides a visible shield behind which the experts can wait for potential friends to come to them. The initial search for data and evaluations is an opportunity to announce the pundit's tentative outline of the course to follow. Official or informal requests for data and consultations provide potential allies with a rough indication of the nature of the experts' preoccupations, a rough sketch of where they might go if support is forthcoming. The argument is simple: the more lead time is available, the more time is available to test out different alternative courses of action and to assess the strength of opposition.

How far initial testing is carried depends on the scope of the policy or plan and the uncertainty of organized reaction. The idea is to map out potential response and identify the centers of power whose position on various issues has to be assured. Theoretically it is an easy problem. It is always possible to find out where people stand; they usually want to tell you. Given time and access to power centers, positions can be reliably identified.

Of course, this sounds easier than it is, because it is easier to write about planning than to do it. Supporters are not found in one day. You do not call strangers on the telephone and ask them how they stand on complex policy issues. It takes a fair amount of trust before the pundit can ask meaningful questions.

A common practice is to circulate papers that are usually called "think pieces." These spell out the pundit's approach to the policy issue. The think pieces are circulated among friends in the profession and colleagues and other experts in universities and think tanks: people who are on similar "wavelengths" and can provide both criticism and the nucleus of professional support. These friends may begin to circulate the paper outside the community to contacts in government and the influential publics. Kathleen Archibald, who studied the way policy experts are oriented to academe or to government, captures this initial stage of the communication process in one of her interviews with an expert in a new policy research field, working in one of the think tanks. He describes his initial audience as "still very narrow."

These "narrow" audiences are beachheads or enclaves in the policy world. These enclaves emerge in other policy research centers where similar research is being initiated: "This kind of research [has developed] elsewhere, and we have reached a point now where there is a fairly good communication among the enclaves. Largely but not completely within the universities"

(Archibald 1970a, p. 11). Thus is the new play initiated, the first themes presented, and the rough script of things to come created.

At this stage, communications outside the narrow audiences are still on a chance basis: the experts wait to see who is interested, who might respond: "We had a mailing list ... at first, they were just names. Frequently we've sent papers *without any explanations* at all.... We've sent an awful lot of stuff, and I'm sure some were bewildered by what we sent" (Quoted in Archibald, p. 11).

In time experts get to know their audiences. Other experts who are further ahead, and whom Archibald identifies as having "strategic orientations," seem to know their relevant supporters in and out of government. At a minimum they know the Prince and the implementers:

> "My main concern is people in and out of government who are concerned with national security policy broadly or military policy specifically...."
> "My audience for many years was primarily just the *top people with the power*, making decisions on the deterrent forces...."
> "I have in mind government people as an audience and I know they will read it, and sometimes it is ... a mimeographed paper to people whom I know will read it because they are interested in the subject or because they know me." (Archibald, pp. 16–17)

Others are aware of beneficiaries and find them useful because "it [is] a good *channel to government.*" One expert even publishes articles (in this case unclassified articles reaching a much larger audience): "The people who read [that journal] are more important in decision making on the whole than those who read regular classified documents of a technical nature ..." (Archibald, p. 17).

In due time the papers are circulated and discussed, and the outline of a potential coalition emerges. Once the potential coalition is identified, it has to be revealed. But even if potential supporters privately favor a new course of action, they are quite unwilling to risk a stand. It is easy enough to assure the pundit of support "in principle," but such support is only a promise of no opposition. The supporter is waiting on the sidelines. The experts have to move some of their supporters one step further. They have to invest political resources in the process.

To achieve this, it will be necessary to convince them that the proposed course of action has a fair chance of success. In other words, at some point the coalition has to become aware that it exists; it has to be brought together and become involved in the elaboration of the policy. Increased involvement and their own commitment of time and staff encourage the supporters to provide more political resources to help the planners. Therefore, conferences and gatherings of supporters provide awareness of strength, particularly if the support comes from widespread areas in and out of government.

This organizing cannot take place if the Prince is suspicious. If he is unsure of the politics of his experts, he may decide to eliminate them before they acquire too much power of their own. There are two alternatives:

1. The Prince can be kept totally unaware of the process until the coalition is a fait accompli. But this, of course, is practically impossible in any public administration. Any Prince worth his salt has his own sources of information; unless the process is rapid enough, he will be able to use his own larger political resources to eliminate any incipient movement he does not favor.

2. The Prince can be kept partially aware of some aspects of this process. He can be brought in early and asked to chair some of the gatherings, thus extending the prestige of his own position to the undertaking. The coalition can be camouflaged by a judicious sprinkling of other uncommitted or potential opponents. Ultimately the Prince's own time constraints will not allow him to oversee the political acts of the expert, who can then create the coalition under the guise of technical consultations.

Getting the Prince to Join

ONCE THE COALITION is organized, it reveals itself. The Prince has been cautiously waiting to see how the planning exercise progresses; he has been waiting for an outcome.

Once an outcome is apparent, the experts attempt to get the Prince's sanction. They know that if the Prince is not convinced, potential supporters will think twice, and the tentative coalition might disintegrate. If the Prince decides to oppose his experts, he is still able to do so. He can clamp secrecy on their exercise, gain time, and even organize a second group of experts to counteract the first. Therefore, the pundit does not contemplate opposing or defeating the Prince without considerable preliminary work.

If the Prince is a single position-holder (e.g., a minister), it is necessary to erode his position by eliminating his lieutenants one by one. The coalition has to be made known to those lieutenants who are most amenable to its pressures. As lieutenants join the coalition, the potential resistance of the Prince may be eliminated.

If the Prince is actually a set of distinct position-holders representing different constituencies—e.g., a city council or a school board—support is acquired gradually from the various members of the organization. On some occasions, the experts have a vocal minority hold the line with their own supporters; they create the impression that if a showdown comes, the outcome will be favorable to their position, and thus are able to swing the other members to their side.

The potential resistance of the Prince depends in part on the content of the proposed policies and in part on the cost of coming up with alternatives, the elaboration time involved, and the implied political cost of postponing action. This is why it is so important for experts to negotiate for lead time from the start, not only to organize support, but also to hinder potential opposition, including any notion the Prince might have of changing experts.

Once the coalition is organized, the experts accentuate time pressures on the Prince: the fact that a decision is about to be taken is leaked out, creating outside pressure for a resolution of the uncertainty surrounding the policy. In this way, experts make the cost of further delays as high as possible. Therefore, the monopolistic position of the experts, together with the support of the coalition, creates pressure on the Prince to act.

Many policy issues involve both the public administration and the private sector. Implementers in government are not the only relevant actors. Implementers and beneficiaries in the private sector have a significant role. Mobilizing private support may be more time-consuming, but it can be an important leverage point for experts working on a recalcitrant Prince.

Outside allies are most useful when time is getting short and secrecy is the only expedient course of action for the Prince. A vocal minority outside can keep the issue alive: secrecy is difficult to maintain inside, and the chain of events initiated inside can be brought to fruition by this small but vocal external support. As long as counterexpertise is difficult to organize and counterproposals difficult to prepare, the minority outside can have considerable leverage because it can publicize the experts' arguments and thus maintain the pressure for decision and new actions.

Once the Prince joins the coalition, the sum of his political assets and those of the pundit's coalition may be sufficient to hold the line against further resistance, in which case the opposition has to reorganize and attack again at a later date. Meanwhile the course of action has been reoriented, and this is all that can be expected: policies and plans are never final; the conflict continues once the opposition is ready to counterattack.

Most experts cannot move a Prince too far. Both Prince and pundits recognize and deal with similar political realities; their political environments, while different, usually have considerable overlap. In fact, as long as we discuss only politics, it is difficult to see how any pundit alters the political situation significantly. But the politics of expertise are based on technical dimensions. The technical argument is the framework of expert power. The politics of expertise are never dissociated from the way ideas, facts, and analysis influence policy support. As we have been saying all along, the art or science consists of integrating the two dimensions. If the integration of the rational calculus and selected supporters is successful, the Prince may be moved a considerable distance: sometimes to success as in the case of the economic policies of the Kennedy administration; sometimes to ultimate failure as in the case of the Vietnam war.

Presenting Results

THE PUNDIT TEAM presents ideas, research results, or policy suggestions to relevant publics on many occasions. Three levels of presentation are relevant: (1) person to person; (2) limited circulation reports and documents; and (3) mass media.

Undoubtedly, the most effective but most costly presentation is person to person, in the form of structured briefings by team members. Any team member can be trained and given the necessary materials to present facts to significant groups, i.e., the Prince, implementers, and beneficiaries. But since time and resources are limited, great care must be taken to identify target audiences and prepare properly trained presentation teams to meet with these groups. It cannot be assumed that the members of the team know how to do this: materials (flip-charts, slides, films, etc.) have to be elaborated, and dry runs of presentations undertaken with mock groups. Then the presentations and materials are evaluated and improved.

The facilities and auspices of existing prestigious institutions are used to give the briefings their greatest appeal. Since curiosity about secret matters is a universal weakness, the briefings go under the cloak of apparent secrecy. Invitations are sent to selected groups of implementers and beneficiaries. As news of the briefing spreads, others who were deliberately omitted want invitations, and these, of course, are issued. The room shown on the invitation is small, but a larger facility is kept on standby. It is better, however, to have a small, packed room than a huge, half-empty auditorium. If the briefing is a success, the news carries throughout the administration; other briefings are arranged in larger facilities. But coalitions are not organized around verbal briefings and meetings. The potential coalition needs written statements as a contract to bring it together. The experts elaborate "limited circulation" reports for this purpose. At first they are think pieces. In due time they become the proposed language of legislation or the outline of the plan, but as long as they are not formally approved, they are for limited access only.

Once a limited circulation report is ready, news of its

availability is leaked. But the report is not circulated widely, because it will not be read unless the recipient wants it. Therefore, the briefings are used to create interest in the report. Some members of the mass media are invited to these briefings, and certain aspects of the report's contents are elaborated in news form, not so much to use the mass media to transmit information about the policy recommendation as to create an interest in the potential coalition. Significant potential allies in and out of the administration have to read the report and understand it if they are to be useful. This is why the reports are so important and great care needs to be taken in their elaboration.

The report reaches a variety of readers:

1. Top policy-makers working under time pressures may read only two or three pages and need to be given a highly condensed statement of the nature of the policy being elaborated, the reasons for it, and its potential impact.

2. The staffs of these policy-makers have more time to evaluate the report. For these, considerable information has to be presented: the results of research, the nature of the policy options, and the logical reasoning leading to a particular choice. Data is included in abbreviated form; as far as possible, it is presented in nontechnical terms to facilitate understanding. Where possible, visual material is presented: e.g., graphs, tables, and photographs.

3. Popularizers—mass-media evaluators for whom press releases have to be elaborated—are used to create interest in the exercise.

It is a waste to elaborate a report that is neither readable nor interesting. From the beginning, editors have to work in close collaboration with the professionals to help them express their ideas as clearly and logically as possible. An art or layout consultant is also useful to present attractive visual material. The pundit uses a qualified production organization so that the reproduction is impeccable, the binding durable, and the package easily processed in the mails. Some experts argue that the report should be issued in a size that fits the standard briefcase (so that it can be taken home to read) but not the standard bookcase (so that it cannot be shelved in the office). But this has its costs: a report that does not fit the standard bookcase has to be disposed of, possibly in the wastepaper basket. It is also argued that the title should appear on the spine. Obviously there are no firm rules on these issues; nevertheless they deserve consideration.

The core team requires its own drafting talent. It cannot rely only on editors. It needs professionals who write rapidly and well, for the success of a coalition depends very much on the way the technical arguments are presented and understood outside expert circles.

Simplification of technical arguments can have unforeseen consequences, particularly when the policy research deals with tentative explanations of causation or with hard-to-understand probability statements about future events. How policy research is interpreted and understood outside expert circles is a field of knowledge in its own right. The expert wants to draft the report in such language that the layman's interpretation approximates the expert's meaning. Drafting is an art acquired with experience; it requires exposure to the realities of policy-making situations and some understanding of how arguments can be used and distorted to support political positions. For example, one widely used tactic is to use language that sounds as conventional as possible: it is easier to organize support if the plan sounds "safe." There is little advantage in scaring friends or enemies. Walter Heller makes this point in his account of the work of the Council of Economic Advisors under presidents Kennedy and Johnson:

> In the search for consensus on responsible use of fiscal and monetary power to achieve growth and stability, both Presidents recognized that it was necessary to make concessions to popular economic ideology and precepts. Their responsibilities as national leaders did not permit them to wait until the economic intelligence gap had been closed. So they drew on what Norton Long calls "the great psychological assets of sailing under the familiar colors." In that vein Sorensen described the economics of Kennedy's New York speech: "It sounded like Hoover, but it was actually Heller." (Heller 1967, pp. 38–39)

Retreat, The Better to Advance

EXPERTS SOMETIMES DISCOVER that the politics of a situation are unclear and that any move on their part seems to elicit a strong negative response. The problem may be linked to larger unresolved issues or the various factions involved may be determined to go to a showdown. Whatever the experts recommend, therefore, is bound to fail, since they cannot create a strong enough coalition of supporters. In these cases, retreat is the wiser course of action. Experts should not waste scarce political resources when there is little or no chance of success. It is preferable to consolidate a position and wait for a more opportune time.

The most elegant retreat position is to provide expert advice that can be used by any political group for its own purposes. Instead of attempting to create a coalition, the experts provide the elements necessary for policy formation without attempting to spell out desirable outcomes. Such advice takes the form of setting forth the probable consequences of a wide variety of courses of action without attempting to select among them. The experts provide as many facts as possible. Instead of working in series, attempting to create consensus for a single solution and only moving from one to another as they attempt to create a coalition, they work in parallel, simultaneously describing many possible solutions without making any attempt at coalition formation.

This exercise has an important heuristic function, and the experts will be stepping back and watching it carefully: it provides new information that may be the basis for future coalition. Since many alternatives are discussed, some are new, and their appeal is unknown. The experts find out how different groups react. But they are careful to avoid any suggestion that a coalition is contemplated. Essentially, they retreat into the technical definition of their role. As one international expert in a country going through political upheaval put it to me: "There is no point in our getting involved. God knows how this mess will come out. We have to help them understand the choices they have to make. But that's all. We give them the facts. If they use them, that's their business. Meanwhile, we watch which way the wind blows...."

Another widely practiced approach is to call for further evaluation, research, and experimentation. It is used to familiarize potential future coalitions with new courses of action. If there is time to wait, the pundit educates his potential allies. For example, when I inquired about the HEW approach to social welfare, an expert serving in the Johnson administration told me:

> For the moment, we are trying to find out what works and what does not. For once we are going to be systematic about this. Lots of people do not like the [present] programs, the way social welfare agencies administer. O.K., that's reality. We are not making new proposals. We want to experiment. Take the negative income tax. We will find out what happens when you use it in a real situation. It has lots of enemies, creates lots of fear. Well, are these based on empirical facts? That's a good question. Do workers with a guaranteed minimum income tend to work less? Do people attempt to cheat? What real problems arise when you try to administer this kind of program? That's the way to approach these problems.

Experiments and pilot projects provide a way to step back and gain time while new facts are discovered and the potential resistance of a strong opposition is gradually eroded. The evident problem with experiments, pilot projects, or more research is that they are also perceived as evasions of decision-making. Some beneficiaries are quick to recognize and resent them, since they oppose delaying tactics. Therefore, the success of the experiment depends first on obtaining the support of outside groups who favor the new approach, and second on internal support. The bureaucracy is always delighted to experiment as long as nothing else is nothing. Those who are familiar with the pitfalls of development in the Third World are aware that it is filled with well-intended pilot projects that never went beyond that stage.

Experts do not underestimate the utility of experiments or pilot projects in resisting future counterattacks: "Opponents say that this approach will not work because clients are expected to cheat. This is not factual. The pilot project indicates that cheating happens rarely—in only 0.2 percent of cases—and is not a significant implementation issue."

One problem with experiments and pilot projects is that they take time and often last longer than the governments who initiate them: "Sure, we undertook three pilot projects and they were successful—but by the time the results were in, the new administration had come in and they did not care about the projects of the previous one—they just forgot about it all...."

Evaluation of past performance provides another important way to wait and see. It provides ammunition for future encounters. But the bureaucracy and the beneficiaries are aware of this and resist it. "They do not want to do anything. They just want to evaluate us to death."

Gambling

ALL THE PANACHE and clever efforts of experts do not alter the fact that they work from a weak political position. The details covered in these last two chapters reveal more about the nature of their weakness than about their strength. Experts do not control votes or vast bureaucracies, and they do not have access to conventional political resources. They have to use their wits, and politically, their wits rarely seem anything like the power of the Prince.

Sometimes they align themselves with political trends and ride the coattails of other developments. Sometimes they become depressed, or at least excessively shy. They find it easier to retreat or to blame others. Too often they are tempted to say they do not know, particularly when they are not certain of their own knowledge. Walter Heller was well aware of the dilemma:

> Staying within the technical limits of his analysis and information is essential to confidence in the adviser. This means that he sometimes has to say "I don't know" even when an educated guess seems a manlier way out.... But it does *not* mean that he has to forswear judgments and advice until all the facts and analyses are in. If it did, he would stand mute a good part of the time. In the course of a hearing before the Joint Committee in 1959, I observed that "policy itself must be made humbly and hesitantly in the light of imperfect knowledge ... policy decisions cannot wait until knowledge is perfect." Senator Douglas quickly replied in the words of Justice Oliver Wendell Holmes: "Every year, if not

every day, we have to wager our salvation upon some prophecy based on imperfect knowledge." (Heller 1969, p. 35)

Academicians are not evaluated positively by their peers when they make generalizations that go beyond the reliability or validity of their findings. Yet policy expertise demands generalizations even when knowledge is not sufficient. Therefore, the gap between academic and policy roles is most severe when the knowledge base is most uncertain and the pundits' reluctance to commit themselves strongest.

Of course, this is role confusion, and for the moment it is unavoidable. But is helps to explain why some physical scientists feel free to give advice in domains that are peripheral to their area of expertise while social scientists are reluctant to plunge.

Often the choice between remaining silent and providing advice and between knowing and not knowing is unclear. There is risk involved, and it is not even clear how advice might influence the course of events, or what might be the nature of possible support and the strength of the opposition. In such situations the policy experts have no way to judge if their advice will strengthen or weaken their new profession. In short, the experts' new role includes gambling. They listen to their intuitions and those of the other members of the team. Often, experts have to act without knowing how they will come out. This is a role they learn to play, and it is possibly the hardest of all.

I conclude this chapter with two mottoes that illustrate an aspect of the reality of planning. The first was given by an experienced planner on a plane between Washington and New York. We were discussing educational aid under the Alliance for Progress. My friend had been consulting right and left with the Agency for International Development, the White House staffs, President Kennedy, and a number of senators. We did not think enough attention was given to education in Latin America, but Washington seemed unresponsive. I was asking how far we should try to move and what principle to adopt. He said: "When in doubt about what to do, do what you think is right."

The other motto comes from a small book by Jean Cocteau that provides good advice to poets, painters, and planners.

Cocteau describes an Indian chief who was invited to the White House: "At the table of President Wilson, his close friends made him understand that he was eating and drinking a little too much. 'A little too much is just enough for me,' the chief answered." Cocteau loves it: "If I had to choose a motto," he says, "I would pick that magnificent statement" (Cocteau 1946, p. 33).

ten

Strategy: What Do We Plan?

WHAT DO WE PLAN? This is the kernel of dispute. When I was involved in planning foreign aid in the late fifties, we argued for the comprehensive approach. At the time, it was evident to me and some of my colleagues that if aid expenditures were formulated in a broader economic context, we could have better and more correct policies. In a book on foreign aid for Africa, we argued that aid could not be divorced from trade and private investment. There was little use in "helping" with one hand and "strangling" with the other; the instruments of external intervention had to be attuned. We wrote the typical experts' admonitions; that is, a blend of sadness at the revealed state of affairs and courageous prescription for others to adopt:

> No adequate studies of the long term outlook for African export trade exist. The information now available suggests that unless deliberate steps are taken to remedy the problem—unless the West adopts policies that recognize the interrelation between trade, aid and investment—the future will not be bright. Western attempts to promote economic development primarily through loans and private investment, while trade remains strangled and fluctuates excessively, will result in great misunderstanding. (Benveniste and Moran 1962, p. 133)

Looking back and knowing that aid, investment, and trade policies are still uncoordinated, I can say only, "Well, it was, or it is, the correct prescription—clearly too early for its time, but we wrote what was right." Right or wrong, the tangible fact is that we did not influence policy.

Did it make sense to argue for the integration of aid, investment, and trade policies? Logically, the answer is yes, but realistically, for the moment, the answer must be no. At best, we wrote a utopian analysis. Kathleen Archibald, whose study of experts we briefly mentioned in the last chapter (Archibald 1970a), describes three types of experts based on their orientations: academic, strategic, and clinical. The first fits us. We were oriented to academic theory, not to strategy of action. We did not care to implement our recommendations; we were telling the world about its "problem," suggesting that the world had better find a way to solve it. Our book contained a fair number of detailed recommendations, but we never attempted to work them out; we simply assumed that our readers would be convinced and become followers. The broader the scope and the larger the vision, we supposed, the more followers could be expected.

The point of all this is that there is a relationship which is rarely made clear between the degree of comprehensiveness of an evaluation, policy, or plan and the process of its implementation.

In this chapter, we discuss the myth of the comprehensive approach. We examine how the selection of time and system boundaries for any expert intervention is guided, in part, by the nature of supportive coalitions and, in part, by the consequences of the intervention for the affected organizations. We provide a theoretical framework to define the extent to which an evaluation, policy, or plan can be comprehensive.

The Myth of the Comprehensive Approach

THE DEGREE OF comprehensiveness of any evaluation, policy, plan, program, etc., is always a matter of debate: "Why did they do a study on foreign aid without saying a word about foreign trade? Why do they not mention foreign investments? All these are linked together, are they not?" "Why do they discuss changes in the governance of the university without discussing changes in society? How can you change universities without changing society?"

These two examples highlight the dilemma of any expert intervention: what is to be included in the analysis and what is not. The comprehensive approach says that analysis has to take the broadest view possible so that the problem can be seen in a new perspective that goes beyond the blinders imposed by the parochial interests of any one individual, office, or organization: "How can you discuss learning in America by just looking at the formal school system? Learning takes place elsewhere—in homes, on the job, through the mass media, peer groups, etc.; therefore, to plan education, you must look beyond the formal school system."

As we suggested in previous chapters, experts use the comprehensive approach to acquire an advantage over the implementers and the lieutenants surrounding the Prince: "Yes, we understand your concern in this department, but yours is a narrow view of the problem. We have to look at it in a broader perspective which explains why we suggest a different course of action. . . ."

As a result, the comprehensive approach is always popular among experts—so much so, that experts tend to lose sight of the relationship between the scope of their interventions and the possibility of implementation.

If you are interested in the unrealistic assumptions of the comprehensive approach, read Charles Lindblom. He is an economist who writes about "disjointed incrementalism" and had the courage to publish a paper on "the science of muddling through" (Lindblom 1959; 1969). On the other side is the normative literature preaching integration, systematic analysis, and the overall view. This approach is so pervasive that, as John Friedmann points out, comprehensive planning "arrived" in the mid-sixties in America, at least for urban metropolitan planning. The Bureau of the Budget issued an official definition (Executive Office Circular No. A-82, 18 December 1967), and federal money supports comprehensive planning in hundreds of cities (Friedmann 1971, p. 315). Interestingly, Friedmann, a regional planner who wrote several years ago that "regional planning strives for comprehensiveness" (Alonso and Friedmann 1964, p. 61), has gone through his own reappraisal which is revealing. In a more recent book, Friedmann is pragmatic: he argues that planning is a learning process that recognizes the competing claims of overlapping interests. Planners should be willing to work at the "interfaces of group conflict": "This new style holds nothing in common with comprehensive planning which may now be seen for what it really was, an old-fashioned static ideology devised chiefly to advance the interest of a few professions in climbing to positions of dominating influence in the society" (Friedmann 1971, pp. 323, 325).

Kathleen Archibald would call it the clinical approach to planning (Archibald 1970a, p. 12): a kind of "what can I do to help to get these various organizations to mesh their work better," more in the tradition of the sociology of organization, planned organizational change (Bennis et al. 1961; 1969), and intervention theory (Argyris 1970).

The debate about the desirability of a comprehensive approach was also sparked by the apparent success of socialist planning, particularly the Soviet experience. After Sputnik, socialist planning, which—until then—had been viewed as utopia or as bête noire, was suddenly viewed in the West as a potential threat. Many feared that the integrated and apparently coherent society (centrally planned) might be more rational, more efficient, and more powerful than the "messy society," and ultimately might bury it.

Meanwhile, to confuse the American or Western discussion about comprehensive planning, the Soviet Union went through a major reform in 1965 which reduced the degree of comprehensiveness of Soviet planning.

Prior to 1965, there had been attempts to decentralize Soviet planning, but the system still operated on the basis of an overall integrative effort going from the bottom to the top and back down again. Planning is initiated at the level of the factory (the bottom), and the plans are gradually brought together at successive levels of integration until they reach the center (the top), where the plan directives and instructions are set and sent back to the bottom.

The degree of comprehensiveness of Soviet planning is illustrated by the number of indicators that are used to plan with. Indicators such as measurements of production output, raw materials to be used per unit output, characteristics of labor that can be employed per unit output, price at which production can be sold are used to control production in factories and other workplaces.

The 1965 reform reaffirmed the need for central planning, but it was accompanied by a significant reduction in the numbers of these centrally set enterprise indicators from approximately forty to eight or nine and by an increase in the powers of industrial managers over personnel, operations, and material resources (Ryavec 1975, p. 3). In other words, the center significantly reduced the scope of its interventions on the way decisions are made in the factories, communes, and other workplaces. While Soviet planning continued, the reduction of comprehensiveness provided more opportunities for innovations and changes to be initiated at the grassroots level.

The Soviet reforms underscore several dimensions of the debate on the advantages and limitations of comprehensive planning:

1. There are limits on the capability of any central planning body to handle large numbers of decisions. Comprehensive planning has to rely on routinization of decision-making. This places sharp limits on the ability of the system to handle many changes or unforeseen events. On the other hand, a central comprehensive planning body can direct national energies toward well-defined goals.

2. Comprehensive planning tends to reduce innovations in the workplace. Some innovations are picked up by the central decision-making apparatus which, in these few instances, is able to move very rapidly. But many innovations cannot be initiated because those who innovate in the workplace are aware of the fantastic effort required to make the innovation known to the center, to have it accepted and implemented.

3. Comprehensive planning has to rely on strict control of performance in the workplace. This is important and needs to be understood. If a large society is going to attempt comprehensive planning, it cannot rely only on the multiplier effect which we discussed in chapter 2. Much of the implementation of the plan has to rely on direct controls. The Prince has to tie rewards and punishments to actual implementation of plan targets. This, of course, is the case in the Soviet Union. Rewards in the form of bonuses to managers and workers are tied to reaching or surpassing planned production targets. Therefore, there is considerable pressure to meet targets. But what are these targets? They are the measurable indicators used by the planning body to control the production of goods and services. This means that certain measurements become very important—possibly more important than the actual service or product. This is a classical problem in any organization. Control of behavior with a measure means that the measure becomes a goal in itself. If you measure learning with the ability to take tests, schools will make every effort to train students to pass tests successfully even if they learn very little. This creates distortions that can be costly.

4. Errors introduced in the planning process are very difficult to correct once the planning machinery is set in motion. Since comprehensive planning relies on tying rewards and punishments to the implementation of plans, any desired alteration in the plan requires a massive bureaucratic effort from the bottom to the top and back down again. This means that, in practice, production managers in the field have considerable trouble handling all the unforeseen eventualities they confront daily (Benveniste 1977, chapter 12).

NEVERTHELESS, at the time Soviet planning was undergoing a reform toward more flexibility, American planning was moving in the opposite direction. As we saw in chapter 5, United States planning is diffuse and centered in organizations. The call for reform in the United States is toward more integration, more comprehensiveness. Each new administration seeks to rationalize the existing or apparent disorder. This explains why, at about the same time the Soviet Union was moving away from an excessively comprehensive approach, the discussion in the United States was for rationalizing decision-making through the introduction of PPB (Program Planning and Budgeting) in public administration. It also explains why Charles Schultze, who was Director of the Budget under President Johnson, could write a book to defend PPB against the arguments of Lindblom. Schultze argued that analysis is important because it relates means to ends, and, of course, this is correct as far as organizations go.

> It may indeed be necessary to guard against the naïveté of the systems analyst who ignores *political* constraints and believes that efficiency alone produces virtue. But it is equally necessary to guard against the naïveté of the decision maker who ignores *resource* constraints and believes that virtue alone produces efficiency. (Schultze 1968, p. 76)

Schultze's points are well taken, but this does not tell us how comprehensive a plan should be. Given that in the United States, planning is diffuse, given that many organizations, government agencies, pressure groups, special interests, and others participate in it, two questions emerge. First, to what extent should the United States move toward more integration, more comprehensiveness? And, second, whose planning is it? Whose political interests are pursued? Whose resources are used? We attempt to provide the basis for answering the first question in this chapter and the second in the last chapter.

How Comprehensive Can Expert Interventions Be?

HOW COMPREHENSIVE CAN an intervention be? This question applies equally well to planning, policy analysis, programming, and evaluation. How far should an evaluation go? Do we simply look at the activities of a specific department in a government agency? Do we ask questions about the goals of this department? about the way the department interacts with the rest of the agency? about the outcomes of its activities on the clients it serves? with the rest of the society?

Any expert intervention requires boundaries. In this chapter, we discuss time horizon, system size, and measurement selection boundaries. The boundaries define the questions that will be asked and those that will remain unanswered: how large a bite does one take at one time?

There is a logic to the way boundaries of any intervention are selected. It is fairly important to understand how this logic relates the technical dimension of the intervention to the political process. In other words, the answer to the question, "Should we have a comprehensive plan?" depends both on technical considerations, i.e, the knowledge available, and on whether the political situation favors a comprehensive approach.

Two considerations come into play. The first is the relationship between boundaries and the consequences for planning and anti-planning factions: how does the choice of boundaries affect implementers and beneficiaries and create political opposition? The second has to do with cost consequences of the choice of boundaries for the implementers.

Let us discuss the perceived reality of the intervention: how does what is analyzed and what is left unanalyzed affect this? How do the boundaries affect the scientific validity of the exercise, and how do they affect the perception of its reality? Our book on foreign aid to Africa was utopian, because its scope was much too large. While it was filled with good advice, it lacked any underpinnings of political support. We consulted implementers of aid, trade, and investment programs, but never attempted to organize a coalition to support our recommendations. The people we interviewed told us what the problem was, and we thought that reporting the facts would be sufficient to create spontaneous action; as we saw in the last chapter, it is not. It was beyond our ability to create a coalition with the resources available to write the book.

The second consideration is somewhat different. The question now is, what happens as a result of an expert intervention? What consequences and costs must be considered?

Policy analysis and planning distort organizational goals or accentuate goal conflict. They distort goals when easy-to-measure target outputs replace more important but hard-to-measure outcomes. They accentuate goal conflict when vague goals everyone agrees with are replaced by specific targets. They can create new avenues of corruption, not only because planning reveals facts that need to be hidden, but also because the facts can be falsified if rewards are related to goal attainment. They can result in excessive paperwork.

Evaluation can have similar consequences for the organizations being evaluated. Again, it may force the organization to pay excessive attention to certain measurable outputs that are only incidental to the activity. It may force the members of organizations to assume the blame for outcomes that are not due to them and it can easily lead to falsification of results.

Undesirable consequences of this kind can result in the demise of experts, the ultimate cost at least from the point of view of the expert.

The conventional wisdom disregards both process and costs. The experts' task is to take these into account. They need to balance an unknown, or at least unmeasured, societal need to reduce uncertainty (benefit of their intervention) against the unforeseen and undesirable side effects of analysis (the cost of expertise).

The problem is not elegant; we cannot quantify any of it. At best, the balancing act is approached by trial and error. But knowing there is a balancing act, the pundit does not assume that a more comprehensive approach is always desirable. Instead, experts select boundaries that are limited not only by the dollar cost of doing research and the availability of facts and knowledge, but also by considerations of process and its consequences.

A Rationale for Discussing Boundaries

WHEN WE THINK about the future we always think in a limited or bounded fashion. As Herbert Simon pointed out some time ago, decision-making and organizational rationality are necessarily a bounded form of rationality (Simon 1965, pp. 81 ff.). There are limits to what we know, and what we do not know impinges on what we know.

It can be argued that in policy, knowledge leads to pessimism:

the more we understand about society, the more we perceive by-products of actions, and the more difficult it becomes to evaluate desirable courses of action. If we know too much, we find it more difficult to decide and act.

More important, if we know much about some factors, and little about others, we overplay the factors we know. The pacification program in Vietnam was introduced with some fanfare, because analysis had a preconceived vision of outcome. They thought they knew what was important in the situation and they acted on their knowledge, yet, according to Daniel Ellsberg, it came out "a rather mangled version of what the analysts thought they were recommending and the decision makers thought they were introducing" (Archibald 1970b, p. 82).

"Optimal ignorance" (Ilchman and Uphoff 1969, pp. 260–62) is the level of information that allows decision-makers to select their preferred course of action. Additional information is irrelevant, either because they cannot use it (they cannot select the best week to visit the Dordogne Valley on the basis of available weather records of last year's rain because they show it rained every week during that summer), or it is too limited (the guidebook tells them what hotels to stay at but not how crowded they are) or too selective (it lists only flashy hotels for tourists, and they still do not know about the little auberge by the river Lot that is only sixty-six kilometers from Souillac [on the Dordogne] and serves the best paté in the region).

From a theoretical point of view, narrowing the boundaries of the analysis does not necessarily result in lowering the quality of decisions. It depends on the nature of the boundaries and the characteristics of the information that is eliminated. In practice, of course, we cannot know when optimal ignorance is reached. Unless we know what the additional information looks like, we cannot guess if it will help or not. Therefore, whenever boundaries are selected for an expert exercise, what is not included is not known and involves an unknown level of incoherence. If we decide to plan the growth of higher education with no reference to the future demand for high-level skills, we give up opportunities for making choices that we do not know exist. All boundaries imply inefficiencies, a lack of articulation, and, therefore, mistakes and uncertainty. But given the necessity for boundaries, the question is not how better choices can be made, but how we can cope with those we make. Knowing all sorts of mistakes will still be made, can we reduce uncertainty sufficiently to manage social life? Can we learn the art of reaching optimal ignorance?

Time Horizon Boundaries

ANY POLICY OR planning exercise defines a relevant time boundary, i.e., six months, one year, five years, ten years, or more. One limit is the cost of information and its reliability. The longer the time horizon, the more alternatives have to be considered, the more expensive the search for information becomes, and the less reliable the results.

Today's beneficiaries or implementers are not necessarily the true representatives of tomorrow's politics. A regime may make plans for succeeding governments only to see its plans repudiated as soon as a new administration takes over (Beneviste 1970, pp. 79–85). As a consequence, the Prince emphasizes short-term planning and budgeting; seeks to minimize his costs, including the devaluation of political resources; and tries to keep his options open. (See chapter 4.)

But the experts are not dealing with the Prince only; they have lieutenants, implementers, and beneficiaries to please, and the selection of time boundaries affects the composition of potential coalitions of supporters. If the time boundary is far off, say ten or fifteen years, the relevant actors are not well known and their participation is difficult to secure. The future implementers and beneficiaries are not yet around, and those who happen to be around are not exercised by long-term issues that do not affect them.

All expert interventions are in fact bound by present time. That is, it is not the future that is being discussed, but the way a vision of the future impinges on today's decisions. Experts select the time horizon that interests existing implementers and beneficiaries. This will usually be the immediate future: next year or two years from now. The longer-term future is only interesting if it can be used to influence today's decisions.

Even if the main focus of attention is on the immediate future, the distant future is searched selectively in areas that do influence today's decisions. This is important. The pundit scans ahead to identify emerging problems no one else is aware of. This new information is an asset in the politics of expertise: emerging problems imply emerging solutions, and these are the basis of durable coalitions.

Experts deal with two time boundaries. One refers to immediate political reality, i.e., the current debate of implementers and beneficiaries. The other consists of longer-term explorations of finite problem areas.

Policy analysis and planning are, to a limited extent, the advocacy of causes that will interest future political actors who are not yet able to make their weight felt. If experts select emerging problems and spend sufficient time educating today's public, they reduce uncertainty by making the political weight of future actors felt in the present. For this, as we said in chapter 8, they need time and resources. But the key to expanding time horizons is to limit them at first, to be selective and gradual in expanding the research, and to select problem areas amenable to meaningful research, i.e., problems that involve uncertainties that are relevant today.

System Size Boundaries

PUBLIC POLICIES AND plans impinge on many different subsystems. Since systems analysts cannot look at everything, an arbitrary choice is made whenever the relevant system is selected, for example, a plan for aid with no reference to trade. This arbitrary choice favors some political actors and downgrades others.

If the system boundary for a policy on national transportation is arbitrarily limited to economic considerations, the impact of investments in bridges, ports, and roads, and of subsidies to railroads, airports, and aircraft companies is measured along a common frame of reference. The apparent rationality of the economic model hides other effects; for example, ecological, cultural, social, and aesthetic effects (e.g, the impact of highways or segregated housing patterns). Economists can handle these problems and convert "externalities" into "internalities," that is, add external costs to their model. But this does not alter the fact that any system definition downgrades certain issues, and therefore the interests of certain actors, while it favors others.

Much of public policy and planning deals with resource allocation between competing claims, and therefore between competing subsystems. Policies have to be established on the basis of intersystem comparisons. Since economics is the social science that provides the more advanced model for intersystem comparisons, economic system boundaries tend to dominate. But the selection of system boundaries also implies a definition of desirable goals and values. That is, economic goals and values dominate policy considerations, not because of their intrinsic values to the actors involved, but because economic analysis provides a rationale for decision-making.

Since this favors some implementers and beneficiaries and downgrades others, the possibility of organizing coalitions is facilitated or hindered depending on the problems and the organizations that deal with them. The experts have to judge whether their choice of relevant boundaries is too narrow in terms of the process of coalition formation. The economic model may be attractive theoretically and impractical politically. For example, in education, the economic model is sometimes too constraining. In some situations, it is useful to have a manpower plan to argue with the finance ministry. That ministry understands the economic argument. In contrast, the manpower plan may be quite misleading and inadequate to work out a coalition of supporters in the ministry of education. This explains in part why educational planning relies on different planning methodologies (e.g., manpower planning, social demand approach, and cost-benefit analysis). Each methodology implies different system boundaries, and each is suited to different kinds of coalitions of supporters.

The manpower approach defines the relevant planning system as the education industry (its inputs and outputs) in relation to the employment market (the manpower inputs in the economy). The social demand approach defines the relevant planning system as a set of school-age cohorts in relation to the education industry. The cost-benefit approach defines the relevant planning system in various ways, depending on how costs and benefits are defined, but usually in terms of the cost of education (salaries of teachers, income forgone by students, and other expenses) versus the benefits of education (increased income of graduates over productive lifetimes). The social demand approach has direct sociological implication. Since education is a "social mobility valve"—in the meritocracy, education is a necessary if not sufficient requirement for advancement—the demand for access to higher levels of education is greater than actual technological need. Moreover, the more education is expanded, the more the social valve is moved upward: where some college or a bachelor's degree was sufficient thirty years ago, today a master's or Ph.D. degree is necessary for certain careers. In a country such as the United States, where the politics of education are decentralized, the social demand for education is politically far more useful to obtain resources for education. Cost-benefit analysis can be used after the fact to show that individuals who acquire an education reap higher lifetime benefits; the analysis may also be used to identify the kinds of education that have low cost-benefit ratios. In contrast, the manpower approach is better suited to centralized educational systems where overall educational resource allocations take place in a single location (e.g., the ministry of finance), because it is directly concerned with the projected employment needs of the economy.

The methodology of the manpower approach is the conscious definition of the future stratification system; i.e., how many chiefs there will be, and how many judges, engineers, accountants, unskilled laborers, etc. In contrast, the social demand approach leaves the definition of the future stratification system in doubt. It is a secret plan in that regard, with all the advantages this implies for educators. These political realities explain why in some countries, such as the United States, educational planners depend mostly on the social demand approach, sometimes on cost-benefit analysis, and very rarely on manpower planning; while in other nations, such as the Soviet Union, they rely mostly on manpower considerations. This is due not only to ideological differences, but also to different organizational arrangements, different political actors, and, therefore, different needs for system boundaries.

The choice of methodologies and system boundaries is closely related to perceptions of plan reality and the multiplier effect. If the boundaries are too large—for example, if the plan attempts to deal with events clearly outside the control not only of the Prince but also of the implementers in the coalition, or with wants outside the predictive knowledge of the experts—doubts arise and the multiplier effect does not operate.

Economic development in poor and small countries depends on export markets totally outside the control of their governments, on international investments of foreign corporations, and on aid policies that are difficult to predict. It is no surprise that national economic plans fail to influence even the investment policies of their own government agencies, not to mention those of local investors. The uncertain environment is overwhelming and the means of national self-determination too weak for planning to succeed in reducing uncertainty. Therefore the scope of such national planning is too large because it includes too many inputs that cannot be controlled or predicted. Turning the problem around, we can still argue that their system boundaries are too small because a small economy—where trade, investments, and aid are a substantial portion of the modern sector of the economy—is too small to plan independently and that if planning is to succeed, it has to become international in scope.

This theory suggests that the choice of time and system boundaries is adapted both to the political characteristics of the situation and the availability of expert knowledge. In the case of poor and small countries, these factors presently dictate a reduction in the scope of national planning to specific public projects and to policies for promoting economic activity, e.g., export promotion and foreign investments.

This is what Albert Waterston calls the "annual-planning-cum-sectoral-programming approach to national planning," which includes:

> 1. The preparation of annual plans in which two basic items [are]: (1) an inventory of current public investment, rationalized by the application of general economic and other criteria and made consistent with available financial resources, and (2) policies for stimulating private investment along appropriate lines.
>
> 2. The improvement of budgetary organization, administration and procedures for (1) linking annual plans with budgets, (2) relating investment and recurrent budgets, (3) controlling expenditures, and (4) reporting on the progress of projects and programs.
>
> 3. The preparation of multi-annual sector programs which concentrate on the identification of a shelf of potentially viable projects in each sector. (Waterston 1969, p. 7)

This theory explains, at least in part, why the study of planning in developing countries we mentioned earlier suggests that all comprehensive long-term horizon planning is a waste of time (Caiden and Wildavsky 1974, pp. 291–322). Caiden and Wildavsky go too far with their recommendations of limiting the time horizon of analysis to that of annual or even semi-annual budgets. Our theory suggests that they underestimate the extent to which very specific analysis into a longer time horizon can alter today's decisions, and they also underestimate the extent to which system boundaries can be extended; that is, government decisions have to take into account probable developments in the private sector. Nevertheless, their point is well taken. There does not exist a universal law about the scope of expert interventions. Each intervention is tailored to the politics of what is possible in a given situation, and much planning can be overambitious.

This theory also explains why those nations, or those regions of the world that have greater control over their economic life—i.e., where external interventions such as trade, aid, and foreign investment represent a small percentage of gross national product—have been, relatively speaking, better able to plan their economies during certain periods of time. But these same countries have moved away from comprehensive planning when external events over which they have less control have impinged on them. In the case of France, national indicative planning during the sixties depended on close contact between the private sector and government, particularly the extent to which government was able to influence the financing of private enterprise through its participation in both banking and insurance. These political realities, together with the dominant influence of the Gaullists and their control of Parliament, made the "inevitability" of the plan what it was.

One could also explain the success of French planning in terms of its scope: it resulted from a political process of planning in which the careful choice of boundaries was related to the process of coalition formation (Bauchet 1962, Cohen 1969, Hackett and Hackett 1965, Ullms 1975). For example, the Plan Organization did limit its interference in educational affairs to overall budget considerations—particularly for new school construction—leaving the intricacies of other educational choices to others, i.e., the Ministry of Education and other relevant institutions. Therefore, while relatively comprehensive, there always were distinct and carefully selected boundaries.

In the seventies, French planning reduced the scope of intervention further (see chapter 7). These actions are due, in part, to external uncertainties such as the energy crisis and the world economic recession of the middle seventies, and, in part, to the difficulties of creating a stable coalition of supporters as French politics became more polarized.

Measurement Selection Boundaries

ANY SYSTEM IS a process with inputs and outputs. An electric generating system is a process taking place in an electric plant. If it is a steam plant, the principal inputs may include gas or coal, cooling water, manpower, and spare parts for maintenance. Outputs include electricity, heat, and chemicals dissipated in the atmosphere. Measures of task performance include output measures (e.g., how much electricity is generated, measured in kilowatt-hours), input measures (i.e., how much fuel, manpower, water, etc., is necessary to produce electricity), and process measures (i.e., measures within the plant, such as amount of steam generated in the boilers, efficiency of the turbines, and pressure in the condensers).

If the relations between the components of the system are well known, we predict output if we know inputs or vice versa. If we know how the steam plant components perform, we predict electric production on the basis of fuel consumption. But the relations between social system components are not usually known in any similar precise manner. Therefore measurements of inputs are only rough indicators of outputs and vice versa. Moreover, the measurements that are used are not necessarily valid reflections of whatever it is the social system consumes or produces. As mentioned previously, an educational system might be intended to produce socially useful and sane citizens who will become considerate partners in marriage and loving parents. But this desired output is not easily measured, or we cannot use available data (e.g., suicide and divorce statistics of high school graduates) because they are difficult to interpret.

What can be measured is the ability to take examinations. Therefore, this instrument displaces other more expensive but more relevant measures. We could argue that a school principal should be evaluated by measures having to do with the difference between the numbers of creative and mentally healthy adolescents coming into and leaving the school. But the principal and the staff are evaluated on the children's ability to take reading tests; before you know it, the school becomes an institution specializing in preparing children and adolescents to take such tests. (We need not digress too long to point out the numerous opportunities for corruption as private companies plunge into the testing business and design programs to fit the tests.)

When output measures are hard to come by, input measures are used instead. In schools we measure numbers and training characteristics of the teachers, size of buildings and classrooms, numbers of books in libraries, numbers of laboratories, and so on. Since we do not know how these inputs relate to the creative abilities and mental health of children, or even to their ability to take examinations, input measures are not sufficient, and the tendency is to go one step further, specifying process behavior and using process measures to ensure task performance.

This means that rules and regulations specify how people are expected to behave. These rules and regulations provide process measures to ensure that task performances are assessed. But if we know very little about the process itself (and we know very little about what makes good and bad teachers), these rules and regulations are only a deterrent to good performance.

As the level of uncertainty rises and planners and other experts are increasingly in evidence, the problem is accentuated. The uncertainty surrounding education results in increased rigidity as the bureaucracy erects protections, i.e., establishes input and process rules. Meanwhile, insistence on inadequate output measures exacerbates goal conflict and leads to goal displacement, falsification of measures, and finally corruption of the system.

I have discussed these problems at greater length elsewhere (Benveniste 1977), but some points of particular interest to the politics of expertise need to be mentioned here.

Faced by an uncertain situation, experts are tempted to force new measures on the reluctant bureaucracy, but the bureaucracy is well aware of the deficiencies. Since the environment is unfriendly, they plan the game of wait-and-see. In due time, the relevant public will recognize the distortions imposed by bad measures. As dissatisfaction with task performance grows, the educational bureaucracy will be quick to place the blame on the planners.

In United States education, there is much talk of accountability. Analysts are easily tempted to talk about program priorities and the widespread use of performance measures. At worst, these approaches only alleviate or hide conflicts in the governance of the schools. At best, they sometimes provide minimal protection for minorities seeking equal treatment. But experts should think twice about notions of accountability when output measures are difficult to come by. They should discuss their measures with the implementers and resist the temptation to force the bureaucracy through remedies that may turn out to be worse than the diseases. They need to select output measures with few opportunities for goal conflict and displacement. For example, they may decide to measure the numbers of graduates, their ethnic composition, and the kinds of jobs or further education they obtain. New policy instruments are not to be forgotten. The wise experts are imaginative, for they know that a new solution may be accepted more readily—if only because potential opponents have not yet understood its impact. But they are careful; they deliberately choose output and policy instruments where goal consensus is easier to achieve, goal displacement and corruption are minimized, and the demise of experts is avoided.

The Cost of Measurements

TWENTY YEARS AGO, we were justifying investments in urban highways on the basis of the savings accrued by the reduction of maintenance expenses of users; today, we have techniques to calculate the value of the time saved by commuters. If we can develop a method to measure how citizens rank their preferences, we have a basis for evaluating how they might support a plan. Therefore, the availability of data and information on preferences is central to the creation of coalitions of implementers and beneficiaries.

This data has a cost, and the cost of making planning decisions cannot be more than the value of the choices. In other words, the cost of research on how citizens will benefit from a new highway cannot exceed the value of that benefit.

Prices in the marketplace, the electoral process, and other indicators are the traditional sources of preference information. But as the system becomes more complex, the need for information multiplies. As a result, there has been—starting in the early sixties—interest in developing social indicators to help policy-making. Most of this work has been done in the United States and, to a more limited extent, in Western Europe (Cazes 1972, pp. 9–11). The focus of attention has been on developing measures in social and economic areas where measures are not available: for example, the measurement of preferences of people for certain policies, the measurement of social costs of innovations and technological changes, the measurement of social ills such as violence on children, the measurement of levels of society-wide performance in broad areas such as health, nutrition, education. The scope of innovation in social measurement is very wide, indeed. In 1966, Raymond Bauer published the first major study of social indicators (Bauer 1966), and a Panel on Social Indicators was created in HEW which led to the publication in 1969 of *Toward a Social Report* (United States Department of Health, Education, and Welfare 1969).

Bauer's study mentions that there is no data, no measurement for four out of ten of the eighty-one domestic goals identified by the President's Commission on National Goals in 1960. This means there are no available indicators to know and "wonder about." Comparing the goal statements of 1960 with those made by a commission appointed by President Hoover in 1933 shows that "for those goal statements made in 1933 which were also restated in 1960, there were indicators for seventy-three percent, while indicators were available for only twenty-five percent of the *new* goals that appeared in the 1960 statement but not in the 1933 statement" (Bauer 1966, p. 24).

Notwithstanding its importance, the social-indicator movement has had its problems. First, the cost of generating new measures; second, the difficulty of generating measures that are meaningful to decision-makers in implementing agencies; third, the difficulty of generating measures that are meaningful to beneficiaries (Angrist et al. 1976).

The complexities involved may be made clearer if we consider what is involved in trying to obtain measures of the felt needs of beneficiaries. How does an analyst know what people want? Usually, the most readily available information is price indicators or electoral information. What people are willing to pay or what they are willing to vote for is an indicator of their preferences.

Market price indicators and electoral information are necessarily fragmented and, at times, distorted. Monopolistic production or its equivalent (e.g., monopolistic patterns of distribution, as when there is only one store in town, and you have no real choices) causes prices to distort preferences (you buy products you do not want because you cannot obtain those you do want). As market prices reflect existing patterns of income distribution, the preferences of citizens reflect the existing power structure. This may be important to an analyst attempting to predict the demand for services that imply a new distribution of income and power. (If you no longer have rich people, the price of caviar goes down; is this a shift of preference, or is it a shift in the absolute amount of money each household can devote to caviar?) In short, the relation between prices and preferences is not devoid of conceptual problems.

Moreover, individual preferences (as revealed by acts) and the collective good are not necessarily the same. There may be undesirable structural effects: I may drive a car because my marginal benefit from driving (rather than taking the streetcar) is much higher for me than the minute difference in my marginal cost from the increase in air pollution caused by my car. Yet, I like clean air and would pay a price if I knew it made a difference. Therefore, as a matter of policy, we cannot use the empirical information derived from my behavior to estimate the value I actually attach to clean air.

Analysts use the concept of shadow prices. Shadow prices are developed either theoretically or empirically to attach a value where market prices are either absent or distorted (e.g., a shadow price for the citizen's willingness to pay for clean air). Empirical shadow prices might be based on actual interviews or questionnaires where ranking of various preferences permits calculation of a shadow price for some.

Correcting for error and distortions, discovering shadow prices, and developing new indicators is a costly activity. In any planning situation, the expense of obtaining facts and figures is a constraint on the pundit's ability to create viable coalitions of supporters. This is why, as we saw in preceding chapters, experts do not rely exclusively on analysis to assure themselves that their plans will receive support. But, in the long run, they have to campaign for more data and better indicators simply because these are the basic tools of both the technical and the political dimensions of their role.

It is somewhat ironic that the movement to improve social

indicators in the United States was so poorly understood in Congress during the sixties and has not changed appreciably since then. Bauer's study to assess the entire set of social indicators used in our society was financed by the National Aeronautics and Space Administration (Bauer 1966). Presumably, since NASA wanted to examine the impact of space programs on our society, it felt it could legitimately finance a study of the social indicators available for this purpose. But Congress had consistently been lukewarm about the idea of improving this kind of information, possibly because Congress fears that improving the pundit's ability to serve his Prince will further reduce its own influence. We will come back to this problem in the following chapter. Meanwhile, we can note that the 1969 HEW study *Toward a Social Report* does not tell us how much was spent for social-indicator research in the United States. But the extent of congressional suspicion was revealed by Congress's opposition to the National Science Foundation's Program of Research Applied to National Needs, which had only a two-million-dollar budget for social-indicator research (*Science* 172, June 1971, p. 131).

ANOTHER DIMENSION OF the cost of measurements is the spiraling cost of expert requirements for specification of goals and achievements of implementing agencies. Each time a new program is enacted and a need assessment is undertaken, the bureaucracy is asked to spell out objectives and procedures. Program plans are elaborated, evaluations are undertaken, measurements are requested, and the paperwork costs of these interventions is considerable: "We do not even know what plans we have elaborated. For each categorical program, we have to have one—this mounts in pounds of paperwork. I cannot even tell you where they are. . . ."

For example, recent testimony in the state legislature in California points out that regulations passed by the State Board of Education require a comprehensive school level plan for all schools receiving categorical funds including Title I, ECE, SB 90/EDY and State Bilingual Education. These school level plans contain (1) goals and objectives which stem from an annual needs assessment, (2) program plans, (3) evaluation procedures, and (4) other required data. Furthermore, this information is presented for every one of eight separate components (reading, language, mathematics, multi-cultural education, staff development, parent participation, parent education, and health/auxiliary services).

Complete plans, typically, are sixty to one hundred pages each, and there are 3,200 consolidated application schools. To give an idea of the volume of paperwork, the Los Angeles Consolidated Application weighed over 1,000 pounds.

Based on information collected at the school site, it is estimated that the preparation of these plans requires one to two hundred hours of professional time per school year, representing a total implied cost statewide of $2.7 to $5.5 million. Most of this time is contributed by teachers and administrators who stay "after hours" to complete the forms. Nevertheless, the magnitude of the effort required raises questions about whether it is the best use of staff time (unpublished testimony of 9 November 1976 to Senate Education Committee, Sacramento, California).

As a result, a new elite emerges within the implementing bureaucracy which keeps track of the paperwork and administers the implementation of programs that require expert intervention: "Here, we have a principal, but he is not very active—and, after all, what can you expect; look at his budget! Miss X, in the program office, is running the programming of all the federal and state categorical programs—she really has the power in this school. . . ."

Experts have to take these costs into account in formulating the boundaries of their interventions. To be sure, the administrative patterns that are generated as a result of expert interventions are not their immediate doing, but the profession has to be concerned with such developments: if the implementers are burdened by excessive paperwork, they will ultimately find a way to do without experts.

Guessing

WHEN EXPERTS UNDERTAKE analysis, they often adopt the posture of "realists." Reality, in this context, is "hard-nosed" reality; it usually involves a simplified image of humanity, say "economic" man and woman or "exchange and power" man and woman. Since experts still think they are agents of efficiency instead of inventors of the future, their calculus of rationality reflects theories of behavior that are necessarily simplified.

In planning, evaluation, or policy analysis, this results in downgrading certain concepts such as aesthetic norms, love, or even ideologies. Experts create their own consensus of relevant values, based on available measures, and judge the past and design images of the future accordingly. The failure of some planners in predicting the outcome of United States action in Vietnam is due to a calculus that underplayed cultural elements, placed the respective ideologies of the contending parties at par, and simplified the characteristics of the conflict by measuring body counts. They disregarded the way planning led to measurement corruption (e.g., including dead civilians in the enemy body count or even killing civilian populations that could be tabulated as killed enemies), and failed to evaluate the resilience of the opposition and the way United States intervention fed the determination to resist.

Disregard for love, poetry, art, ideology, or other cultural attachments results in images of the future in which love, poetry, and art play a minimal part. (They may be an item of consumption in the economy but not a principle central to explaining preferences.) Since images of the future serve to orient action and thus become self-fulfilling prophecies, the architects of the future assume less than is wanted or possible. The social edifice is gradually built on limited assumptions, and, increasingly, a limited and possibly quite unattractive social world is created.

Some experts are aware of this. For example, there is a movement to reintroduce the "human element" in environmental planning, to make architects and city planners more responsive to the ways people want to live instead of relying exclusively on design considerations that fail to account for that factor (Perin 1970). This movement is a response to planning failures arising from insufficient information or simplified assumptions about the need for space and shelter. Similarly, policy planning for the longer-term future is now undergoing important changes as planners sense that they are also rejected because of their own sterility and lack of imagination. To think about different ways of life and preferences means guessing, yet guessing is an unavoidable dimension of planning, because information is insufficient and invention continues unabated. The more the rate of invention is accelerated (i.e., the more resources go into research and development), the more guessing is needed to approximate future reality.

A plan or policy without imagination is further away from the possible than one with it. But the guessing must be perceived as legitimate. Therefore, guessing takes social forms: brainstorming, the "Delphi" technique, alternative futures, scenario writing, and science fiction. In short, guessing is still expert judgment of what may happen (Adelson 1968, Jantsch 1966).

I will give only one example. The "Delphi" technique is a method of obtaining consensus among "oracles." A questionnaire is sent to a number of experts. It asks the respondents whether they agree or disagree with statements about the distant future. If they disagree, they are asked to reword the statements. The statements deal with relevant topics: urban problems, family structure, the economy, education, leisure, values and mores, and so on. Consensus is achieved by going through a number of rounds with the questionnaire. Once the first set is in, the researchers collate the responses and communicate them to the respondents. Reasons for extreme positions are included. With this information respondents alter their judgments when persuaded by the judgments of others. The images of the future are collected and used to generate scenarios of alternative long-term futures that are used to work backward to less distant study-time horizons. The Delphi method includes variants such as the cross-impact matrix, which is used to discover how experts evaluate future probabilistic relations between events: i.e., the experts are asked if the occurrence of one event would affect the probability of another event's occurring and the direction of influence. Key events can be extracted and the matrix used to assess the effect of that event's absence on the other events, thereby generating other alternative scenarios. A relevance tree may be used. This is a model of the process that serves as a cross-reference system to make sure that questionnaires, matrices, and scenarios are complete (Helmer 1966).

It is sometimes argued by those who do not see any need for them, that experts cannot succeed because the data are bad, the statistics inadequate. But as we suggested earlier, it is the lack of data and knowledge that brings about the need for experts. Planning is brought about by a relative absence of information. Therefore, there is always need for guessing, and the pundit has to learn how to practice the art. Frederick Crew in his humorous account of the Patch Commission is not far from reality when he has one of the three commissioners explain the difference between systems and operations analysis:

> "I mean something a little exact by Systems Analysis.... Systems Analysis is when you ought to be maximizing your decision reliability by computerizing all contingencies, but the breadth of problems and lack of data mean you have to make up all the figures out of your head. Operations Analysis is when you've actually got some figures to play with. Systems Analysis is riskier, more abstract, a lot more fun." (Crew 1968, p. 13)

eleven

Experts and the Democratic Process

THIS BOOK ON the politics of expertise began with a dilemma of the modern Prince: his or her increasing dependence on the advice of experts. We explored the ways these pundits participate in the intrigues of the palace. We saw them in various functions: holding trial balloons that test the next audacious venture of the Prince; suffering as scapegoats when the Prince is in defeat; standing as symbols of the Prince's pretended concern in the affairs of state when the Prince is enchanted only by his amusements, including the hunt.

We also saw them in another, more essential function: relieving the Prince and his subjects of the excessive uncertainties caused by the multiplicity of alternatives possible with technology and the interdependence of differentiated subunits in complex societies.

We described various tasks undertaken by experts: first, evaluation of past activities and, second, the linked stages of policy analysis, programming, and planning to help select and decide among options for future action. We discussed implementation—if the future described by experts is not implemented, it is either trivial or utopian and does not reduce uncertainty. We presented two principles of implementation: first, the power of the Prince—his ability to tie rewards and punishments to the implementation of the recommendations of experts; second, the multiplier effect—how shared beliefs about the future lead many independent implementers to reorient their actions to fit the recommendations of experts.

We stressed the importance of the multiplier effect in societies where planning is diffuse and decentralized. We saw how the Soviet model of planning relies more on the first principle of implementation, and we alluded to some of the costs involved.

The discussion of the multiplier effect led us to understanding the importance of coalition formation. We decided that experts play a new social role that is poorly understood. They provide a new language for policy-making and planning—a language that becomes the basis for limiting or enlarging the policy discourse and the entourage of the Prince and also defines the place, time, and terrain of negotiations.

We saw how the allocation of resources for policy research and planning is dominated by organizational imperatives rather than overall consideration of the needs of citizens. Since what is good for organizations is not necessarily good for citizens, we suggested that laissez-faire in planning is dysfunctional within a democracy and leads to the corporate state. We saw why experts are more concerned with implementers than with beneficiaries. The logic of creating a coalition of supporters in a limited time period makes the implementers the center of expert attentions. Beneficiaries are relevant when they are organized and can exercise political muscle upon the implementing bureaucracies.

IN TECHNOLOGICAL SOCIETIES, the more the system is developed, the more it is composed of many different subunits, each specializing in a limited domain, each articulated to and relying upon others and in turn being relied upon by its own consumers. This complex articulated system goes beyond national boundaries. For example, we are aware of the extent to which individuals and organizations in the United States are dependent on resources, products, and services coming from every part of the globe and how, in turn, individuals and organizations elsewhere are dependent on what happens in the United States.

Such a worldwide system of individuals and organizations is highly susceptible to changes taking place anywhere in the system. The energy crisis illustrates the nature of the dependencies involved. Changes take place in other countries or closer to home. They can be natural accidents but are mostly the consequences of human decisions, particularly the result of technological innovations and rising levels of consumption.

Since the system is highly complex and the components are articulated among themselves, changes anywhere in the system result in what I call articulation errors (Benveniste 1977, p. 172). Articulation errors happen any time an individual or an organization finds that the resources it needs or the services or products it produces are either unavailable or not wanted. Articulation errors are often severely punished: you train to be a school teacher, go to college for four years and take a one-year credentialing program only to find out there are no openings for teachers. Your training was, at least in part, a waste of time and resources.

In all bureaucracies, there is much fear of articulation errors because these affect the survival of one's unit or one's career. Therefore, all bureaucracies engage in defensive strategies, one of which is the use of experts to help reduce the level of uncertainty. I have discussed these bureaucratic symptoms at greater length in *Bureaucracy* (Benveniste 1977). Here we focus on some effects of the politics of expertise on the democratic processes.

AS THE LEVEL of organizational uncertainty rises in democratic technological societies, there is an increasing demand for the services of experts. There is more demand for rationality, accountability, and centralization; more calls for evaluation, policy analysis, programming, and planning. The call for centralized comprehensive planning is made anew as if the deficiencies, fears, and general malaise that prevail in the organizations of a democratic technological society could be resolved by adopting centralized controls and planning practices that are already encountering problems of their own in one-party socialist countries.

To plan from the bottom up, as is done in the Soviet Union, requires a single ideological purpose to restrict alternative courses of action. As already mentioned, Soviet planning is initiated at the level of the factory (the bottom), and the plans are gradually brought together at successive levels of integration until they reach the center (the top), where the plan directives and instructions are set and sent back to the bottom.

Units at the bottom and at intermediary levels are able to undertake a step-by-step resolution of conflict and common-interest aggregation, because a single political party controls ideology. In such circumstances, national planning allows participation, while a selective flow of information goes upward toward successive stages of integration and coherence.

The Soviet model has the apearance of rationality because it allows for a comprehensive approach. But interest aggregation from the bottom up takes place within system boundaries provided by the ideology of the one-party structure. Divergences are legitimately eliminated, because ideological control provides a basis for keeping many alternatives out of consideration.

The ideology and its social consequences (full employment, redistribution of income) should not be underestimated, but it is not the planning structure that makes these possible. Full employment and income redistribution are feasible under any planning arrangement; they are possible in the United States. It is ideological control that permits comprehensive planning, and the costs are evident.

The major cost is bureaucratic inertia and commitment to the status quo. It is not without significance that Soviet planning is heavily influenced by developments outside the socialist countries. Changes in production, pricing, and consumption are generated both internally and externally. External influences, i.e., what happens in market societies, provide external guidelines for Soviet planning. In fact, it is debatable whether the Soviet model would continue to exist as it is if external stimulation were eliminated.

There are distinct advantages to a planning system that ensures that all the graduates of all the schools in the country always find relevant employment because national norms of production and employment are established beforehand and are articulated with established school production targets. This level of coherence implies that all individuals share an assurance of employment that should not be undervalued. But it is easy to make errors in the choice of norms of production and their manpower implications. This is particularly true if comparisons with market economies cannot be made. Also, the long and tedious process of planning and articulating a complex manpower apparatus has costs not easily measured. More important, there exist overall advantages to the flexibility of the United States system in the form of opportunities for inventing new roles and life styles and for self-determination.

If comprehensive planning is not a solution to our problems of planning, what is? Apparently, United States planning leads to the corporate state, in which policy and planning decisions are made by the organized corporate political forces of the state (i.e., the military, industry, banking, at times labor, and whatever groups have the resources to exert direct influence on the planners and through them on the executive). Political parties and legislative processes are bypassed or co-opted, and the courts alone are left with the impossible task of defending democracy. What is to be said about the gradual demise of legislative bodies?

The problem before us has been called anomic democracy (Crozier, Huntington, and Watanuka 1975). Anomic democracy is the result of a situation where consensus about what to do does not exist and where the existing political institutions are unable to resolve conflicts openly and achieve consensus:

> Without common purpose, there is no basis for common priorities, and without priorities, there are no grounds for distinguishing among competing private interests and claims. Conflicting goals and specialized interests crowd in one upon another, with executives, cabinets, parliaments, and bureaucrats lacking the criteria to discriminate among them. The system becomes one of anomic democracy, in which democratic politics becomes more an arena for the assertion of conflicting interests than a process for the building of common purposes. (p. 161)

The authors spell out the consequences of anomic democracy: the delegitimation of authority (people do not trust government); the overloading of government (nevertheless, people expect government to handle every conceivable ill and place too many demands upon it); the disaggregation of interests (the political parties are no longer aggregating conflicting interests and cannot function properly). They ask:

> How viable is democratic government without parties or with greatly weakened and attenuated parties? (p. 166)

THIS CHAPTER ADDRESSES itself to two aspects of these issues. First, we review ways experts can reduce excessive fears generated by articulation erors while limiting the scope of their interventions. In other words, how can decision-making be decentralized and democratic participation increased without the benefits and costs of heavy centralized control? Second, we address ourselves to the issue of participation. In democratic societies, the participation of citizens in decisions is protected, in part, by the election of representatives and the creation of political parties. We therefore discuss the role of experts vis-à-vis legislative bodies. To what extent can experts improve the analytical capabilities of elected representatives and their political parties?

Errors and Remedies

THE DILEMMA OF any technological society is like eating your cake and keeping it: the more productive a society is, the more alternatives are possible. But the more society is productive, the more it is differentiated and needs articulation and conformity. This dichotomy is resolved either by comprehensive planning and ideological conformity, which means alternatives are lost, or by a limited form of planning with system boundaries, which means errors arise from a lower level of articulation. We have these in the United States and other non-socialist countries in the form of unemployment, unsold stocks, and unfinished projects or inadequate facilities, sold-out services, crowded highways, and exhausted supplies. We see them when school graduates cannot find employment for which they are trained, the unskilled cannot learn skills, and an affluent society cannot provide amenities of life that are common in less affluent countries.

American planning is informal—made up of many subplans with different boundaries and different coalitions of supporters. Some plans are more influential because those who support them have learned the complex skills of the art and have found that not all implementers and beneficiaries are needed, only enough of them to create a belief in what is to come and to entice others to align themselves with what appears to be a more probable future. But the level of articulation is far from perfect; the alignments still reflect individual preferences, competitive subplans, and non-plans. United States planning is overlapping but incomplete, connected and split, and meshed together by the accidents of informal professional networks and the limited influence of an elite of experts serving an elite of Princes, each in pursuit of his pleasures, budget, and organizational survival.

Since errors are inevitable and excessive, remedies are sought. At present, the obvious remedy is government intervention. Government interventions of all sorts—protection of consumer interests, control of safety and environmental conditions, controls of inflation, etc.—result from the fear of articulation errors. In this respect, it is somewhat ironic that such government intervention is often referred to as "creeping socialism" when in fact it is the exact opposite of the kind of intervention that socialist planning calls for, since socialist planning involves different kinds of errors and costs. Yet, while there is a call for government intervention, there is also a very real fear that it will result in inefficiencies and waste, that it weakens the fabric of capitalism, and that it ultimately leads to a planning structure that requires ideological conformity and state control of the means of production.

Actually this fear hides another fear—the fear that a socialist system is better able to mobilize resources and to control and orient the purposive actions of its citizens and therefore is more efficient, rational, and powerful. We are familiar with the next stage of this process of thought: "To survive, capitalism must divert itself from sentimentality and exercise power. The poor and the misfit are not important, because they are a load on the productive members of society and capitalism cannot afford inefficiencies. The insurgents are misguided, and the liberals too weak for the challenge. A strong and vigorous capitalism need have no fear of exercising its police. Law and order are more important than justice. Since the enemy is at the gates, we must trim the fat. Therefore, impose bureaucratic conformity; fire the dissenters." "It is arrogant of individuals to think they know what is right," the head of a think tank reportedly commented when the ex-expert Ellsberg undertook the 1971 leak and publication of the secret Pentagon documents (*Washington Post,* 7 August 1971).

Socialist planning has boundaries of conformity and bureaucratic apathy: it downgrades serendipity. It is doubly ironic that some of those who propose to defend capitalism from the apparent power of socialist planning would erode the fascinating creativity of democratic societies—their principal raison d'être and unique strength. The call for centralization and accountability often masks simple misguided fears and oversimplified solutions. As we saw in this book, rationality is often more apparent than real, and any successful approach to the current dilemma of democratic institutions does not consist in adopting the ideology, language, and practices of hierarchical organizations. One does not insure artistic and scientific creativity by imposing strict bureaucratic controls. Experts in the hire of a Prince in fear can as easily extinguish new ideas as they can help propagate them.

It is therefore necessary to attack the fundamental underlying cause of the excessive fears that prevail in all the organizations that compose a democratic society. This is not done by imposing more centralized planning but by correcting the consequences of errors that penalize certain individuals and organizations.

The weakness of democratic planning systems that are diffuse is that some individuals or organizations are bound to be treated unjustly in a system that nevertheless benefits the aggregate. This is not admissible in an affluent society. It is the cause of the present malaise and the collapse of most of our institutions, because these errors do not arise from individual defects or weaknesses but from a collective pattern of action. It is the system of planning that is at fault, not the individuals who make unavoidable errors. American planning has obvious advantages, but it is not strengthened by emulating the defects of socialist planning; it is strengthened by avoiding cruel treatment of those who suffer from articulation errors. When it is said that government welfare programs support the weak and inefficient, we must answer, "Nonsense"; government help to individuals seeking employment or in training or retraining, government financing of continued education for those who wish to redefine their role in society, and government supports to agencies or corporations caught in planning errors are all part and parcel of improving a planning system that suits a nation where there is a value in diversity.

This does not mean that all welfare programs or government financing of large corporations near bankruptcy are desirable, or that their expansion should be unchecked. It means that in a complex technological society it is necessary to create institutions that are specifically charged with providing remedies for unforeseen errors. In *Bureaucracy* I have proposed the creation of Professional Governors to protect the interests of individuals within organizations (they would guarantee employment and retraining); Professional Courts to protect consumers and the public at large; and Councils charged with protecting any organization caught in a major articulation error (Benveniste 1977, chapter 13). I do not see these specific proposals as any final solution to the dilemma—but I have made them to highlight the characteristics of the problem and the elements of corrective action.

There is an important link between the idea of providing remedies for the consequences of articulation errors and planning, democratic participation, and innovation. If it is known that there exists an institution to correct errors after they happen, excessive fear in organizations might be eliminated. To achieve this, it is still necessary to plan, but the scope of expert interventions could then be sharply limited: since errors would be corrected after they happen, it would be less necessary to try to plan everything ahead of time.

If planning is bounded and remedies for errors are available, subunits can experiment and adopt their own life styles and ideological commitments. Democratic participation in decisions is possible because of decentralization and the impact of planning on the democratic political process is attenuated. For example, the American schools have certainly become rigid and sterile, but all the brave words about innovations and flexibility carry little hope in the context of inadequate planning and remedies for planning errors. Without remedies for errors, the call for innovation is a sterile call for those innovations that are guaranteed ahead of time to succeed. Unless we can make mistakes we will not really try to innovate, because we fear risks.

In a more perfect planning system, the schools might receive most of their financing from the states or the federal government, but they would be quite free to introduce new programs. For example, there would be no fear of introducing innovations in schools and universities if the relevant public wanted to do so. Considerable latitude would be left at the grass roots to try new approaches agreeable to participants in local decisions. The administration and actual teaching and learning would no longer take place in an unbearably threatening environment: a limited set of understandable targets, together with needed resources, would be given to each school. Other decisions, arrangements, and innovations would be matters to be resolved at the operating level. Reliance on process rules and excessive attention to inadequate and misleading output measures would no longer be needed to justify budgets, because the units would know beforehand that as long as they met a limited set of targets they could do as they pleased.

Of course, errors would be made. Many false starts and unsuccessful innovations would take place. But these would be in no way comparable to the costs of the sorry waste and lack of hope that prevail in our educational system.

Since errors would be made, and innovations encouraged, it would still be necessary to reduce the probability that they would lead to undesirable consequences. A consciously limited form of planning, together with remedies for individual errors, has to be tied to an extensive program of scanning and forecasting. Moreover, the choice of time and system boundaries must be flexible and reflect the results of these forecasts. In other words, if undesirable collective consequences of actions can be discerned, these must be integrated in future planning. The formula is simple: choices are left to individuals and sub-units as long as public costs are not excessive.

Assume we create a national educational planning system that prescribes a budget and a target output for each unit (e.g., each school is supposed to graduate so many people coming from different ethnic and social backgrounds), but does not specify what skills are to be taught or how they are to be imparted. Scanning is necessary to see the consequences of the decisions being taken at the local level. As long as enough doctors are produced, there is no problem; if too many doctors are produced, some leeway exists; past a certain limit, corrections are applied, although it is known that doctors who cannot find employment will be helped in one way or another. But if scanning suggests that not enough doctors are being produced, incentives or other planning interventions are applied.

Limited planning cannot remain limited when the public costs of individual decisions are excessive. At that point the plans are expanded, and there must be mechanisms to do this. Does this scheme seem impossible? I think not. Of course, all this is utopian and well in advance of reality. But the image is interesting, even disturbing, because it is not impossible. If we cannot grasp it as yet, it is simply because we do not understand our role, perceive the wrong explanations, downgrade what experts can do, and assume ourselves to be prisoners of bureaucracies when we need not be.

Let us turn to the issue of laissez-faire in planning and the supremacy of the corporate state. Our utopian design makes little sense in the context of existing planning structures, if only because laissez-faire does not provide legitimate institutions or the resources required to undertake the political dimension of the planning we allude to. But laissez-faire as we know it in the United States is not an intractable problem: the genius of our government provides balances that are adaptable to the modern requirements of governance and to a more perfected form of planning.

WE HAVE SAID very little about legislatures or about political parties. Yet, since legislatures are political bodies and planning is a political process, there is no fundamental reason why legislative planning cannot correct or at least reduce some of the more overt deficiencies we have discussed—no fundamental reason, that is, if we accept the notion of partisan legislative planning.

Partisan Legislative Planning

PROFESSOR CARL FRIEDRICH writes that "right policies are policies which seem right to the community at large and at the same time do not violate 'objective' scientific standards. Only thus can public policy contribute to what the people consider their happiness" (Friedrich 1969, p. 425). But pundits have too many opportunities to define scientific standards and too few occasions to assess what seems right to the community at large. With laissez-faire, even if they do not serve their Prince, they serve lesser vassals in his entourage. In any case, they usurp power intended for elected representatives. Our emerging corporate state is not subservient to the elected for the simple reason that it does not have to be. Thus, the weakening of legislative bodies has roots in the power held by government and private organizations and the way they use it to control planning and analysis.

It is sometimes argued that United States planning, for example, the introduction of PPB or other schemes to reinforce central control in the federal administration, reinforces the democratic process: since the president is elected, and since PPB and other schemes reinforce the presidency, it follows that these reinforce the democratic process. Even if we disregard the impact of United States planning on Congress, there is some doubt that the presidency is reinforced by PPB. There is always a question about who serves the president and who serves other interests (Huitt 1968). It is not necessarily the president who ensnares the pundits; the heads of bureaucratic empires with access to economic resources may hire pundits to ensnare the president.

To be sure, most planners are opposed to the notion of a "hidden corporate state." But the logic of the planning process is not modified by the ideology of planners. Even if they are committed to achieving more democratic balances of power and influence, it is the coalitions of selected implementers and beneficiaries that come to dominate the elaboration of plans and policies. We have tried to show how experts acquire elbow room of their own, but we never suggested they could do this alone. This means that if they do not work for the Prince, they work for others, and these others happen to be those who make a difference.

The weakening of legislatures has not passed unnoticed, and the call for legislative reform is not new. Given the emergence of a corporate state, and assuming that experts and the bureaucracy dominate the legislatures, is there no reaction? What happens to the planning capability of legislatures and more particularly of Congress? If experts serve an emergent corporate state, why do they not also serve the elected representatives?

Aaron Wildavsky explains this in his study of the federal budget process (Wildavsky 1964, pp. 128–34). The reason Congress did not attempt to have an overview of the federal budget, but approached it in piecemeal fashion, was not ignorance or stupidity; it was simply that any budget is only the visible portion of the iceberg of power and influence in the society:

> It makes no sense to speak as if one could make drastic changes in budgeting without also altering the distribution of influence. But this task is inevitably so formidable . . . that most adversaries prefer to speak of changing the budgetary process, as if by some subtle alchemy the intractable political element could be transformed into a more malleable substance. (Wildavsky 1964, pp. 131–32)

Congressional failures to control the Council of Economic Advisors and the Budget Bureau arose from these conditions. Until 1974, when Congress reformed its budgetary practices, there was no cohesive group in Congress capable of using these government agencies to affect decision-making by imposing its preferences on a majority of its members (Wildavsky 1964, p. 134). Therefore, it follows, as Arthur Maas shows in the case of water resources (Maas 1965), that members of Congress were more concerned with shifting the opinions of the experts in the Corps of Engineers than with attempting to contradict them. Prior to 1974, Congress was fragmented and at the mercy of those who had access to both information and power. As a consequence, Congress was suspicious of experts and sought only to reduce or eliminate the budgets of the think tanks (*Science* 174, 1971, p. 1008).

This phenomenon is not peculiar to Congress but is symptomatic of most elected governing bodies. On one hand we have the administrative and executive branch depending more and more on the expertise of its agencies, gathering information about its own activities and formulating its own plans for the future, and on the other side we have elected bodies which are intended to defend the interests of the electorate, but which are unable to govern because they do not have the expertise to deal with the recommendations of the executive. Thus, power is transferred from the legislative branch or from governing boards to the executive or administrative bodies they are supposed to control.

Why are legislators or elected boards unable to cope with the expertise of executive and administrative bodies? Why is Congress unable to use analysis? Several explanations can be mentioned:

—Congress cannot adequately use the result of analysis because very few members are trained to do so: Paul de Forest, who studies the role of social scientists in congressional foreign policy committees, shows in a neat little table (de Forest 1969, p. 141) that very few members of these committees have any training and expertise in the social sciences. Therefore, they rarely contract for policy research and their principal contact with experts is at hearings. But we can assume that experts who testify at hearings are often in the service of other Princes, and any Prince is pleased to have his pundits fight his battles "on the hill."

—Congress cannot adequately use analysis because it distrusts analysts and social scientists. Congressional suspicions of the social sciences have often been documented (Lyons 1969,

Robinson 1967). These include distrust of the advice given, lack of interest in the assumptions underlying the advice given, and simply lack of relevance of advice to policy issues.

—Congress cannot adequately use analysis because of the time constraints imposed by the decision-making process. Under the best of circumstances, there is not enough time to digest the relevant information. The advice comes at the wrong time. It is too late to act.

—Congress cannot adequately use analysis because the analysis is perceived to have a political bias and politicians do not agree with the political assumptions made in the analysis. We will return to this issue, which may be most important.

—Lastly, Congress cannot adequately use analysis because it does not spend enough to do so. Not enough analysis is undertaken to help the decision-making process.

This last explanation received much attention during the late sixties and early seventies, and calls for reform of the congressional budget process continued. Suggestions ranged from creating an equivalent of the English royal commission under congressional auspices (Hansen 1969) to enlarging the staff of committees to include systems analysts (Hirsch 1969) or improving the data-processing ability of Congress to provide members with "a logical way to comprehend and respond" to Program Planning and Budgeting (Chartrand 1968, p. 6).

Yet, it is revealing that a Special Commission on the Social Sciences of the National Science Board, which addressed itself to the question of improving the nation's use of the social sciences, had not a single word to say about the potential role of the social sciences in Congress. The 1969 report *Knowledge into Action* talked about social-science advisors in the White House and government agencies, improving social science data and business and labor's "association" with the social sciences, more analysis of the role of social sciences in community organizations, more money for social science education, and creation of social problem research institutes since "mobilization of social science for solutions to social problems customarily has been ineffective because the problems themselves do not fall solely within the traditional areas of a given social science" (National Science Foundation 1969, p. xix). But there was no mention of Congress or of any legislative bodies. That commission seems to have given up on the legislative branch of government.

Legislative or governing bodies are never completely at the mercy of the analysis of the executive or administrative branch, and, in the United States and other countries, they exercise most of their analytical control through the processes of approving and auditing the budgets of the agencies they are supposed to guide or govern. Modern analytical capabilities within legislatures or governing bodies usually emerge from this auditing function. For example, in the Congress we find the General Accounting Office (GAO), which was established in 1921 and had in 1976 a staff of slightly more than five thousand people—a considerable expert capability, trained, usually, in the traditions of accounting control—which are not necessarily those of analysis and planning—but capable of broadening and therefore initiating such analysis. It is therefore not surprising that these auditing capabilities have evolved over time, and in some instances these bodies have undertaken analysis. The best-known example is the Office of Legislative Analyst of the State of California, an innovation initiated in 1941 which has been adopted in one form or another in many other states. Its original name was Office of the Legislative Auditor; it was renamed in 1957. Today, the Office of the Legislative Analyst in California has a staff of about fifty technical analysts whose main function is to analyze the budget proposed by the governor of the state before it is submitted to the legislature. The staff prepares a written "Analysis of the Budget Bill" which is a basis for budget hearings. The Office of Legislative Analyst is now distinct from the auditing function, which is carried by an audit bureau established in 1955.

The analytical strength of the Office of the Legislative Analyst derives in part from the fact that this analytical group can take an overall view of the budget and in part from the known fact that it can make recommendations to the legislature.

Similarly, the 1974 reforms of the budgetary process in Congress were a conscious attempt to improve the overall analytical capability of Congress through the creation of the Congressional Budget Office (CBO) and the establishment of Senate and House budget committees which can take an overall view of the budget. The CBO had an initial professional staff of about a hundred, which has increased to an estimated two hundred in 1977 (Schick 1976, Thurber 1976). These reforms were reinforced by other developments during the mid-seventies. There were continued attempts to reduce the total number of congressional committees to reduce congressional fragmentation. The General Accounting Office (GAO) was asked to undertake analysis for CBO, thus increasing its analytical strength. Other analytical capabilities were created or expanded. Committee staffs, which did not really exist before 1946, grew so that by 1976 the total staff of all committees of the House of Representatives numbered more than fifteen hundred persons (Malbin 1976). The old legislative reference service of the Library of Congress was renamed the Congressional Research Service (CRS) and handled about two thousand inquiries a year. The Office of Technology Assessment, established in 1972, had by the mid-seventies a professional staff of about fifty and a budget of some five million dollars.

These reforms force an open discussion of priorities and provide Congress with a greater ability to take an overview of the budget. How far and how effective the reforms will be is difficult to evaluate. On one hand, it is clear that these centralized capabilities permit legislatures to confront the executive with their own analytical strength and, therefore, to recapture the control of the purse to some extent. But on the other side of the coin, we know that the analysis has to remain in a terrain that is as politically neutral as possible. The analysts cannot take any political stand, and just to give an example, it is very significant that several influential members of Congress questioned the policy stands taken by the CBO during the 1976 appropriation hearings (Thurber 1976, p. 213).

Any analytical group serving an eminently political body composed of many political factions has to remain as neutral and safe as possible. The Prince in this case is a composite of political forces, and the politics of expertise we described in this book cannot take place easily or at least can take place only where considerable consensus exists. The Office of the Legislative Analyst in California or the CBO in Washington cannot appear to make any political choices. This is why these experts tend to have to take cautious or conservative stances or have to limit themselves to an analysis that presents as many facts as possible without attempting to go beyond them. This does not undervalue the importance of facts and the contribution such analysis makes. But it highlights the inherent limitation of the approach.

On one hand we have the executive branch where analysis emerges from agency interests and we see the domination of corporate organizational politics, and on the other hand we have legislatures attempting to represent the interests of citizens but only able to muster a conservative, cautious analytical strength which responds to or at best only attempts to control the executive.

It is necessary to emphasize that legislative bodies are not conventional hierarchical organizations. They are aggregations of political interests. Confronted by the power of the executive, reformers of legislatures attempt to pattern the organization of Congress or other legislatures on the organization of the executive. But, whereas this leads to some control over the executive, it also imposes the structure of the executive on legislatures, an analytical structure which is not appropriate to a political body. Yet, this is the repetitive pattern, and report after report makes the same suggestion: for example, the 1975 Commission on the Organization of the Government for the Conduct of Foreign Policy suggests that Congress create a Joint Committee on National Security:

> It should perform for the Congress the kinds of policy review and coordination now performed in the executive branch by the National Security Council, and provide a central point of linkage to the President and to the officials of that Council. In addition, it should take responsibility for Congressional oversight of the Intelligence Community. (Commission on the Organization of the Government for the Conduct of Foreign Policy 1975, pp. 208).

Attempts to pattern the analytical capability of legislatures on the hierarchical pattern of the executive or administrative branch are inadequate because political bodies are by definition composed of different interest groups, different political parties that aggregate interest groups pursuing different objectives. Since analysis is politically valuable, it is to be expected that it is always suspect when it is not directly controlled by political interests. In other words, analysis within legislatures or governing boards cannot be limited to central services but needs to be tailored to the needs of the political factions that compose these bodies.

This book suggests why committee reorganizations and the centralization of budget analysis are not sufficient and why the suspicions of Congress are not unfounded. Once you accept the political dimension of expertise, the solutions adopted are simply too aseptic and unreal. It is all well and good to have Congress as a body or committees of Congress use systems analysis as if this analysis were impartial and were helping all members of Congress. But this has nothing to do with the partisan nature of the enterprise. Congress is rightly suspicious of letting in the enemy. Increasing the staffs of committees also reduces the influence of elected members. Data banks and computerized information can increase the research capability of the Library of Congress or of the Congressional Budget Office, and individual members of Congress can avail themselves of these services, but this will not improve the planning capability of the Congress sufficiently. Eminently political bodies can only use expertise if expertise is partisan. This has to be recognized from the start.

If advocacy planning can help the poor in their dealings with the experts, partisan legislative planning can help legislators in their dealings with the executive and the private sector. Of course, any budget reveals the nature of existing influence groups, but a link is missing from that argument. Some influence groups have acquired excessive power because they control the experts. Elected representatives do not always pursue the strategies they want to pursue, because they do not know the alternatives. Partisan legislative planning would remedy excesses and distortions. It would not replace politics with rationality; it would use a rational language to allow politics to take place again.

Both the left and the right have been suspicious of experts. The result is visible: legislatures have lost ground. If the left and most of the right do not wish to give up to an emerging corporate state, they have to learn to use experts and in so doing reestablish their intended role.

This means that analysis must be undertaken not only for the legislature as a whole but for the political parties that compose these legislatures. The revitalization of democratic processes depends on the revitalization of political parties. These institutions, which seem to serve well in gathering votes and raising funds for political campaigns, need to acquire a greater capability in dealing with the political content of analysis.

An idea of the dimension of the problem is illustrated by the Democratic Study Group in the House of Representatives. Created in 1959 to bring together liberal members of the Democratic Party, it had some 150 members in the early seventies. The Study Group raises funds from contributions of members and other donors to undertake, among other activities, studies of policy issues. But in the early seventies, the analytical strength of this politically committed group was provided by a small staff of only twelve persons (Stevens et al. 1974, p. 669). This is not the only source of politically committed analytical strength in the Congress, but its size does illustrate the orders of magnitude separating the capabilities of the executive and those of partisan legislative planning.

MODERN DEMOCRATIC SOCIETIES need new institutions to cope with the consequences of technology. If democratic values are to emerge again, the institutions of democracy have to be protected. The role confusion that surrounds experts has resulted in the growth and strength of the executive vis-à-vis elected representatives. We have seen how policy analysis, accountability, and planning logically lead to a corporate state—a mild form of fascism where the organized implementers and a few beneficiaries exercise political muscle. If experts are not to be the agents of a corporate state, they need to campaign for an adequate level of partisan legislative policy analysis and planning. This means that political parties need to be able to raise the necessary resources to finance this activity at a level sufficient to permit the legislative branch to deal with the executive and with the private sector. This applies to Congress and to all other government bodies from state legislatures to school boards.

Moreover, if legislative planning is to influence executive and private planning, it should not duplicate it. It should rely on the powers of the legislature in contrast to the powers of the executive or the private sector.

There are three levels of partisan legislative planning: (1) monitoring, (2) forecasting, and (3) research for legislation.

Monitoring is the use of extensive resources to provide facts to partisan groups in the legislatures regarding the work of systems analysts and other planners in government agencies and in the private sector. This first level of legislative planning provides access to information about planning exercises while they are under way and before change becomes impossible. Much of Congress's impotence stems from the simple tactic of presenting congressional committees with a fait accompli or, in the better situations, with many related decisions that have already been made, thus providing Congress with nothing but the opportunity of approving the only course of action that can still be taken.

We know that executive planning is concerned with the present; the Congress is also. But in its confrontations with the executive and the private sector, Congress has more to gain from using a long-term perspective as a tool to influence the present. In contrast to executive or corporate planning, which orients action to defend past bureaucratic achievement, legislative planning reflects legislators' concern with new realizations. There is more to gain from using long-term intelligence to create new programs than from using it to protect old ones.

Forecasting is the use of extensive resources to undertake long-term review of particular problem areas. For example, as the rate of change continues to accelerate, the long-term technical feasibility of many programs and activities reaches finite limits imposed by the conditions of life on earth. Therefore, one source of legislative power arises from a better awareness of these limits and from using this knowledge for new legislation.

Finally, legislative planning is the application of systems analysis to the elaboration of legislative programs. The results of monitoring executive planning together with the insights of its own long-term forecasting can be used by Congress to orient, redirect, or even stop actions of the executive or the private sector that it can and wishes to control.

This does not prove that legislatures can acquire control over the emerging corporate state, but it suggests that they might not be totally at its mercy. A legislature with facts, television, and other means of communication is not necessarily at the mercy of the centers of influence that surround its own fragmented community. There are always other centers of influence that can be mobilized if the facts are made known. Expertise, together with the prestige and legitimacy of the legislature, is a new political asset that can be used in the emerging restructuring of society. Congress will not abolish the experts; the world is much too uncertain and planners are needed. It might learn instead to use their talent and imagination.

Whose interests do experts serve? Are they to be hired by those who have power, to defend that power? Or are they to strengthen democratic institutions? As we saw, experts have a limited power of their own and are never totally at the mercy of the Prince who hires them. But there are many Princes and some are closer to democratic values than others. With laissez-faire, the tendency has been toward the use of experts to strengthen bureaucratic empires. For this and other reasons, anomic democracy prevails. But experts can act and have commitments of their own. It is possible to strengthen democratic institutions and the future need not be bleak or despairing. Social invention is possible.

References

ADELSON, Marvin. 1968; *The Technology of Forecasting and the Forecasting of Technology.* Santa Monica, Calif.: Systems Development Corp.

ALLISON, Graham T. 1971. *Essence of Decision: Explaining the Cuban Missile Crisis.* Boston: Little, Brown & Co.

———. 1975. Implementation analysis: the "missing chapter" in conventional analysis. A teaching exercise. In Richard Zeckhauser et al., eds., *Benefit-Cost and Policy Analysis,* 1974. Chicago: Aldine Publishing Co.

ALMOND, Gabriel A., and Verba, Sydney. 1965. *The Civic Culture.* Boston: Little, Brown & Co.

ALONSO, William. 1968. Beyond the inter-disciplinary approach to planning. Berkeley, Calif.: Center for Planning and Development, University of California.

ALONSO, William, and Freidmann, John, eds. 1964. *Regional Development and Planning.* Cambridge, Mass.: MIT Press.

ALTSHULER, Alan A. 1965. *The City Planning Process: A Political Analysis.* Ithaca, N.Y.: Cornell University Press.

ANGRIST, Shirley S.; Belkin, Jacob; and Wallace, William. 1976. Social indicators and urban policy analysis. *Socio-Economic Planning Sciences* 10, pp. 193–98.

ARCHIBALD, Kathleen. 1970a. Alternative orientations to social science utilization. *Social Science Information* 9 (April), pp. 7–34.

———. 1970b. Three views of the expert's role in policy-making: systems analysis, incrementalism and the clinical approach. *Policy Sciences* 1, pp. 73–86.

ARGYRIS, Chris. 1970. *Intervention Theory and Method—A Behavioral Science View.* Reading, Mass.: Addison-Wesley Publishing Co.

ARMSTRONG, John A. 1973. *The European Administrative Elite.* Princeton, N.J.: Princeton University Press.

ARNDT, Hans-Joachim. 1966. *West Germany: The Politics of Non-Planning.* Syracuse, N.Y.: Syracuse University Press.

AZRAEL, Jeremy R. 1966. *Managerial Power and Soviet Politics.* Cambridge, Mass.: Harvard University Press.

BARBER, Richard J. 1966. *The Politics of Research.* Washington, D.C.: Public Affairs Press.

BARDACH, Eugene. 1974. Gathering data for policy research. *Urban Analysis* 2, pp. 117–44.

———. 1977. *The Implementation Game.* Cambridge, Mass.: MIT Press.

BAUCHET, Pierre. 1962. *La Planification Française.* Paris: Éditions du Seuil.

BAUER, Raymond A., ed. 1966. *Social Indicators.* Cambridge, Mass.: MIT Press.

BEALS, Ralph L. 1969. *Politics of Social Research.* Chicago: Aldine Publishing Co.

BEHAVIORAL and Social Sciences Survey Committee. 1969. *The Behavioral and Social Sciences.* New York: Prentice-Hall.

BELL, Daniel. 1973. *The Coming of Post-Industrial Society: A Venture in Social Forecasting.* New York; Basic Books.

BENNIS, Warren G.; Benne, Kenneth D.; and Chin, Robert, eds. 1969. *The Planning of Change.* 2d ed. New York: Holt, Rinehart & Winston.

BENVENISTE, Guy. 1970. *Bureaucracy and National Planning: A Sociological Case Study in Mexico.* New York: Praeger Publishers.

———. 1977. *Bureaucracy.* San Francisco: Boyd & Fraser Publishing Co.

BENVENISTE, Guy, and Ilchman, Warren F., eds. 1969. *Agents of Change: Professionals in Developing Countries.* New York: Praeger Publishers.

BENVENISTE, Guy, and Moran, William E., Jr. 1962. *Handbook of African Economic Development.* New York: Frederick A. Praeger.

BERREMAN, Gerald. 1969. Not so innocent abroad. *The Nation,* 10 November, pp. 505–8.

BETTELHEIM, Charles. 1959. *Studies in the Theory of Planning.* Bombay: Asia Publishing House.

BLAU, Peter. 1964. *Exchange and Power in Social Life.* New York: John Wiley & Sons.

BOGUSLAW, Robert. 1965. *The New Utopians: A Study of System Design and Social Change.* Englewood Cliffs, N.J.: Prentice-Hall.

BOULDING, Kenneth E. 1966. The ethics of rational decision. *Management Science* 12, pp. 161–69.

BROOKS, Harvey. 1969. The scientific adviser. In Thomas E. Cronin and Sanford D. Greenberg, eds., *The Presidential Advisory System.* New York: Harper & Row.

———. 1976. The federal government and the autonomy of scholarship. In Charles Frankel, ed., *Controversies and Decisions.* New York: Russell Sage Foundation, pp. 235–57.

CAIDEN, Naomi, and Wildavsky, Aaron. 1974. *Planning and Budgeting in Poor Countries.* New York: John Wiley & Sons.

CAZES, Bernard. 1972. The development of social indicators: a survey. In Andrew Shonfield and Stella Shaw, eds., *Social Indicators and Social Policy.* London: Heinemann Educational Books, pp. 9–22.

CHARTRAND, Robert L., et al., eds. 1968. *Information Support Program Budgeting and the Congress.* New York: Spartan Books.

CHURCHMAN, C. West. 1968. *The Systems Approach.* New York: Dell Publishing Co.

COCTEAU, Jean. 1946. *Poésie Critique.* Paris: Éditions des Quatre Vents.

COHEN, Stephen. 1969. *Modern Capitalist Planning: The French Model.* Cambridge, Mass.: Harvard University Press.

COLEMAN, James S. 1965. *Education and Political Development.* Princeton, N.J.: Princeton University Press.

———. 1972. *Policy Research in the Social Sciences.* Morristown, N.J.: General Learning Press.

COOMBS, Phillip H. 1967. What do we still need to know about educational planning? In George Z. F. Bereday, Joseph A. Lauwerys, and Mark Blaug, eds., *The World Year Book of Education, 1967: Educational Planning.* New York: Harcourt, Brace & World.

COOPER, Michael H. 1973. *Social Policy: A Survey of Recent Developments.* Totowa, N.J.: Robertson, Martin & Co.

CREW, Frederick. 1968. *The Patch Commission.* New York: E. P. Dutton & Co.

CROZIER, Michel. 1964. *The Bureaucratic Phenomenon.* Chicago: University of Chicago Press.

CROZIER, Michel; Huntington, Samuel P.; and Watanuki, Joji. 1975. *The Crisis of Democracy.* New York: New York University Press.

DAVIDOFF, Paul. 1965. Advocacy and pluralism in planning. *Journal of the American Institute of Planners* 31, pp. 331–37.

DAVIDSON, Phillip W. 1967. Foreign policy. In Paul F. Lazarsfeld et al., eds., *The Uses of Sociology.* New York: Basic Books.

DAVIS, Abraham L., ed. 1975. *The U.S. Supreme Court and the Uses of Social Science Data.* New York: Mss Information Corp.

DEDIJER, Stevan. 1965. Research and the developing countries: problems and possibilities. In Norman Kaplan, ed., *Science and Society.* Chicago: Rand McNally & Co.

DE FOREST, Paul. 1969. The social sciences in the foreign policy subsystem of Congress. In Elizabeth T. Crawford and Albert D. Biderman, eds., *Social Scientists and International Affairs.* New York: John Wiley & Sons.

DERTHICK, Martha. 1972. *New Towns In-Town.* Washington, D.C.: The Urban Institute.

DOGAN, Mattei, ed. 1975. *The Mandarins of Western Europe: The Political Role of Top Civil Servants.* New York: John Wiley & Sons.

ETZIONI, Amitai. 1971. Policy research. *American Sociologist* 6 (Supplementary Issue), pp. 8–12.

FRANKEL, Charles, ed. 1976. *Controversies and Decisions.* New York: Russell Sage Foundation.

FRIEDMANN, John. 1971. The future of comprehensive urban planning: a critique. *Public Administration Review* 31 (May–June), pp. 315–26.

———. 1973. *Retracking America: A Theory of Transactive Planning.* Garden City, N.Y.: Doubleday.

FRIEDMANN, John, and Hudson, Barclay. 1974. Knowledge and action: a guide to planning theory. *Journal of the American Institute of Planners* 40, pp. 2–16.

FRIEDRICH, Carl J. 1969. Public policy and the nature of administrative responsibility. In Alan A. Altshuler, ed., *The Politics of the Federal Bureaucracy.* New York: Dodd, Mead & Co.

GALBRAITH, John Kenneth. 1968. *The New Industrial State.* New York: Signet Books.

———. 1969. *Affluent Society.* 2d ed. Boston: Houghton Mifflin.

GEHLEN, Michael P. 1969. *The Communist Party of the Soviet Union: A Functional Analysis.* Bloomington, Ind.: Indiana University Press.

GLAZER, Nathan. 1969. On task forcing. *The Public Interest* 15 (Spring), pp. 40–45.

GOODWIN, Leonard. 1975. *Can Social Science Help Resolve National Problems? Welfare, a Case in Point.* Riverside, N.J.: Free Press, a division of Macmillan Co.

GREENBERG, D. S. 1969. European science: financially, politically, it has trouble too. *Science* 166, pp. 1122–23.

GUTTENTAG, Marcia, and Struening, Elmer L., eds. 1975. *Handbook of Evaluation Research, Vols. 1 and 2.* Beverly Hills, Calif.: Sage Publications.

HACKETT, John, and Hackett, Anne-Marie. 1965. *Economic Planning in France.* Cambridge, Mass.: Harvard University Press.

254 *References*

HANSEN, Charles J. 1969. Royal commissions for the U.S. In Thomas E. Cronin and Sanford D. Greenberg, eds., *The Presidential Advisory System*. New York: Harper & Row.

HARGROVE, Erwin C. 1975. *The Missing Link: The Study of the Implementation of Social Policy*. Washington, D.C.: The Urban Institute.

HAVILAND, Field H. 1976. Federal-academic relations in social science research. In Charles Frankel, ed., *Controversies and Decisions*. New York: Russell Sage Foundation, pp. 219–34.

HELD, Virginia. 1968. PPBS comes to Washington. In Fremont Lyden and Ernest Miller, eds., *Planning Programming Budgeting: A Systems Approach to Management*. Chicago: Markham Publishing Co.

HELLER, Walter W. 1967. *New Dimensions of Political Economy*. New York: W. W. Norton & Co.

———. 1969. Economic policy advisers. In Thomas E. Cronin and Sanford D. Greenberg, eds., *The Presidential Advisory System*. New York: Harper & Row.

HELMER, Olaf. 1966. *Social Technology*. New York: Basic Books.

HIRSCH, Werner Z. 1968. Congress and program budgeting: problems and potentials. In Robert L. Chartrand et al., eds., *Information Support Program Budgeting and the Congress*. New York: Spartan Books.

HOOS, Ida R. 1972. *Systems Analysis in Public Policy: A Critique*. Berkeley, Calif.; University of California Press.

HOROWITZ, Irving L. 1967. *The Rise and Fall of Project Camelot*. Cambridge, Mass.: MIT Press.

———. 1969. Engineering and sociological perspectives on development: interdisciplinary constraints on social forecasting. *International Social Science Journal* 21, pp. 545–56.

HUITT, Ralph. 1968. Political feasibility. In Austin Ranney, ed., *Political Science and Public Policy*. Chicago: Markham Publishing Co.

ILCHMAN, Warren F., and Uphoff, Norman T. 1969. *The Political Economy of Change*. Berkeley, Calif.: University of California Press.

JANTSCH, Erich. 1967. *Technological Forecasting in Perspective*. Paris: Organization for Economic Cooperation and Development.

KOCH, Susan J. 1976. Nondemocratic nonplanning: the French experience. *Policy Sciences* 7, pp. 371–85.

KRAMER, Fred A. 1975. Policy analysis as ideology. *Public Administration Review* 35, pp. 509–17.

LASSWELL, Harold. 1951. The policy orientation. In Daniel Lerner and Harold D. Lasswell, eds., *The Policy Sciences*. Stanford, Calif.: Stanford University Press.

LAUTMAN, Jacques, and Thoenig, Jean-Claude. 1966. *Planification et Administrations Centrales*. Paris: Centre de Sociologie des Organisations.

LEPAWSKY, Albert. 1971. The progressives and the planners. *Public Administration Review* 31 (May–June), pp. 297–302.

LEVINE, Robert A. 1972. *Public Planning: Failure and Redirection*. New York: Basic Books.

LEWIS, Oscar. 1959. *Five Families*. New York: Basic Books.

———. 1961. *The Children of Sanchez*. New York: Random House.

LINDBLOM, Charles E. 1959. The science of muddling through. *Public Administration Review* 19 (Spring), pp. 79–88.

————. 1965. *The Intelligence of Democracy: Decision Making through Mutual Adjustment.* New York: Macmillan Co.

LYONS, Gene M. 1969. *The Uneasy Partnership: Social Science and the Federal Government in the Twentieth Century.* New York: Russell Sage Foundation.

————, ed. 1975. *Dartmouth-OECD Conference: Social Science Research and Public Policies.* Hanover, N.H.: University Press of New England.

MAAS, Arthur A. 1965. Congress and water resources. In Francis E. Rourke, ed., *Bureaucratic Power in National Politics.* Boston: Little, Brown & Co.

MACHIAVELLI, Niccolò. 1952. *The Prince.* New York: Mentor Books. (Written in 1513.)

MALBIN, Michael J. 1976. Congressional staffs—growing fast—but in different directions. *National Journal* 8, pp. 958–65.

MANNHEIM, Karl. n.d. *Man and Society in an Age of Reconstruction.* New York: Harcourt, Brace & World. (First published in German in 1935.)

MARGOLIS, Howard. 1973. *Technical Advice on Policy Issues.* Beverly Hills, Calif.: Sage Publications.

MARRIS, Peter, and Rein, Martin. 1969. *Dilemmas of Social Reform: Poverty and Community Action in the United States.* New York: Atherton Press.

MARTIN, C. J. 1969. A conference note: crisis in planning. *International Development Review* 11 (December), pp. 40–41.

MASSÉ, Pierre. 1962. *Histoire, Méthode et Doctrine de la Planification Française.* Paris: La Documentation Française.

MELTSNER, Arnold. 1976. *Policy Analysts in the Bureaucracy.* Berkeley, Calif.: University of California Press.

MEYNAUD, Jean. 1964. *La Technocratie.* Paris: Éditions Payot.

MILLETT, John D. 1947. *The Process and Organization of Government Planning.* New York: Columbia University Press.

MISHAN, Ezra J. 1967. *The Costs of Economic Growth.* New York: Frederick A. Praeger.

MOORE, Wilbert E. 1966. The utility of utopias. *American Sociological Review* 31, pp. 765–72.

MYRDAL, Gunnar. 1968. *Asian Drama.* New York: Random House.

NATIONAL Academy of Science. 1968. *The Behavioral Sciences and the Federal Government.* Washington, D.C.: Government Printing Office.

NATIONAL Goals Research Staff. 1970. *Toward Balanced Growth: Quantity with Quality.* Washington, D.C.: Government Printing Office.

NEWHOUSE, John. 1973. *Cold Dawn: The Story of SALT.* New York: Holt, Rinehart & Winston.

NIEBURG, H. L. 1966. *In the Name of Science.* Chicago: Quadrangle Books.

ORLANS, Harold. 1973. *Contracting for Knowledge: Values and Limitations of Social Science Research.* San Francisco: Jossey-Bass, Publishers.

PERIN, Constance. 1970. *With Man in Mind: An Interdisciplinary Prospectus for Environmental Design.* Cambridge, Mass.: MIT Press.

PIOUS, Richard W. 1975. Sources of domestic policy initiations. In Harvey C. Mansfield, ed., *Congress against the President.* New York: Praeger Publishers, pp. 98–111.

PLATT, John. 1969. What we must do: a large scale mobilization of scientists may be the only way we may be able to solve our crisis problems. *Science* 166, p. 1115.

POLAK, Fred. 1973. *The Image of the Future.* New York: Elsevier Scientific Publishing Co.

PRESSMAN, Jeffrey L., and Wildavsky, Aaron. 1973. *Implementation*. Berkeley, Calif.: University of California Press.

RIVLIN, Alice M. 1971. *Systematic Thinking for Social Action*. Washington, D.C.: Brookings Institution.

RIVLIN, Alice M., and Timpane, Michael P. 1975. *Ethical and Legal Issues of Social Experimentation*. Washington, D.C.: Brookings Institution.

ROBINSON, James A. 1967. *Congress and Foreign Policy-Making*. Homewood, Ill.: Dorsey Press.

ROSZAK, Theodore. 1969. *The Making of a Counter Culture: Reflections on the Technocratic Society and Its Youthful Opposition*. Garden City, N.Y.: Doubleday & Co.

RYAVEC, Karl W. 1975. *Implementation of Soviet Economic Reforms: Political, Organizational, and Social Processes*. New York: Praeger Publishers.

SCHICK, Allen. 1973. A death in the bureaucracy: the demise of federal PPB. *Public Administration Review* 33, pp. 146–56.

———. 1976. The supply and demand for analysis on Capitol Hill. *Policy Analysis* 2, pp. 215–34.

SCHULTZE, Charles L. 1968. *The Politics and Economics of Public Spending*. Washington, D.C.: Brookings Institution.

SENNETT, Richard. 1970. An urban anarchist—a review of *The Economy of Cities* by Jane Jacobs. *New York Review of Books*, 1 January.

SHELLING, Thomas C. 1963. *The Strategy of Conflict*. New York: Oxford University Press.

SHONFIELD, Andrew. 1965. *Modern Capitalism: The Changing Balance of Public and Private Power*. New York: Oxford University Press.

SIMON, Herbert A. 1965. *Administrative Behavior*. 2d ed. New York: Free Press.

SMITH, Trevor. 1975. Britain. In Jack Hayward and Michael Watson, eds., *Planning, Politics, and Public Policy: The British, French, and Italian Experience*. Cambridge: Cambridge University Press, pp. 52–69.

SOREL, Georges. 1950. *Reflections on Violence*. New York: Macmillan Co., Collier Books. (First published in French in 1908.)

SPECIAL Commission on the Social Sciences of the National Science Board. 1969. *Knowledge into Action: Improving the Nation's Use of the Social Sciences*. Washington, D.C.: National Science Foundation.

STANFORD Research Institute. 1959. *Possible Nonmilitary Scientific Developments and Their Potential Impact on Foreign Policy Problems of the United States*. Washington, D.C.: Government Printing Office.

STEVENS, Aurthur G., et al. 1974. Mobilization of liberal strength in the House 1955–1970: The Democratic Study Group. *American Political Science Review* 68, pp. 667–81.

STEWART, Frances. 1975. A note on social cost-benefit analysis and class conflict in LDCs. *World Development* 3, pp. 31–39.

SUCHMAN, Edward A. 1967. *Evaluative Research*. New York: Russell Sage Foundation.

THOENIG, Jean-Claude. 1973. *L'Ère des Technocrates: Le Cas des Ponts et Chaussées*. Paris: Les Éditions d'Organisation.

THURBER, James A. 1976. Congressional budget reform and new demands for policy analysis. *Policy Analysis* 2, pp. 197–214.

TOFFLER, Alvin. 1970. *Future Shock*. New York: Random House.

TRIBE, Lawrence H. 1972. Policy science: analysis or ideology? *Journal of Philosophy and Public Affairs* (January), pp. 66–110.

TRIST, Eric. 1970. Social research institutions: types, structures, scale. *International Social Science Journal* 22, pp. 301–24.

ULLMO, Yves. 1975. France. In Jack Hayward and Michael Watson, eds., *Planning, Politics, and Public Policy: The British, French, and Italian Experience.* Cambridge: Cambridge University Press, pp. 22–51.

UNITED States Department of Health, Education, and Welfare. 1969. *Toward a Social Report.* Washington, D.C.: Government Printing Office.

WATERSTON, Albert. 1965. *Development Planning: Lessons of Experience.* Baltimore: Johns Hopkins Press.

———. 1969. An operational approach to development planning. *International Development Review* 11 (September), pp. 6–12.

WEBER, Max. 1947. *The Theory of Social and Economic Organization.* Translated by A. M. Henderson and Talcott Parsons. New York: Free Press. (First published in German in 1924.)

WILDAVSKY, Aaron. 1964. *The Politics of the Budgetary Process.* Boston: Little, Brown & Co.

WILENSKY, Harold L. 1956. *Intellectuals in Labor Unions.* Glencoe, Ill.: Free Press.

———. 1967. *Organizational Intelligence.* New York: Basic Books.

WILLIAM, W. 1975. *Social Policy Research and Analysis: The Experience in Federal Social Agencies.* New York: Elsevier Publishing Co.

WORTHLEY, John A. 1974. PPB: dead or alive? *Public Administration Review* 34, pp. 392–94.

ZNANIECKI, Florian. 1965. *The Social Role of the Man of Knowledge.* New York: Octagon Books. (First published in 1940.)

Selected Bibliography

This is not an attempt at comprehensive analysis. I refer the reader to the bibliographical material in Toffler, Alvin, *Future Shock* (see References), pp. 461–83; Wilensky, Harold, *Organizational Intelligence* (see References), pp. 193–207; Crawford, E. T., and Biderman, A. D., *Social Scientists and International Affairs* (New York: John Wiley & Sons, 1969), pp. 285–324; Dror, Yehezkel, *Public Policymaking Reexamined* (San Francisco: Chandler Publishing Co., 1968), pp. 327–56; Benveniste, Guy, *Bureaucracy and National Planning* (see References), pp. 133–36; and Caiden, Naomi, and Wildavsky, Aaron, *Planning and Budgeting in Poor Countries* (see References), pp. 325–56.

In addition, the following are useful: Branch, Melville C., *Comprehensive Urban Planning: A Selected Annotated Bibliography with Related Materials* (Beverly Hills, Calif.: Sage Publications, 1970); Gittinger, J. P., *The Literature of Agricultural Planning* (Washington, D.C.: Planning Association, 1966); and Spitz, Allen A., *Developmental Change: An Annotated Bibliography* (Lexington, Ky.: University of Kentucky Press, 1969).

The New Books

BARDACH, Eugene. *The Implementation Game.* Cambridge, Mass.: MIT Press, 1977.

BREWER, Garry D. *Politicians, Bureaucrats and the Consultant.* New York: Basic Books, 1973.

CAIDEN, Naomi, and Wildavsky, Aaron. *Planning and Budgeting in Poor Countries.* New York: John Wiley & Sons, 1974.

CHAPMAN, Richard A., ed. *The Role of Commissions in Policy-Making.* London: George Allen & Unwin, 1973.

COOPER, Michael H. *Social Policy: A Survey of Recent Developments.* Totowa, N.J.: Robertson, Martin & Co., 1973.

DALKEY, Norman C., ed. *Studies in the Quality of Life: Delphi and Decision Making.* Lexington, Mass.: Lexington Books, 1972.

DOGAN, Mattei, ed. *The Mandarins of Western Europe: The Political Role of Top Civil Servants.* New York: John Wiley & Sons, 1975.

FORBES, Jean, ed. *Studies in Social Science and Planning.* New York: John Wiley & Sons, 1974.

FRIEDMANN, John. *Retracking America: A Theory of Transactive Planning.* Garden City, N.Y.: Doubleday, 1973.

HAYWARD, Jack, and Watson, Michael, eds. *Planning, Politics, and Public Policy: The British, French, and Italian Experience.* Cambridge, Mass.: Cambridge University Press, 1975.

HOOS, Ida R. *Systems Analysis in Public Policy: A Critique.* Berkeley, Calif.: University of California Press, 1972.

LA PORTE, Todd R., ed. *Organized Social Complexity.* Princeton, N.J.: Princeton University Press, 1975.

LYONS, Gene M., ed. *Dartmouth-OECD Conference: Social Science Research and Public Policies.* Hanover, N.H.: University Press of New England, 1975.

MARGOLIS, Howard. *Technical Advice on Policy Issues.* Beverly Hills, Calif.: Sage Publications, 1973.

MELTSNER, Arnold. *Policy Analysts in the Bureaucracy.* Berkeley, Calif.: University of California Press, 1976.

ORLANS, Harold. *Contracting for Knowledge: Values and Limitations of Social Science Research.* San Francisco: Jossey-Bass Publishers, 1973.

PODGÓRECKI, Adam. *Practical Social Sciences.* London: Routledge & Kegan Paul, 1975.

POLACK, Fred. *The Image of the Future.* New York: Elsevier Scientific Publishing Co., 1973.

RIVLIN, Alice M. *Systematic Thinking for Social Action.* Washington, D.C.: Brookings Institution, 1971.

SHONFIELD, Andrew, and Shaw, Stella, eds. *Social Indicators and Social Policy.* London: Heinemann Educational Books, 1972.

THEOBALD, Robert. *Beyond Despair: Directions for America's Third Century.* Washington, D.C.: New Republic Book Co., 1976.

THOENIG, Jean-Claude. *L'Ère des Technocrates: Le Cas des Ponts et Chaussées.* Paris: Les Éditions d'Organisation, 1973.

WILDAVSKY, Aaron. *Budgeting: A Comparative Theory of Budgetary Processes.* Boston: Little, Brown & Co., 1975.

WILLIAM, W. *Social Policy Research and Analysis: The Experience in Federal Social Agencies.* New York: Elsevier Publishing Co., 1975.

ZECKHAUSER, Richard, et al., eds. *Benefit-Cost and Policy Analysis 1974.* Chicago: Aldine Publishing Co., 1975.

The Old Books

BERNAL, J. D. *The Social Function of Science.* London: Routledge & Kegan Paul, 1939.

COLE, G. D. H. *Economic Planning.* New York: Alfred A. Knopf, 1935.

DEVONS, Ely. *Planning in Practice.* London: Cambridge University Press, 1950.

DOOB, Leonard W. *The Plans of Men.* New Haven, Conn.: Yale University Press, 1940.

CALLOWAY, George B., and associates, eds. *Planning for America.* New York: Henry Holt & Co., 1941.

HARRIS, Seymour E., ed. *Economic Planning: The Plans of Fourteen Countries, with Analyses of the Plans.* New York: Alfred A. Knopf, 1949.

HAYEK, Friedrich A. *The Road to Serfdom.* Chicago: University of Chicago Press, 1944.

HOLCOMBE, A. N. *Government in a Planned Democracy.* New York: Norton, 1935.

JEWKES, John. *Ordeal by Planning.* London: Macmillan & Co., 1948.

KNIGHT, Frank H. The planful act. In *Freedom and Reform*. New York: Norton, 1935.

LANDAUER, Karl. *Theory of National Economic Planning*, Berkeley, Calif.: University of California Press, 1944.

LERNER, Daniel, and Lasswell, Harold D., eds. *The Policy Sciences*. Stanford, Calif.: Stanford University Press, 1951.

LORWIN, Lewis. *Postwar Plans of the United Nations*. New York: Twentieth Century Fund, 1943.

MANNHEIM, Karl. *Man and Society in an Age of Reconstruction*. New York: Harcourt, Brace & World, n.d. (First published in German in 1935: translated, revised, and considerably enlarged in 1940.)

———. *Freedom, Power, and Democratic Planning*. London: Routledge & Kegan Paul, 1965. (First published in 1951.)

ROBBINS, Lionel. *Economic Planning and International Order*. London: Macmillan & Co., 1937.

SOULÉ, George H. *A Planned Society*. New York: Macmillan Co., 1932.

STALEY, Eugene. Economic planning and free institutions. *Plan Age*, February 1940.

———. *The Future of Underdeveloped Countries*. New York: Harper & Bros., 1954.

WOOTTEN, Barbara. *Plan or No Plan*. New York: Farrar & Rinehart, 1935.

ZNANIECKI, Florian. *The Social Role of the Man of Knowledge*. New York: Octagon Books, 1965. (First published in 1940.)

Future, Uncertainty, and Utopias

ADELSON, Marvin. *The Technology of Forecasting and the Forecasting of Technology*. Santa Monica, Calif.: Systems Development Corp., 1968.

ALONSO, William. Predicting with imperfect data. *Journal of the American Institute of Planners* 34 (1968), pp. 248–55.

BELL, Daniel. Twelve modes of prediction. *Daedalus* 93 (1964), pp. 845–80.

BELL, Wendell, and Mau, J. A., eds. *The Sociology of the Future*. New York: Russell Sage Foundation, 1971.

BOULDING, Kenneth E. *The Image: Knowledge in Life and Society*. Ann Arbor, Mich.: University of Michigan Press, 1956.

BOWMAN, Mary Jean, ed. *Expectations, Uncertainty and Business Behavior*. New York: Social Science Research Council, 1958.

CARTER, C. P.; Meredith, G. P.; and Shackle, G. L. S., eds. *Uncertainty and Business Decisions*. Liverpool: Liverpool University Press, 1962.

COHEN, J. *Behavior in Uncertainty*. London: George Allen & Unwin, 1964.

DE JOUVENEL, Bertrand. Utopia for practical purposes. *Daedalus* 94 (1965), pp. 437–65.

———. Political science and prevision. *American Political Science Review* 59 (1965), pp. 29–38.

———. *The Art of Conjecture*. New York: Basic Books, 1967.

DUVEAU, Georges. *Sociologie de l'Utopie*. Paris: Presses Universitaires de France, 1961.

ELLUL, Jacques. *The Technological Society*. New York: Alfred A. Knopf, 1964.

FRAISE, Paul. *The Psychology of Time*. New York: Harper & Row, 1963.

FRASER, J. T., ed. *The Voices of Time*. New York: George Braziller, 1966.

HETMAN, François. *The Language of Forecasting*. Paris: Futuribles, 1969.

HUBER, Bettina J., and Bell, Wendell. Sociology and the emergent study of the future. *American Sociologist* 6 (1971), pp. 287–95.

JANTSCH, Erich. *Technological Forecasting in Perspective.* Paris: Organization for Economic Cooperation and Development, 1967.

———. *Perspectives of Planning.* Paris: Organization for Economic Cooperation and Development, 1969.

KAHN, Herman, and Wiener, Anthony J. *The Year* 2000. New York: Macmillan Co., 1967.

KNIGHT, Frank H. *Risk, Uncertainty and Profit.* New York: Harper & Row, Harper Torchbooks, 1965. (First published in 1921.)

LECHT, Leonard A. *Goals, Priorities, and Dollars: The Next Decade.* New York: Free Press, 1966.

MANNHEIM, Karl. *Ideology and Utopia.* New York: Harcourt, Brace & World, Harvest Books, 1965. (First published in 1936).

MASSÉ, Pierre. *Les Réserves et la Régulation de l'Avenir dans la Vie Économique.* Paris: Hermann, 1946.

MCHALE, John. *The Future of the Future.* New York; George Braziller, 1969.

MICHAEL, Donald N. *The Next Generation: Problems of Youth in the Next Twenty Years.* New York: Random House, 1965.

———. *The Unprepared Society: Planning for a Precarious Future.* New York: Basic Books, 1968.

———, ed. *The Future Society.* Chicago: Transaction Books, 1970.

MOORE, Wilbert E. *Man, Time and Society.* New York: John Wiley & Sons, 1963.

———. The utility of utopias. *American Sociological Review* 31 (1966), pp. 765–72.

———. *Order and Change.* New York: John Wiley & Sons, 1967.

MUMFORD, Lewis. *The Story of Utopias.* New York: Viking Press, 1963. (First published in 1922.)

OZGA, S. A. *Expectations in Economic Theory.* Chicago: Aldine Publishing Co., 1965.

POULET, George. *Studies in Human Time.* New York: Harper & Row, Harper Torchbooks, 1959.

RIESMAN, David. Some observations on community plans & utopia. In *Individualism Reconsidered.* New York: Doubleday & Co., Anchor Books, 1954.

SHACKLE, G. L. S. *Decision Order and Time in Human Affairs.* Cambridge: Cambridge University Press, 1961.

TOFFLER, Alvin. *Future Shock.* New York: Random House, 1970.

WHEELER, Harvey. *The Politics of Revolution.* Berkeley, Calif.: Glendessary Press, 1971.

Science, Change, Planning

BARBER, Bernard. *Science and the Social Order.* Glencoe, Ill.: Free Press, 1952. Rev. ed. New York: Macmillan Co., Collier Books, 1962.

BARBER, Richard J. *The Politics of Research.* Washington, D.C.: Public Affairs Press, 1966.

BEALS, Ralph L. *Politics of Social Research.* Chicago: Aldine Publishing Co., 1969.

BELL, Daniel, and Olson, Mancur. Toward a social report. *The Public Interest* 15 (1969), pp. 72–105.

BENNIS, Warren. *Changing Organizations.* New York: McGraw-Hill, 1966.
BENNIS, Warren; Benne, K.; and Chin, R., eds. *The Planning of Change.* New York: Holt, Rinehart & Winston, 1969.
BOULDING, Kenneth E. *The Impact of the Social Sciences.* New Brunswick, N.J.: Rutgers University Press, 1966.
BUCHANAN, James S., and Tullock, Gordon. *The Calculus of Consent: Logical Foundations of Constitutional Democracy.* Ann Arbor, Mich.: University of Michigan Press, 1965. (First published in 1962.)
CROZIER, Michel. *Le Phénomène Bureaucratique.* Paris: Éditions du Seuil, 1963. (Translated by the author and published as *The Bureaucratic Phenomenon.* Chicago: University of Chicago Press, 1964.)
DAHL, Robert, and Lindblom, Charles E. *Politics, Economics, and Welfare: Planning and Politico-Economic Systems Resolved into Basic Social Processes.* New York: Harper & Row, Harper Torchbooks, 1963. (First published in 1953.)
DOWNS, Anthony. *An Economic Theory of Democracy.* New York: Harper & Bros., 1957.
———. *Inside Bureaucracy.* Boston: Little, Brown & Co., 1967.
DROR, Yehezkel. *Policy Analysis: A Theoretic Framework and Some Basic Concepts.* Santa Monica, Calif.: RAND Corp., July 1969 (Report P4156).
———. *Alternative Domestic Politics Futures: Research Needs and Research Designs.* Santa Monica, Calif.: RAND Corp., February 1970 (Report P4306).
———. *Policy Sciences: Developments and Implications.* Santa Monica, Calif.: RAND Corp., March 1970 (Report P4321).
———. *From Management Sciences to Policy Sciences.* Santa Monica, Calif.: RAND Corp., May 1970 (Report P4375).
———. Systems analysis and national modernization decisions. *Academy of Management Journal* 13 (1970), pp. 139–52.
———. A policy sciences view of future studies. *Technological Forecasting* 2 (1970), pp. 3–16.
———. *Ventures in Policy Sciences.* New York: American Elsevier Publishing Co., 1971.
DRUCKER, Peter F. The sickness of government. *The Public Interest* 14 (1969), pp. 3–23.
ETZIONI, Amitai. *The Active Society: A Theory of Societal and Political Processes.* New York: Free Press, 1968.
FRIEDEN, Barnard J., and Morris, Robert, eds. *Urban Planning and Social Policy.* New York: Basic Books, 1968.
FRIEDMAN, Milton. *Capitalism and Freedom.* Chicago: University of Chicago Press, 1962.
GANS, Herbert. *People and Plans: Essays on Urban Problems and Solutions.* New York: Basic Books, 1968.
GOULDNER, Alvin W., and Miller, S. M., eds. *Applied Sociology: Opportunities and Problems.* New York: Free Press, 1965.
HAGEN, Everett E. *On the Theory of Social Change.* Homewood, Ill.: Dorsey Press, 1963.
HOROWITZ, Irving Louis. *Three Worlds of Development.* New York: Oxford University Press, 1966.
ILCHMAN, Warren F., and Uphoff, Norman T. *The Political Economy of Change.* Berkeley, Calif.: University of California Press, 1969.

KAPLAN, Norman, ed. *Science and Society*. Chicago: Rand McNally, 1965.

LAZARSFELD, Paul F.; Sewell, William H.; and Wilensky, Harold L., eds. *The Uses of Sociology*. New York: Basic Books, 1967.

MACHLUP, F. *The Production and Distribution of Knowledge in the U.S.* Princeton, N.J.: Princeton University Press, 1962.

MENDÈS-FRANCE, Pierre, and Ardant, Gabriel. *Economics and Action*. Paris: UNESCO, 1955.

MENKE-GLUKERT, Peter. Mankind in the world tomorrow: the changing environment. *Technological Forecasting and Social Change* 2 (1971), pp. 231–35.

MERTON, Robert K. The role of applied social science in the formation of policy. *Philosophy of Science* 16 (1949), pp. 161–81.

MESTHENE, Emmanuel G. *Technological Change: Its Impact on Man and Society*. Cambridge, Mass.: Harvard University Press, 1970.

MORRIS, Robert, ed. *Centrally Planned Change: Prospects and Concepts*. New York: National Association of Social Workers, 1964.

RICHTA, Radovan. *Civilization at the Crossroads: Social and Human Implications of the Scientific and Technological Revolution*. Prague: International Arts & Sciences Press, 1969.

ROGOW, Arnold A., ed. *Politics, Personality and Social Science in the Twentieth Century*. Chicago: University of Chicago Press, 1969.

SHONFIELD, Andrew. *The Attack on World Poverty*. New York: Vintage Books, 1962.

——. *Modern Capitalism: The Changing Balance of Public and Private Power*. New York: Oxford University Press, 1965.

VICKERS, Sir Geoffrey. Ecology, planning, and the American Dream. In L. J. Duhl, ed., *The Urban Condition*. New York; Basic Books, 1963.

——. *The Art of Judgment: A Study of Policy Making*. New York: Basic Books, 1965.

WEBBER, Melvin M. Comprehensive planning and social responsibility. *Journal of the American Institute of Planners* 29 (1963), pp. 232–41.

Planning, Politics, Process

ALTSHULER, A. A. *The City Planning Process*. Ithaca, N.Y.: Cornell University Press, 1965.

ANDERSON, Stanford, ed. *Planning for Diversity and Choice*. Cambridge, Mass.: MIT Press, 1968.

ARCHIBALD, Kathleen. Alternative orientations to social science utilization. *Social Science Information* 9 (April 1970), pp. 7–34.

——. Three views of the expert's role in policymaking: systems analysis, incrementalism and the clinical approach. *Policy Sciences* 1 (1970), pp. 73–86.

BANFIELD, Edward C. Ends and means in planning. *International Social Science Journal* 11 (1959), pp. 361–68.

——. *Political Influence*. Glencoe, Ill.: Free Press, 1961.

BAUER, Raymond A. Social psychology and the study of policy formation. *American Psychologist* 21 (1966), pp. 933–42.

BAUER, Raymond, and Gergen, K., eds. *The Study of Policy Formation*. New York: Free Press, 1968.

Selected Bibliography265

BOGUSLAW, Robert. *The New Utopians: A Study of System Design and Social Change.* Englewood Cliffs, N.J.: Prentice-Hall, 1965.
BRAYBROOKE, David, and Lindblom, Charles E. *A Strategy of Decision: Policy Evaluation as a Social Process.* New York: Free Press, 1963.
COSTELLO, Timothy W. Psychological aspects: the soft side of policy formation. *Policy Sciences* 1 (1970), pp. 161–68.
DAHL, Robert. The politics of planning. *International Social Science Journal* 11 (1959), pp. 341–50.
DAVIDOFF, Paul. Advocacy and pluralism in planning. *Journal of the American Institute of Planners* 31 (1965), pp. 331–38.
DAVIDOFF, Paul, and Reiner, Thomas A. A choice theory of planning. *Journal of the American Institute of Planners* 28 (1962), pp. 103–15.
DROR, Yehezkel. The planning process: a facet design. *International Review of Administrative Sciences* 19 (1963), pp. 46–58.
———. *Public Policymaking Reexamined.* San Francisco: Chandler Publishing Co., 1968.
DYCKMAN, John W. The practical uses of planning theory. *Journal of the American Institute of Planners* 35 (1969), pp. 298–301.
FRIEDMANN, John. A conceptual model for the analysis of planning behavior. *Administrative Science Quarterly* 12 (1967), pp. 225–52.
———. The future of comprehensive urban planning: a critique. *Public Administration Review* 31 (May–June 1971), pp. 315–26.
GALBRAITH, John K. *Economic Development in Perspective.* Cambridge, Mass.: Harvard University Press, 1962.
———. *Economics and the Art of Controversy.* New York: Vintage Books, 1965.
GEIGER, Theodore, and Solomon, Leo, eds. *Motivations and Methods in Development and Foreign Aid.* Washington, D.C.: Society for International Development, 1964.
GLASS, Ruth. The evaluation of planning: some sociological considerations. *International Social Science Journal* 11 (1959), pp. 393–409.
GROSS, Bertram M. National planning: some fundamental questions. *American Behavioral Scientist* 8 (1964), pp. 7–15.
———. National planning: findings and fallacies. *Public Administration Review* 25 (1965), pp. 263–73.
———, ed. *Action under Planning: The Guidance of Economic Development.* New York: McGraw-Hill, 1967.
———, ed. *Social Intelligence for America's Future.* Boston: Allyn & Bacon, 1969.
———. Planning in an era of social revolution. *Public Administration Review* 31 (1971), pp. 259–96.
HIRSCHMAN, Albert O., and Lindblom, Charles E. Economic development, research and development, and policy making: some converging views. *Behavioral Science* 7 (1962), pp. 211–12.
HOROWITZ, Irving Louis. Social science mandarins: policymaking as a political formula. *Policy Sciences* 1 (1970), pp. 339–60.
KAHN, Alfred J. *Studies in Social Policy and Planning.* New York: Russell Sage Foundation, 1969.
LINDBLOM, Charles E. The science of muddling through. *Public Administration Review* 19 (Spring 1959), pp. 79–88.
———. *The Intelligence of Democracy: Decision Making through Mutual Adjustment.* New York: Macmillan Co., 1965.
———. *The Policy Making Process.* Englewood Cliffs, N.J.: Prentice-Hall, 1968.

LYDEN, Fremont J., et al., eds. *Policies, Decisions and Organizations.* New York: Appleton-Century-Crofts, 1969.

MARRIS, Peter, and Rein, Martin. *Dilemmas of Social Reform.* New York: Atherton Press, 1969.

MAU, James A. *Social Change and Images of the Future.* Cambridge, Mass.: Schenkman Publishing Co., 1968.

MILLER, George A.; Galanter, E.; and Pribram, K. H. *Plans and the Structure of Behavior.* New York: Holt, Rinehart & Winston, 1960.

MYRDAL, Gunnar. *The Political Element in the Development of Economic Theory.* London: Routledge & Kegan Paul, 1953.

———. *Beyond the Welfare State: Economic Planning and Its International Implications.* New Haven, Conn.: Yale University Press, 1960.

OLSON, Mancur, Jr. *The Logic of Collective Action.* Cambridge, Mass.: Harvard University Press, 1965.

PETERSEN, William. On some meanings of "planning." *Journal of the American Institute of Planners* 32 (1966), pp. 130–42.

REIN, Martin. Social planning: the search for legitimacy. *Journal of the American Institute of Planners* 35 (1969), pp. 233–44.

SCHOEFFLER, S. Toward a general definition of rational action. *Kyklos* 7 (1954), pp. 245–371.

SHELDON, Eleanor Bernert, and Moore, Wilbert E. *Indicators of Social Change: Concepts and Measurements.* New York: Russell Sage Foundation, 1968.

TULLOCK, Gordon. *The Politics of Bureaucracy.* Washington, D.C.: Public Affairs Press, 1965.

WEBBER, Melvin M. The prospects for policies planning. In L. J. Duhl, ed., *The Urban Condition.* New York: Basic Books, 1963.

———. The roles of intelligence systems in urban-systems planning. *Journal of the American Institute of Planners* 31 (1965), pp. 289–96.

WILDAVSKY, Aaron. *The Politics of the Budgetary Process.* Boston: Little, Brown & Co., 1964.

———. Rescuing policy analysis from PPBS. *Public Administration Review* 29 (1969), pp. 189–202.

Role of the Expert

BENVENISTE, Guy, and Ilchman, Warren, eds. *Agents of Change: Professionals in Developing Countries.* New York; Praeger Publishers, 1969.

BOULDING, Kenneth E. The ethics of rational decision. *Management Science* 12 (1966), pp. 161–69.

CRAWFORD, E. T., and Biderman, A. D. *Social Scientists and International Affairs.* New York: John Wiley & Sons, 1969.

DOWNS, Anthony. Some thoughts on giving people economic advice. *American Behavioral Scientist* 9 (1965), pp. 31–32.

DUHL, L. J., and Volkman, Q. Participant democracy: networks as a strategy for change. *Urban and Social Change Review* 3 (1970), pp. 11–14.

DYCKMAN, John W. Social planning, social planners, and planned societies. *Journal of the American Institute of Planners* 32 (1966), pp. 66–76.

ELSNER, Henry, Jr. *The Technocrats: Prophets of Automation.* Syracuse, N.Y.: Syracuse University Press, 1967.

GOULDNER, Alvin W. The sociologist as partisan: sociology and the welfare state. *American Sociologist* 3 (1968), pp. 103–16.

HIRSCH, Walter. *Scientists in American Society.* New York: Random House, 1968.

HOROWITZ, I. L. The academy and the polity: interaction between social scientists and federal administrators. *Journal of Behavioral Science* 5 (1969), pp. 309–36.

JÖHR, W. A., and Singer, Hans W. *The Role of the Economist as Official Advisor.* London: George Allen & Unwin, 1955.

KORNHAUSER, W. *Scientists in Industry.* Berkeley, Calif.: University of California Press, 1962.

LYONS, Gene M. *The Uneasy Partnership: Social Science and the Federal Government in the Twentieth Century.* New York: Russell Sage Foundation, 1969.

MERTON, R. K. The role of the intellectual in public bureaucracy. *Social Forces* 23 (1945), pp. 405–15.

MEYNAUD, Jean. *La Technocratie.* Paris: Éditions Payot, 1964.

RANSOM, Harry Howe. *The Intelligence Establishment.* Cambridge, Mass.: Harvard University Press, 1970.

SCHOOLER, Dean, Jr. Political arenas, life styles and the impact of technologies on policy making. *Policy Sciences* 1 (1970), pp. 275–88.

———. *Science, Scientists and Public Policy.* New York: Free Press, 1971.

WHEATON, William L. C. Public and private agents of change. In M. M. Webber et al., eds., *Explorations into Urban Structure.* Philadelphia: University of Pennsylvania Press, 1963.

WILENSKY, H. L. *Intellectuals in Labor Unions: Organizational Pressures on Professional Roles.* Glencoe, Ill.: Free Press, 1956.

ZNANIECKI, Florian. *The Social Role of the Man of Knowledge.* New York: Octagon Books, 1965. (First published in 1940.)

Technical, Analytical

ACKOFF, R. L. *Scientific Method: Optimizing Applied Research Decisions.* New York: John Wiley & Sons, 1962.

———. *A Concept of Corporate Planning.* New York: John Wiley & Sons, 1970.

ANTHONY, Robert A. *Planning and Control Systems.* Boston: Harvard Business School, 1965.

ARROW, Kenneth J. *Social Choice and Individual Values.* 2d ed. New York: John Wiley & Sons, 1964.

BARSOV, A. A. *What Is Linear Programming.* Boston: D. C. Heath & Co., 1964.

BAUER, Raymond A., ed. *Social Indicators.* Cambridge, Mass.: MIT Press, 1966.

BETTELHEIM, Charles. *Studies in the Theory of Planning.* Bombay: Asia Publishing House, 1959.

BOBROW, Davis B., and Schwartz, Judah L. *Computers and the Policy Making Community.* Englewood Cliffs, N.J.: Prentice-Hall, 1968.

BROSS, Irwin D. J. *Design for Decision.* New York: Macmillan Co., 1953.

CAIDEN, Naomi, and Wildavsky, Aaron. *Planning and Budgeting in Poor Countries.* New York: John Wiley & Sons, 1974.

CARLSON, Sune. *Development Economics and Administration.* Stockholm: Scandinavian University Books, 1964.

CHAMBERLAIN, Neil W. *Private and Public Planning.* New York: McGraw-Hill, 1965.

CHASE, Samuel B., ed. *Problems in Public Expenditure Analysis.* Washington, D.C.: Brookings Institution, 1968.

CHURCHMAN, C. West. *Prediction and Optimal Decision: Philosophical Issues of a Science of Values.* Englewood Cliffs, N.J.: Prentice-Hall, 1961.

———. *Challenge to Reason.* New York: McGraw-Hill, 1968.

———. *The Systems Approach.* New York: Delacorte Press, 1968, and Dell Publishing Co., 1968.

CHURCHMAN, C. West, et al. *Introduction to Operations Research.* New York: John Wiley & Sons, 1957.

DORFMAN, Robert, ed. *Measuring Benefits of Government Investments.* Washington, D.C.: Brookings Institution, 1965.

GOODE, Robert. *System Engineering.* New York: McGraw-Hill, 1957.

HITCH, Charles J., and McKean, Roland N. *The Economics of Defense in the Nuclear Age.* Santa Monica, Calif.: RAND Corp., 1960.

HOOS, Ida R. Information systems and public planning. *Management Science* 17 (1971), pp. 658–71.

ISARD, Walter, and Cumberland, John, eds. *Regional Economic Planning.* Paris: Organization for Economic Cooperation and Development, 1961.

KING, J. A., ed. *Economic Development Projects and Their Appraisal.* Baltimore: Johns Hopkins Press, 1967.

KÖHLER, Heinz. *Welfare and Planning: An Analysis of Capitalism vs. Socialism.* New York: John Wiley & Sons, 1966.

LEWIS, J. Arthur. *The Principles of Economic Planning.* London: Dobson, Allen & Unwin, 1949.

———. *Development Planning: The Essentials of Economic Policy.* New York: Harper & Row, 1966.

LYDEN, Fremont J., and Miller, Ernest G., eds. *Planning Programming Budgeting: A Systems Approach to Management.* Chicago: Markham Publishing Co., 1968.

MASON, Edward. *Economic Planning in Underdeveloped Areas: Government and Business.* New York: Fordham University Press, 1958.

McKEAN, Roland. *Efficiency in Government through Systems Analysis.* New York: John Wiley & Sons, 1958.

MEIER, Richard. *Developmental Planning.* New York: McGraw-Hill, 1965.

MISHAN, Ezra J. *The Costs of Economic Growth.* New York: Frederick A. Praeger, 1967.

MONTGOMERY, John D., and Siffin, William J. *Approaches to Development: Politics, Administration and Change.* New York: McGraw-Hill, 1966.

MORGENSTERN, Oskar. *The Accuracy of Economic Observations.* Princeton, N.J.: Princeton University Press, 1963.

NOVICK, David, ed. *Program Budgeting: Program Analysis and the Federal Government.* Cambridge, Mass.: Harvard University Press, 1965.

PIATIER, André. *Equilibre entre Développement Économique et Développement Social.* Paris: Éditions Genin, 1962.

QUADE, E. S., and Boucher, W. I. *Systems Analysis and Policy Planning: Applications in Defense.* New York: Elsevier Publishing Co., 1968.

RAIFFA, Howard. *Decision Analysis.* Reading, Mass.: Addison-Wesley, 1968.

REUTLINGER, Schlomo. *Techniques for Project Appraisal under Uncertainty.* Baltimore: Johns Hopkins Press, 1970.

RUDWICK, Bernard H. *Systems Analysis for Effective Planning.* New York: John Wiley & Sons, 1969.

SCHELLING, Thomas C. *The Strategy of Conflict.* New York: Oxford University Press, 1963.

STEINER, George A. *Top Management Planning.* New York: Macmillan Co., 1969.

TINBERGEN, Jan. *The Design of Development.* Baltimore: Johns Hopkins Press, 1958.

_____. *Central Planning.* New Haven, Conn.: Yale University Press, 1964.

UNITED Nations. *Administration of National Development Planning: Report of a Meeting of Experts Held at Paris, France, 8–19 June 1964.* New York: United Nations, 1964 (ST/TAO/M/27).

_____. *The Administration of Economic Development Planning: Principles and Fallacies.* New York: United Nations, 1966 (ST/TAO/M/32).

UNITED States Government. *Organization, Planning, and Programming for Economic Development.* Papers prepared for the U.N. Conference on the Application of Science and Technology for the Benefit of the Less Developed Areas. Washington, D.C.: Government Printing Office, 1962.

VON NEUMANN, John, and Morgenstern, Oskar. *Theory of Games and Economic Behavior.* New York: John Wiley & Sons, 1964.

WALINSKY, Louis J. *The Planning and Execution of Economic Development.* New York: McGraw-Hill, 1963.

Cases, Experience, Description

AKZIN, Benjamin, and Dror, Yehezkel. *Israel: High Pressure Planning.* Syracuse, N.Y.: Syracuse University Press, 1966.

ARNDT, Hans-Joachim. *West Germany: The Politics of Non-Planning.* Syracuse, N.Y.: Syracuse University Press, 1966.

ASHFORD, Douglas E. *Morocco-Tunisia: Politics and Planning.* Syracuse, N.Y.: Syracuse University Press, 1965.

AZRAEL, Jeremy R. *Managerial Power and Soviet Politics.* Cambridge, Mass.: Harvard University Press, 1966.

BALDWIN, G. B. *Planning and Development in Iran.* Baltimore: Johns Hopkins Press, 1967.

BANFIELD, Edward C., and Wilson, James. *City Politics.* Cambridge, Mass.: Harvard University and MIT Presses, 1963.

BAUCHET, Pierre. *La Planification Française.* Paris: Éditions du Seuil, 1962.

_____. *Economic Planning: The French Experience.* London: William Heinemann, 1964.

BENVENISTE, Guy. *Bureaucracy and National Planning: A Sociological Case Study in Mexico.* New York: Praeger Publishers, 1970.

BERNARD, Philippe J. *Planning in the Soviet Union.* New York: Pergamon Press, 1966.

BETTELHEIM, Charles. *L'Économie Soviétique.* Paris: Recueil Sirey, 1950.

BEVERIDGE, Sir William H. *Planning under Socialism.* New York: Longmans, 1936.

BONILLA, Frank, and Silva Michelena, José A. *The Politics of Change in Venezuela.* Cambridge, Mass.: MIT Press, 1967.

BOULDING, Kenneth E., ed. *Peace and the War Industry.* Chicago: Aldine Publishing Co., 1970.

BROWN, Lester A. *Seeds of Change: The Green Revolution and Development in the 1970's.* New York: Praeger Publishers, 1970.

BURKE, Fred G. *Tanganyika: Pre-Planning.* Syracuse, N.Y.: Syracuse University Press, 1965.

CERYCH, Ladislav. *Problems of Aid to Education in Developing Countries.* New York: Frederick A. Praeger, 1965.

COHEN, Stephen. *Modern Capitalist Planning: The French Model.* Cambridge, Mass.: Harvard University Press, 1969.

CRONIN, Thomas E., and Greenberg, Sanford D., eds. *The Presidential Advisory System.* New York: Harper & Row, 1969.

CROZIER, Michel. Pour une analyse sociologique de la planification française. *Revue Française de Sociologie* 6 (1965), pp. 147–63.

CURLE, Adam. *Planning for Education in Pakistan: A Personal Case Study.* Cambridge, Mass.: Harvard University Press, 1966.

DALAND, Robert T. *Brazilian Planning: Development Politics and Administration.* Chapel Hill, N.C.: University of North Carolina Press, 1967.

DEGRAS, Jane, and Nove, Alec, eds. *Soviet Planning: Essays in Honor of Naum Jasny.* Oxford, England: Basil Blackwell, 1964.

DEVONS, Ely. *Planning and Economic Management.* Manchester, England: Manchester University Press, 1970.

DE WITT, Nicholas. *Education and Professional Employment in the USSR.* Washington, D.C.: National Science Foundation, 1961.

FENNO, Richard F., Jr. *The President's Cabinet.* New York: Vintage Books, n.d. (First published by Harvard University, 1959.)

FRANKEL, C. *High on Foggy Bottom: An Outsider's Inside View of the Government.* New York: Harper & Row, 1968.

FREIDIN, Seymour, and Bailey, George. *The Experts.* New York: Macmillan Co., 1968.

FRIEDMANN, John. *Venezuela: From Doctrine to Dialogue.* Syracuse, N.Y.: Syracuse University Press, 1965.

———. Planning as innovation: the Chilean case. *Journal of the American Institute of Planners* 32 (1966), pp. 194–203.

GANS, Herbert J. *The Urban Villagers.* New York: Free Press, 1962.

GEERTZ, Clifford. *Peddlers and Princes.* Chicago: University of Chicago Press, 1963.

GETTINGER, J. Price. *Planning for Agricultural Development: The Iranian Experience.* Washington, D.C.: National Planning Association, 1965.

HACKETT, John, and Hackett, Anne-Marie. *Economic Planning in France.* Cambridge, Mass.: Harvard University Press, 1965.

HAGEN, Everett E., ed. *Planning Economic Development.* Homewood, Ill.: Richard D. Irwin, 1963.

HAGEN, Everett E., and White, Stephanie F. T. *Great Britain: Quiet Revolution in Planning.* Syracuse, N.Y.: Syracuse University Press, 1965.

HANSEN, Niles M. *French Regional Planning.* Bloomington, Ind.: Indiana University Press, 1968.

HANSON, A. H. *The Process of Planning: A Study of India's 5-Year Plans 1950–1964.* London: Oxford University Press, 1966.

HELLER, Walter W. *New Dimensions of Political Economy.* New York: W. W. Norton & Co., 1967.

HIRSCH, Hans. *Quantity Planning and Price Planning in the Soviet Union.* Philadelphia: University of Pennsylvania Press, 1961.

HIRSCHMAN, Albert O., ed. *Latin American Issues.* New York: Twentieth Century Fund, 1961.

————. *Journeys towards Progress: Studies in Economic Policy Making in Latin America.* New York: Twentieth Century Fund, 1963.

————. *Development Projects Observed.* Washington, D.C.: Brookings Institution, 1967.

HOSELITZ, Bert F. *Sociological Aspects of Economic Growth.* New York: Free Press, 1960.

HOSELITZ, Bert F., and Moore, Wilbert E., eds. *Industrialization and Society.* Paris: UNESCO, 1963.

HUNTER, Guy. *Education for a Developing Region.* London: George Allen & Unwin, 1963.

KAUTSKY, John H., ed. *Political Change in Underdeveloped Countries.* New York: John Wiley & Sons, 1962.

KRISHNAMACHARI, V. T. *Fundamentals of Planning in India.* Calcutta: Orient Longmans, 1962.

LA PALOMBARA, Joseph. *Italy—The Politics of Planning.* Syracuse, N.Y.: Syracuse University Press, 1966.

LAUTMAN, Jacques, and Thoenig, Jean-Claude. *Planification et Administrations Centrales.* Paris: Centre de Recherches de Sociologie des Organisations, 1966.

————. La planification, agent de changement dans quelques administrations françaises. In *Analyse et Prévision.* Paris: Futuribles, 1966.

LEDERMAN, Leonard, and Windus, Margaret. *Federal Funding and National Priorities.* New York: Praeger Publishers, 1971.

LE GUAY, F. *La Planification en France.* Paris: Institut National de la Statistique et des Études Économiques, 1963.

LEWIS, John P. *Quiet Crisis in India: Economic Development and American Policy.* Garden City, N.Y.: Doubleday & Co., 1964.

LYONS, Raymond, ed. *Problems and Strategies of Educational Planning: Lessons from Latin America.* Paris: UNESCO, 1965.

MASSÉ, Pierre. *Histoire, Méthode et Doctrine de la Planification Française.* Paris: La Documentation Française, 1962.

MEISTER, Albert. *Socialisme et Autogestion: L'Experience Yougoslave.* Paris: Éditions du Seuil, 1964.

MEYERSON, Martin, and Banfield, Edward C. *Politics, Planning, and the Public Interest: The Case of Public Housing in Chicago.* New York: Free Press, 1964. (First published in 1955.)

MICHAL, Jan H. *Central Planning in Czechoslovakia.* Stanford, Calif.: Stanford University Press, 1960.

MONTIAS, John M. *Central Planning in Poland.* New Haven, Conn.: Yale University Press, 1962.

MYRDAL, Gunnar. *Asian Drama.* New York: Random House, 1968.

NEUSTADT, Richard E. *Presidential Power.* New York: John Wiley & Sons, 1960.

NOVE, Alec. *The Soviet Economy.* New York: Frederick A. Praeger, 1961.

NOZHKO, et al. *Educational Planning in the USSR.* Paris: UNESCO, 1968.

PAAUW, Douglas S. *Development Planning in Asia.* Washington, D.C.: National Planning Association, 1965.

PAIGE, Glenn D. *The Korean Decision.* New York; Free Press, 1968.

PERROUX, François. Le IVème Plan Française (1962–1965): en quoi consiste notre planification indicative? *Économie Appliqué* 11 (1962), pp. 1–65.

PYE, Lucian W. *Politics, Personality and Nation Building.* New Haven, Conn.: Yale University Press, 1964. (First published in 1962.)

RABINOVITZ, Francine F. *City Politics and Planning*. New York: Atherton Press, 1969.

RAINWATER, Lee, and Yancey, William L. *The Moynihan Report and the Politics of Controversy*. Cambridge, Mass.: MIT Press, 1967.

ROBOCK, Stefan H. *Brazil's Developing Northeast: A Study of Regional Planning and Foreign Aid*. Washington, D.C.: Brookings Institution, 1963.

RODWIN, Lloyd, and associates, eds. *Planning Urban Growth and Regional Development*. Cambridge, Mass.: MIT Press, 1969.

SELZNICK, Philip. *TVA and the Grass Roots: A Study in the Sociology of Formal Organizations*. New York: Harper & Row, 1966. (First published in 1949.)

SHAFER, Robert J. *Mexico: Mutual Adjustment Planning*. Syracuse, N.Y.: Syracuse University Press, 1966.

SHEEHAN, Neil, et al., eds. *The Pentagon Papers*. New York: Bantam Books, 1971.

STUPAK, Ronald J. *The Shaping of Foreign Policy: The Role of the Secretary of State as Seen by Dean Acheson*. New York: Odyssey Press, 1969.

SUNDQUIST, James L. *Politics and Policy: The Eisenhower, Kennedy and Johnson Years*. Washington, D.C.: Brookings Institution, 1968.

THOENIG, Jean-Claude. Le P.P.B.S. et l'Administration Publique. Paris: Centre de Sociologie des Organisations, 1971; mimeographed.

UL HAQ, Mahbub. *Strategy of Economic Planning: A Case Study of Pakistan*. Karachi: Oxford University Press, 1963.

WALINSKY, Louis J. *Economic Development of Burma 1951–1960*. New York: Twentieth Century Fund, 1962.

WATERSTON, Albert. *Planning in Morocco: Organization and Implementation*. Baltimore: Johns Hopkins Press, 1962.

———. *Planning in Yugoslavia: Organization and Implementation*. Baltimore: Johns Hopkins Press, 1962.

———. *Planning in Pakistan: Organization and Implementation*. Baltimore: Johns Hopkins Press, 1963.

———. *Development Planning: Lessons of Experience*. Baltimore: Johns Hopkins Press, 1965.

WILENSKY, H. L. *Organizational Intelligence: Knowledge and Policy in Government and Industry*. New York: Basic Books, 1967.

WILES, Peter. *The Political Economy of Communism*. Cambridge, Mass.: Harvard University Press, 1962.

Index

273